HE HAD IT COMING

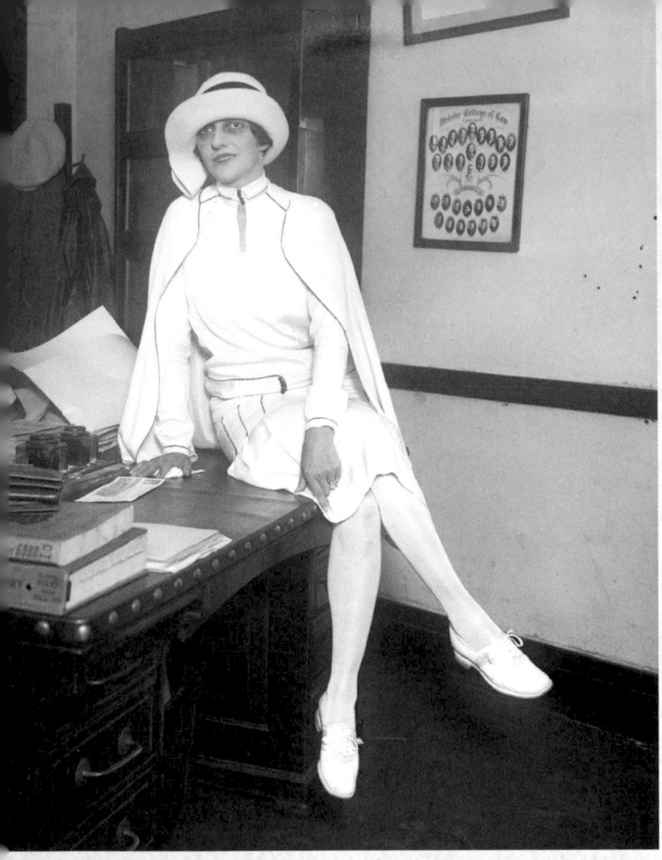

HE HAD IT COMING

FOUR MURDEROUS WOMEN AND THE REPORTER WHO IMMORTALIZED THEIR STORIES

KORI RUMORE
MARIANNE MATHER

Chicago Tribune

MIDWAY

AN AGATE IMPRINT

CHICAGO

Chicago Tribune: R. Bruce Dold, Publisher & Editor-in-Chief; Peter Kendall, Managing Editor; Christine W. Taylor, Managing Editor; Amy Carr, Director of Content/Life + Culture; Todd Panagopoulos, Director of Content/Photography; Jonathon Berlin, Director of Content/Dataviz; Jennifer Day, Books Editor; Kathleen B. O'Malley, Content Editor

Printed in China

10 9 8 7 6 5 4 3 2 1   19 20 21 22 23 24

He Had It Coming
ISBN-13: 978-1-57284-277-9
ISBN-10: 1-57284-277-6

Cover design and art direction by Morgan Krehbiel
Cover photo: *Chicago Herald and Examiner*

Midway Books is an imprint of Agate Publishing. Agate books are available in bulk at discount prices. For more information, visit agatepublishing.com.

CONTENTS

PRELUDE

By Rick Kogan

THE FIRST MURDER in the notoriously bloody history of Chicago took place on June 17, 1812, when a quarrel broke out between two fur traders. They were Jean La Lime and John Kinzie. The latter fatally stabbed the former, fled to Canada, got away with the crime and became one of the city's most prominent early residents.

Over the next century and beyond, most of our local murderers have been men. So were most of their victims. But women began to get into this nasty business soon enough, and by the 1920s they were sufficient in number to occupy their own section in the Cook County Jail.

This was a decade thick with larger-than-life characters living in a world of gangland violence, bootleg liquor, celebrity, sex, art and music. Morals were loosening, societal bonds relaxing, and the combination of bootleg gin and guns was becoming an increasingly dangerous one.

There were plenty of stories to fill the pages of the many daily and weekly newspapers in the city, all of them fighting for readers and for those unusual stories—*man bites dog*—that would grab their eyes.

Female killers perfectly fit that bill. You would have heard then, as you can now, that female murderers are rare. True enough, and that is why the media (which in the 1920s meant exclusively newspapers) eagerly sensationalized their crimes.

Facing page: The male-dominated *Chicago Tribune* newsroom at Madison and Dearborn streets in an undated photo.

"Chicago's frightful lead in the homicides of the world in 1924" shows a comparison of the number of murders in major cities.

(The latest available statistics from the U.S. Department of Justice, covering the years 2003 to 2012, show that eighty-eight percent of homicides are committed by men.)

In this remarkable book you will read about some of the more "interesting" of these women, a group that comprised "Murderess Row," a then-new section of the county jail reserved for women waiting to stand trial for murder. In 1924, there were more than a dozen women there, most accused of killing a husband or lover. And, thanks to the deep and vivid archives of the *Chicago Tribune*, you will see them too.

In general, the mood from cell to cell was surprisingly sunny. The women received fan mail and flowers. Some cut one another's hair, gave one another manicures and discussed cosmetics and fashion. These "damsels" did not feel in any great distress, knowing there was a long-standing tradition of all-male juries failing to convict attractive females of murder, despite what was often a mountain of evidence.

As uncommon as were female killers, so were female newspaper reporters. Newspapering at the time was a raucous and male-dominated realm, slowly crawling its way from the dusty past into the fast-moving modern century.

At the dawn of the 1920s, city delivery of the *Tribune* was still accomplished with more horse-drawn wagons (sixty-eight) than motorized trucks (forty-eight).

As uncommon as were female killers, so were female newspaper reporters in 1924.

But newspapers, specifically this one, had begun to get with the times. Some of that came in efforts to offer stories aimed at female readers, especially in the Sunday editions. Female editors and writers were hired in the hope that they could provide stories from a woman's perspective for this new female audience.

Fanny Butcher became the paper's literary editor in 1913, and Mary King was named the Sunday editor two years later. Slowly—fueled in part by the success of the women's suffrage movement that gave women the right to vote in 1920 and the *what-does-it-all-mean?* psychological restlessness in the wake of the horrors of World War I—the newsroom began to feature more women, and some started to do more than fetch coffee or run errands for the "guys."

Though many female reporters still wrote primarily for the society sections, a few worked their way onto the front page. Into this male milieu in February 1924 walked Maurine Dallas Watkins. She distinguished herself from the outset, especially when—editors thinking the assignment too "boring" for their male reporters—she traveled south to visit Murderess Row. The women she met, the trials she covered and what she later made of it all is detailed on the following pages. It is a great story, and Maurine is as interesting and enigmatic as any character she met in jail.

She was not in town long, but did cover a sensational murder that would come to be known as the "Crime of the Century"—the beating death of fourteen-year-old Bobby Franks by two wealthy University of Chicago students, Nathan Leopold and Richard Loeb.

Maurine left Chicago later in 1924, shortly after the departure of another of the city's legendary reporters, Ben Hecht. It is not known if Maurine and Hecht ever met. But both were deeply inspired by what they saw on the streets of the city. Hecht and his newspaperman pal Charles McArthur wrote "The Front Page," the play that forever defined the rough-and-tumble newspaper business. Maurine wrote "Chicago."

It seems somehow fitting that she beat the boys to the stage: "Chicago" premiered on Broadway in 1926, "The Front Page" two years later.

FOREWORD

By Heidi Stevens

Tʜᴇ sᴛᴏʀʏ ʙᴇʜɪɴᴅ ᴛʜᴇ sᴛᴏʀʏ that eventually became the movie "Chicago" could, itself, be a movie.

The inquisitive photo editor, staked out in the *Chicago Tribune*'s bone-chilling basement (affectionately known as "the morgue"), combing through the newspaper's prodigious archives, stumbling suddenly and fortuitously upon a box labeled, in pencil . . .

Zoom in for close-up:

"Kitty Malm."

Marianne Mather is the inquisitive photo editor, and Katherine "Kitty Malm" Baluk was one of the four women whose real-life murder trials inspired Maurine Watkins, a one-time *Chicago Tribune* reporter, to pen the play "Chicago," which would, in turn, become the musical "Chicago" and the movie "Chicago."

Kitty Malm was Go-To-Hell Kitty in "Chicago."

"Packed a gat where most girls harbor their love letters," the *Tribune* wrote about her on October 16, 1927. "A life-timer at Joliet."

The box—two boxes, it turned out—marked "Kitty Malm" were filled with photo negatives made of glass and stored in sleeves. The sleeves contained very little information—no dates, no context. Mather took the boxes back to the newsroom, digitized the images and started researching Kitty's story.

Facing page: The boxes containing the glass-plate negatives of Katherine "Kitty Malm" Baluk, along with the other women on Murderess Row, are carefully stored in the *Tribune's* archive.

She quickly discovered Kitty's connections to Chicago—both the city and the musical. This led her to search for—and find—the other three women whose stories would, eventually, become "Chicago." They were Beulah Annan, who inspired the character Roxie Hart; Belva Gaertner, who inspired the character Velma Kelly; and Sabella Nitti, who inspired the character Hunyak.

The *Tribune* had glass-plate negatives of all of them.

Mather teamed up with *Tribune* graphic artist Kori Rumore to research the women's stories as well as the story of Maurine Watkins, the writer who brought them—or some approximation of them—to the stage and screen.

"It seems possible Beulah and Belva committed the crimes they were accused of," Mather said. "It's not obvious for the other two."

Their research spanned four years and uncovered layers that never made it into the film and theatrical versions of "Chicago."

"When I tell people I found these photos of the real women that the 'Chicago' women are based on, they say, 'Oh, those were real women?'" Mather said.

"All of these women came to Chicago from someplace else, and they all ended up going somewhere after here," Rumore said. "They all have back stories."

"I guess I want people to know their real stories," Mather said. "And when I go through their stories, I feel like this could still happen today."

Perhaps we—we, the culture; we, the media—would parse our words more carefully today when speaking of four women, each arrested and accused of shooting a man to death.

"Belva Gaertner, another of those women who messed things up by adding a gun to her fondness for gin and men, was acquitted last night at 12:10 o'clock of the murder of Walter Law," Maurine Watkins wrote on June 6, 1924. "So drunk she didn't remember whether she shot the man found dead in her sedan."

Perhaps we wouldn't.

Swirling in the background as Mather and Rumore conducted their yearslong research were the rumblings and reverberations of the #MeToo movement, a presidential candidate bragging on tape about grabbing women by their genitals, that same presidential candidate leading his supporters in chants of "Lock her up!" against his opponent, a country bitterly divided over a Supreme Court nominee accused of sexual assault and the eventual swearing-in of that nominee.

"So much of what we've been finding feels like it hasn't changed," Rumore said.

The accused women being described first and foremost by their appearance.

"I carry these women around with me on a daily basis. . . . Whenever I see a famous woman on screen, I think about the way people shape and use their image." —MARIANNE MATHER

The accused women with a pleasing appearance having a far easier time winning over the public and their juries. The accused women struggling to make their authentic voices heard above the din of a media-driven narrative.

I asked Mather and Rumore if the women stayed with them—whether and when they found their thoughts turning to Belva and Beulah, Kitty and Sabella, Maurine Watkins.

"I think about Maurine a lot," Rumore said. "There's so much about her we don't know. She never married. She never had kids. She never followed the traditional path. She had an advanced education, and it seemed like, at first, with the success of 'Chicago,' she had every resource at her disposal to do further work of that same caliber. But it just didn't happen. I think about what happens when the first thing you write is the most successful thing you'll ever write in your lifetime. Where do you go from there?"

"I carry these women around with me on a daily basis," Mather said. "Whenever I see an immigration rally, I think about Sabella and the Sabellas of today and how they're maybe not being heard or not being understood."

Sabella was born and raised in Bari, Italy. She was compared to a farm animal in news coverage. At the time of her trial, she spoke and read almost no English. When she was convicted, she didn't understand the words spelling out her fate.

"I think about how we get the Sabellas into boardrooms and meeting rooms to make sure these types of things don't happen again," Mather said. "I think about that a lot. I also think about the Beulahs and the Belvas of the world. Whenever I see a famous woman on screen, I think about the way people shape and use their image."

In the media, Rumore said, but also on Instagram. On Facebook and Twitter.

"Can you imagine if Belva and Beulah had Instagram?" Mather said. "So many selfies in those jail cells!

"It all feels relevant today," Mather added.

Relevant and revealing. I think you'll agree.

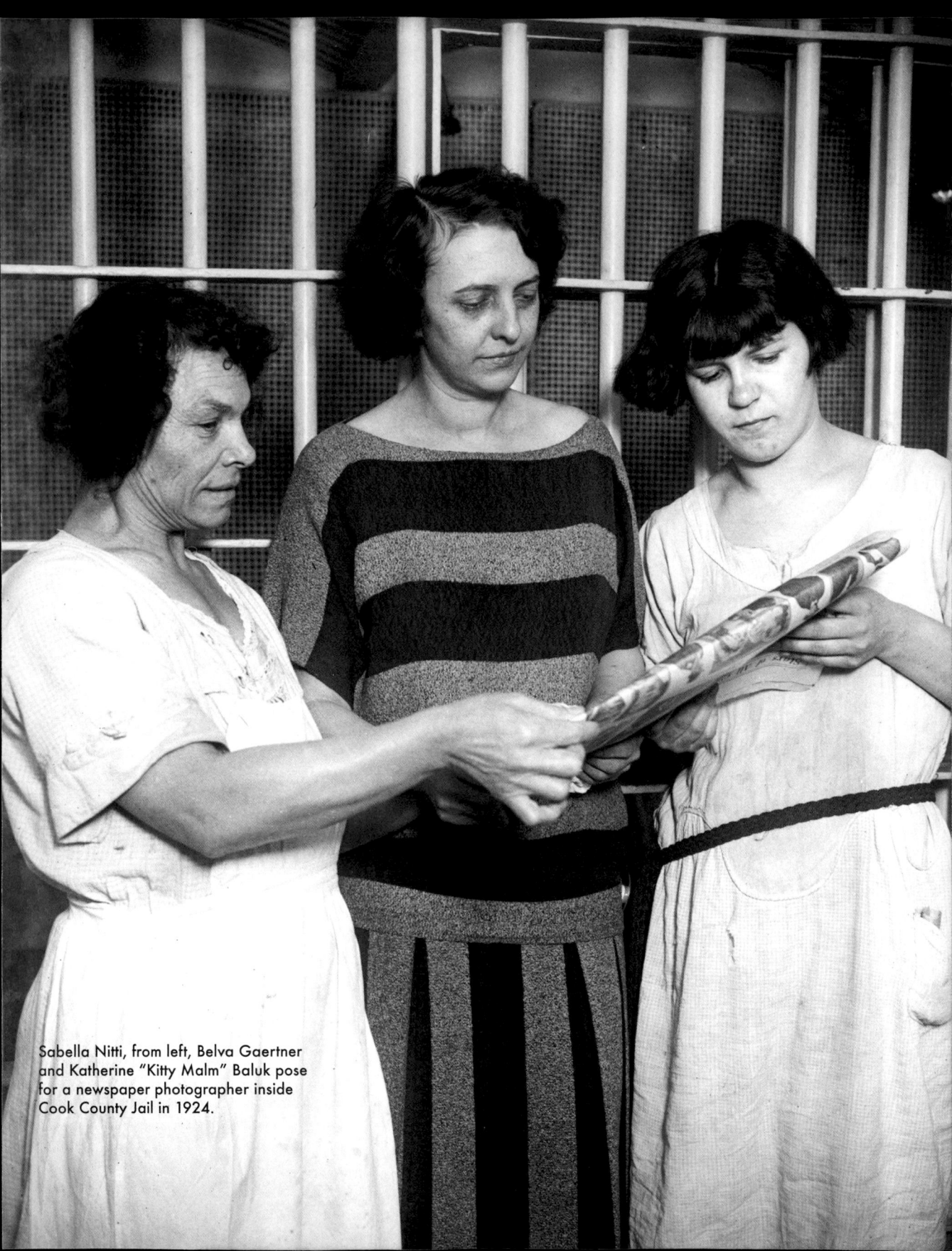

Sabella Nitti, from left, Belva Gaertner and Katherine "Kitty Malm" Baluk pose for a newspaper photographer inside Cook County Jail in 1924.

CHAPTER ONE

THE WOMEN OF 'CHICAGO'

USTICE,
BEAUTY
DEFEN
PLE

ct of Pretty Fac

Prosecutions, Q

Indicate

Harry Kalsted
dah Annan kill
killed him in
do not want
mitted because
etty face. We
die; and justice w
ung woman."

hat was the statem
ott Stewart, attorne
olah Annan, beautif
a who went on trial
illiam J. Lindsay in
urt today on the ch
arry Kalstedt, her
artment at 817 E. 1
a quarrel after a gl

SKS MURDER PEN

Prosecutor McLaug
ening statement, de
mand the penalty f
l not qualify his sta
cate whether he

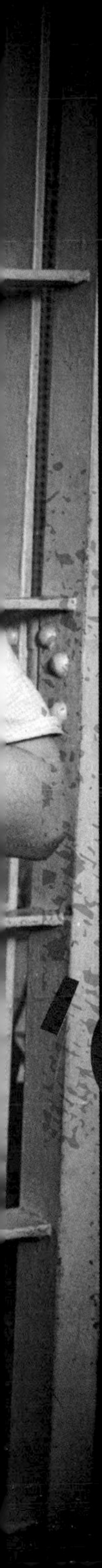

M AURINE WATKINS WAS HIRED as a reporter for the *Chicago Tribune* in February 1924—without any previous professional journalism work to her credit. As Maurine explained in a 1928 interview with Lillian G. Genn:

> I wrote a letter to the city editor of the Chicago Tribune and he asked me to call. The first question he shot at me was whether I had had experience or had ever worked on a newspaper before. I told him I hadn't and he wanted to know what made me think I could work on one. That flustered me a bit and, a little too frightened to answer, I arose to go. But he snapped at me to sit down—and gave me a job!

For the next eight months, Maurine covered a string of sensational crimes, headlined by four murder cases perpetrated by women. These women, brought together under the tabloid glare, form the basis for what has become "Chicago": a $2 billion entertainment franchise featuring A-list celebrities, a hit, Tony Award-winning Broadway musical and an Oscar-winning movie.

Maurine drew on her access to women accused of murder inside Cook County Jail as the inspiration for a three-act play, "A Brave Little Woman," the first play she wrote at the Yale School of Drama in 1926. It was renamed "Chicago" when it debuted on Broadway later that year.

The experiences of the play's lead character, Roxie Hart, closely resembled the same plot twists that played out during the real-life trial of Beulah Annan: a pregnancy claim; a defense built on both the murderess and her lover reaching for a gun; an acquittal from a sympathetic, all-male jury; and reporters and photographers at the ready to record the day's drama.

Velma Kelly's exploits mirrored those of Belva Gaertner, a wannabe cabaret dancer who claimed to be too drunk to remember shooting her lover in the head.

Go-To-Hell Kitty makes a brief yet memorable appearance as a tough-talking stick-up artist who "carried a gun where most girls carry a powder-puff." She's based

Facing page: Beulah Annan, left, and Belva, right, were both on trial for murder in 1924. Beulah, considered the most beautiful woman on Murderess Row, and Belva, called the most stylish woman, were acquitted in speedy trials.

Katherine, right, holds up a playing card—the ace of hearts—as she poses with Belva for a newspaper photographer while in Cook County Jail in 1924.

Why Did Five Chicago Women Commit Murder?

MRS. MALM

MRS. NITTI-CRUDELLE

MRS. KAVANAGH

MRS. ANNAN

MRS. GAERTNER

Muncie Evening Press, April 25, 1924

> "I got so I prayed for murders. Not that you ever have to pray long for murders in Chicago, but I prayed for 'good' murders and then I prayed that I would be sent to cover them."
>
> —MAURINE WATKINS, *SUCCESS MAGAZINE*

on Katherine "Kitty Malm" Baluk, a woman who left her abusive husband to provide a better life for her two-year-old daughter, only to wind up with a convicted murderer who framed her for murder after a robbery attempt went wrong.

And Moonshine Maggie, or Hunyak, a woman who couldn't speak English yet was convicted of murdering a man after selling him tainted booze, is largely based on Italian immigrant Sabella Nitti. Sabella was sentenced to hang for killing her husband, but the decision was reversed after a team of attorneys of Italian ancestry pleaded her innocence before the Illinois Supreme Court.

Maurine left journalism after only eight months of work at the *Chicago Tribune*.

"I got so I prayed for murders," she told Clare Ogden Davis in an interview for *Success Magazine*. "Not that you ever have to pray long for murders in Chicago, but I prayed for 'good' murders and then I prayed that I would be sent to cover them. Finally, I got out of it all. I had to. I was afraid I would let my whole life be influenced by murders—murders by and of other people."

Today, aside from her byline on stories in the paper's archives, there's no indication Maurine ever worked for the *Chicago Tribune*. When she died on August 10, 1969, the paper didn't even run an obituary. If not for the musical adaptation of "Chicago," her name might have been forever lost to history.

"Chicago the Musical" has played on Broadway for more than nine thousand three hundred performances since it premiered on November 14, 1996, yet not many people know about the real women who inspired the characters of Roxie Hart, Velma Kelly and others. Here they are, for the first time in almost a century, illustrated by photos and stories uncovered in the *Chicago Tribune*'s archives.

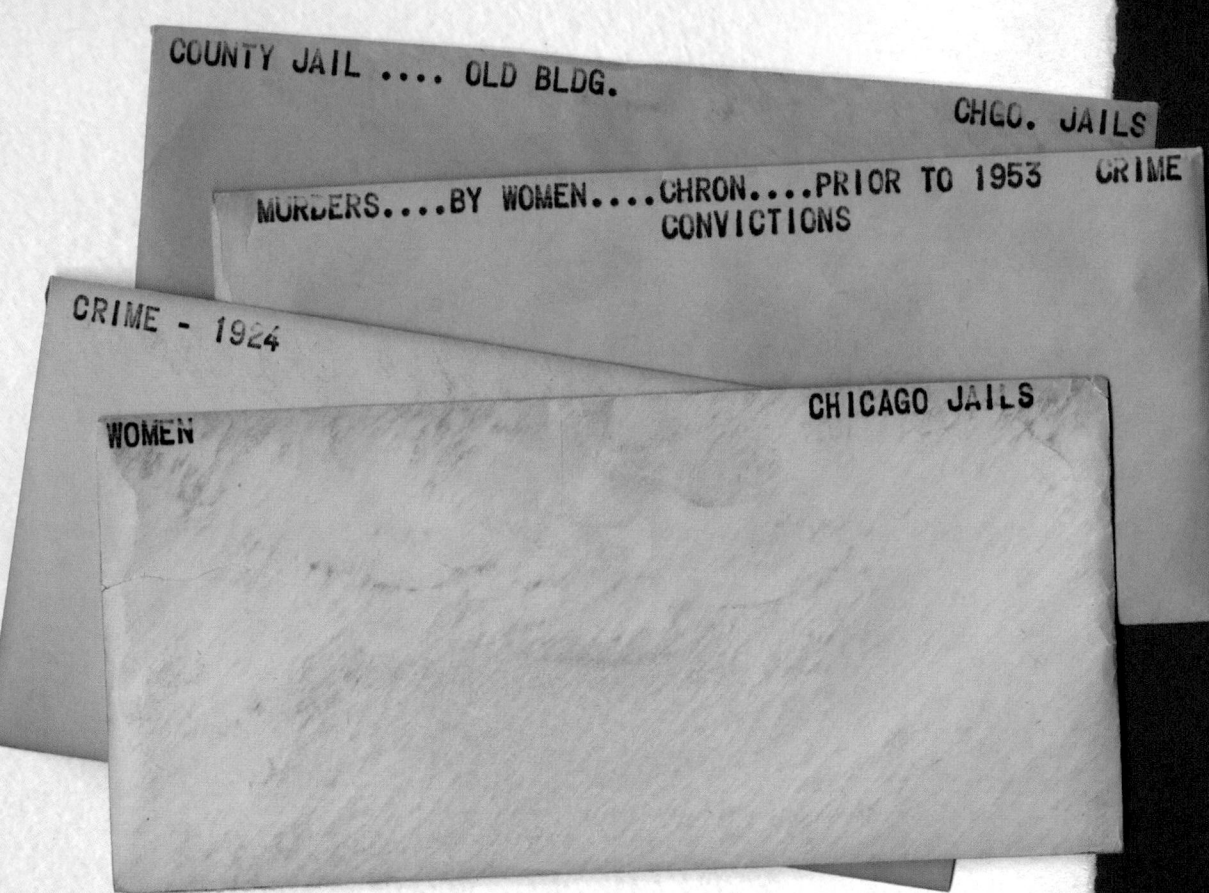

COUNTY JAIL .... OLD BLDG.

CHGO. JAILS

MURDERS....BY WOMEN....CHRON....PRIOR TO 1953   CRIME
CONVICTIONS

CRIME - 1924

CHICAGO JAILS

WOMEN

These newspaper clippings—and the envelopes they were housed in—were gathered from the *Tribune*'s sub-basement archive, stored away like a time capsule by *Tribune* librarians. The clippings are mainly from the *Chicago Tribune* but are also taken from other local newspapers that long ago closed their doors. You will find that many of the historical photos in this book have deteriorated over time, so you'll see cracks, scratches, fingerprints and dust on the photos. Some of them have paint on them from photo retouchers. Due to the cameras and technology of the time period, many of the photos are posed, staged or re-created. We've scanned the beautiful artifacts completely as we found them, as if the person who developed or clipped them all those years ago has just stepped away from his or her desk.

In researching the content for this book, we've done our best to verify the spelling of names, ages, dates and places through the gathering of vital records, newspaper clippings and other documents. Some of the official documentation, however, has been lost to time—including the birth records for Maurine Watkins and Beulah and marriage records for Belva.

IS WALTER LAW;
HOLD DIVORCEE

Mrs. B...

**MURDERESS ROW
LOSES CLASS AS
BELVA IS FREED**

Four Obscure "Girl"
Killers in Jail.

S. GAERTNER
"CLASS" AS
SHE FACES JURY

Demure but with an "Air"
at Murder Trial.

FULL OF GIN
AND CANNOT
REMEMBER,

"TIGER GIRL," ON
STAND, ACCUSES
...ALM OF KILLING

...ith Him

**JURY FINDS
MRS. GAERTNER
NOT GUILTY**

Verdict Found After
Eight Ballots.

NO SWEETHEART
WORTH KILLING—
MRS. GAERTNER

Belva Hopes for Jury of
"Liberal" Men.

...man Plays
...zz Air as
...ictim Dies

For more than two hours yesterday
...ly young wife, played a foxtrot record
named "Hula Lou" in her little apartment at 817 East 46th str...
she telephoned her husb...
ported that she had kill...
"tried to make love" to...
The Hawaiian tune...
song of Harry Kolste...
of 808 East 46th st...
Annan shot because...
their little wine pa...
that he was thro...
body lay hunche...
her bedroom as...
over and over...
When taken...
tion by the...
tearfully th...
to save he...

**SELF-DEFENSE
PLEA GAINS
HER FREEDOM**

**DEMAND NOOSE
FOR 'PRETTIEST'
WOMAN SLAYER**

Mrs. Annan Held on
Murder Charge.

...TY MALI
HUSBAND

JUSTICE,
BEAUTY,
DEFENSE
...LEA

...Each Mem-
...r Verdict.

...E WATKINS.
...whose pursuit of
...z music was inter-
...ss with the trigger
...reedom last night
...f" jury.
...From Judge Lind-
...d at 10:20 brought
...guilty" on the
...r of the mur-
...arry Kalstedt, in
...East 46th street,
...fendant thanked
...assisted by her
...ou!" she said,
...ch one as she
...u don't know,
...felt sure that
...pealing glance
...ercome,
...stood by her
...und the m...
...ASKS

BRUNE: APRIL 6,

**BEULAH ANNAN
SOBS REGRET FO
LIFE SHE TOO...**

Lives Through Crime Agai...
as She Awaits Trial.

BY MAURINE WATKINS.
"Of course I'm sorry. I'd give m...
life to have Harry Kolstedt all...
again! And I never said I was glad
Why, I couldn't. Why——" and tea...
filled the eyes of Mrs. Beulah Ma...
Annan, the "prettiest murderess,"
held to the grand jury for shootin...
her sweetheart in a drunken quarr...
at her apartment on Thursday.
Thursday night, a mad, hysteric...
frenzy, when she babbled conflictin...
accounts of the murder. Friday,...
daze that left her cold and unmove...
But yesterday afte...

BY MAURINE WATKINS.
(Pictures on back page)
Beulah May Annan, the 23 year old
wife who shot "the other man" Thursday afternoon to the tune of her husband's phonograph, was held to the
grand jury yesterday afternoon by a
coroner's jury, which charged her with
the murder of Harry Kolstedt. Assistant State's Attorneys Bert Cronson,
Roy Wood, and William McLaughlin
are preparing to rush the case to an
early trial, at which they will ask the
death penalty.
Thursday afternoon Mrs. Annan
played "Hula Lou" on the phonograph
while the wooer she had shot during
a drunken quarrel lay dying in her bedroom at 817 East 46th street. And yesterday afternoon the chapel organ at
Boydston's undertaking parlors played
"Nearer, My God to Thee" for an old
soldier's funeral, while she waited for
the inquest to start.
Changes Her Story.
Thursday night at the Hyde Park
...she insisted that Kolstedt's ad-

...OVE
...SET F
...SELF WO

...y'll Not Take He
...Says Malm Who T
...Her Killing 2

WAITED DEPUTY W

Presence of Little Si...
From Shooting...
...Laid t

...verruled a...
...McCarthy...
...sentenced
...guilty to t...
...d Spirits.
...owed little e...
...e court. She...
...than at any...
...sted, and relter...
...pected to be ha...
...py when the jury...
...ent that she fainte...
...ut State's Attorney...
...and Robert E. McM...
...gainst the motion to...

NO HAPPY
...halm, tiger woman c...

Beulah Annan
poses doe-eyed
for a cameraman
after admitting she
murdered her lover,
Harry Kalstedt, in
April 1924.

CHAPTER TWO

BEULAH ANNAN

"Too beautiful to work in a laundry, but a sufficiently good shot to get her man with one bullet in the back."

—*CHICAGO TRIBUNE*, OCTOBER 16, 1927

I f Belva Gaertner brings the dazzle to "Chicago," then Beulah Annan is the razzle. The story of the tall, slim woman with auburn, bobbed hair and blue eyes—whose first name means "married" in Hebrew—just couldn't be true.

Already twice married and a mother by the age of twenty-four, neither marriage nor motherhood seemed to satisfy Beulah. She met Harry Kalstedt—a married man who had a six-year-old daughter—at work. Walks together quickly progressed to drinks at her apartment while her husband, Albert Annan, was away working. The pair were intimate on at least three occasions, she would later admit.

During a daytime rendezvous at the apartment on April 3, 1924, Beulah shot Kalstedt with her husband's revolver, causing newcomer *Chicago Tribune* reporter Maurine Watkins to name her "the prettiest woman ever accused of murder in Chicago."

After the shooting, Beulah couldn't get her story straight. Maybe that's why she waited hours to call her husband. Did she realize her phonograph was playing the same Hawaiian-inspired tune, "Hula Lou," over and over again while she contemplated her next steps? Unclear. Just before 6 p.m., she phoned the garage where her husband worked, saying, "I've shot a man, Albert. He tried to make love to me."

Annan rushed home in a taxi, found his wife covered in blood and called the police—despite her urging him not to. But it was too late; Sergeant John O'Grady at the Wabash Avenue station was already on the other end of the line.

"I've just killed my husband!" Beulah shrieked into the receiver, then hung up the phone.

To speed up her trial, Beulah made an announcement a little more than a month following her arrest: She was pregnant. Was there any way a jury composed of all white men would convict a pregnant woman? Not likely, and she knew it. Her plan worked. She was found not guilty. And a baby never materialized.

Beulah's infidelity would lead to Prohibition-era notoriety. Maurine used her real exploits—the affair, the shooting, the trial, the aftermath—to craft the character of Roxie Hart and provide the basis for "Chicago."

Facing page: Beulah, shown after her trial, was careful to craft her image for the press.

BIOGRAPHICAL DETAILS

Domestic turmoil marked Beulah's childhood. Her parents—Utica, Kentucky, farmer John Sheriff and his wife, Mary—separated just after Beulah's eighth birthday. One of the local newspapers, the *Owensboro Messenger*, reported that Mary filed for divorce after John kicked her and their child out of the family's home. Mary claimed that "for some time before their separation, (John) treated her cruelly and displayed such an outrageous temper as to indicate that her safety and possibly her life were endangered." She petitioned the court for $25 in temporary alimony (or about $670 in today's dollars) and $1,000 in permanent alimony (almost $27,000 in today's dollars). Nothing was said regarding who would get custody of the child.

Beulah married for the first time when she was just fifteen, crossing the Ohio River by boat to marry twenty-two-year-old *Owensboro Inquirer* mechanical department staffer Perry Stephens in Rockport, Indiana, on February 11, 1915. It's likely Beulah lied about her age on the marriage certificate, adding four years to avoid an Indiana requirement for parental consent for marriage for those under age eighteen.

Beulah gave birth to a son, Perry Stephens Jr., on August 8, 1916. Divorce soon followed, however. The child went to live with his paternal grandparents, who threw an outdoor party for his second birthday at their home. "Games and music were enjoyed," according to the August 13, 1918, *Owensboro Inquirer*. A noted absence from that party's guest list: Beulah.

In an interview late in his life, Perry Stephens Jr. said he didn't have any recollection of his mother. "She was never mentioned in my presence."

Beulah had moved on—to Chicago. She was married again, this time to a mechanic named Albert Annan. They met in Louisville, Kentucky, and became husband and wife in Cook County on March 29, 1920. Annan, who was seven years older than Beulah, worked long hours and earned up to $60 a week (or about $880 today). They shared a small apartment in the 800 block of East Forty-Sixth Street, in today's Bronzeville neighborhood.

Facing page: Beulah, right, and her mother, Mary Neel, pose for a staged photo in 1924 during Beulah's trial for Kalstedt's murder.

SCHEDULE No. 1.—POPULATION.

State Kentucky
County Daviess

Supervisor's District No. 2
Enumeration District No. 34
Sheet No. 19

Township or other division of county Magisterial District No. 5 Vanover   Name of Institution,

Name of incorporated city, town, or village, within the above-named division,   Ward of city,

Enumerated by me on the 30th day of June, 1900, Columbus M. Murphy, Enumerator.

Name	Relation	Nativity (birthplace)	Occupation
Sheriff, John R.	Head	Kentucky / Wales / Wales	Farmer
— Mary	Wife	Kentucky / Kentucky / Kentucky	
— Beulah	son	Kentucky / Kentucky / Kentucky	
Sheriff, Henry B.	Head	Kentucky / Kentucky / Kentucky	Farmer
— Thornton	Brother	Kentucky / Kentucky / Kentucky	Farm Laborer
— Porter	Brother	Kentucky / Kentucky / Kentucky	Farm Laborer
— Nancy	Mother	Kentucky / Kentucky / Kentucky	
Nicely, Malon	Head	Tennessee / Tennessee / Tennessee	Farmer
— Frances	Wife	Tennessee / Tennessee / Tennessee	
— James	Son	Kentucky / Tennessee / Tennessee	Farm Laborer
— Jesse	Son	Kentucky / Tennessee / Tennessee	Farm Laborer
— Louis	Son	Kentucky / Tennessee / Tennessee	Farm Laborer
— Winford	Son	Kentucky / Tennessee / Tennessee	Farm Laborer
— Iva	Daughter	Kentucky / Tennessee / Tennessee	
— Tony	son	Kentucky / Tennessee / Tennessee	
Wright,	Head	Kentucky / Kentucky / Kentucky	Farmer

Beulah Sheriff (in row three), along with her mother, Mary, and father, John, is listed in the twelfth census of the United States, from 1900. She is erroneously listed as a son.

A CLOSER LOOK

LOCATION	NAME	RELATION	PERSONAL DESCRIPTION
352 / 252	Sheriff, John R.	Head	W M Jun 1873 28 M H
	Mary	Wife	W F July 1879 20 M 4 1 1
	Beulah	son	W M Nov 1858

NATIVITY			CITIZENSHIP	OCCUPATION	EDUCATION	OWNERSHIP OF HOME
Kentucky	Wales	Wales		Farmer		R F 314
Kentucky	Kentucky	Kentucky				
Kentucky	Kentucky	Kentucky				

Application is hereby made for a license for the marriage of

MALE *Perry W. Stephens* to *Beulah M. Sheriff.* FEMALE

UPON THE FOLLOWING STATEMENT OF FACTS RELATIVE TO SAID PARTIES:

1. The full christian and surname of the man is...........
2. Color *white*
3. Where born *Hopville Tenn.* (Town, County, State or Country)
4. When born *Jan 4" 1893.* (Day, Month, Year)
5. Present residence *Owensboro Ky*
6. Present occupation *Painter*
7. If no occupation, what means has the male contracting party to support a family?
8. Is the male contracting party of nearer blood kin to the female contracting party than second cousin? *No.*
9. Full christian and surname of father *W. L. Stephens*
10. His color *white*
11. His birthplace *Kentucky*
12. His occupation *Book Keeper*
13. His residence *Owensboro Ky*
14. Full christian and maiden name of mother *Margarete Wilson*
15. Her color *white* 16. Her occupation *House Keeper*
17. Her birthplace *Kentucky*
18. Her residence *Owensboro Ky*
19. Has the male contracting party been an inmate of any county asylum or home for indigent persons within the last five years? *No*
20. If so, is he now able to support a family and likely to so continue?
21. Is this his first marriage? *Yes* 22. If not, how often has he been married?
23. Has such prior marriage, or marriages been dissolved?
24. If so, how? 25. When?

1. The full christian and surname of the woman is...........
2. Color *white*
3. Where born *Kentucky* (Town, County, State or Country)
4. When born *1896. Nov. 17"* (Day, Month, Year)
5. Present residence *Owensboro Ky*
6. Present occupation *Housekeeper*
7. Full christian and surname of father *John Sheriff*
8. His color *white*
9. His birthplace *Kentucky*
10. His occupation *Farmer*
11. His residence *Owensboro Ky*
12. Full christian and maiden name of mother *Mary Stone*
13. Her color *white*
14. Her occupation *Housekeeper*
15. Her birthplace *Kentucky*
16. Her residence *Owensboro Ky*
17. Has the female contracting party been an inmate of any county asylum or home for indigent persons within the last five years? *No*
18. Is this her first marriage? *Yes*
19. If not, how often has she been married?
20. Has such prior marriage, or marriages been dissolved?
21. If so, how and when?
22. Is the female contracting party afflicted with epilepsy, tuberculosis, venereal or any

---

Married I Rockport.

Mr. Perry W. Stevens and Miss Beulah Sheriff, surprised their friends by going to Rockport yesterday morning and getting married. Rev. Barble, pastor of the Rockport Christian church, performed the ceremony. Mr. Stevens and his bride were accompanied to Rockport by Mrs. Raymond C. Hicks. The young couple returned to Owensboro yesterday afternoon, and for the present will be guests of Mr. and Mrs. Hicks, at their home, No. 214 Center street.

Owensboro Messenger-Inquirer, February 12, 1915

● ● ●

A lawn party was given in honor of the second birthday of Perry Stephens Jr., Thursday, August 8, at the home of his grandparents, Mr. and Mrs. W. L. Stephens, on East Second street. Games and music were enjoyed and ices were served the following: Misses Josephine and Eleanor Barr, Gwendolyn Crabtree, Dorothy Gordon, Helen Lynch and Willie Lee Stephens. Masters Kenneth Barr, Billy Jean McDonald, of Evansville, Ind., Herndon Stephens and Perry Stephens, Jr.

● ● ●

Owensboro Messenger-Inquirer, August 13, 1918

It's likely Beulah lied about her age on the marriage certificate, adding four years to avoid an Indiana requirement for parental consent for marriage for those younger than eighteen.

A birthday party announcement for Beulah's son, Perry Stephens Jr., had a noted absence from the party's guest list: Beulah.

"For more than two hours yesterday afternoon Mrs. Beulah Annan, a comely young wife, played a foxtrot record named 'Hula Lou' in her little apartment at 817 East 46th Street. Then she telephoned her husband and reported that she had killed a man who 'tried to make love' to her." —*CHICAGO TRIBUNE*, APRIL 4, 1924

THE INCIDENT

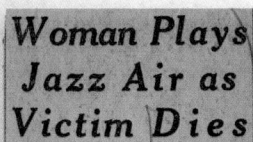

Chicago Tribune, April 4, 1924

The news of Kalstedt's murder made the front page of the next day's *Chicago Tribune* with the headline "Woman Plays Jazz Air as Victim Dies." It was next to a tale of three Chicago police officers who responded to a call of "something's doing" only to discover it was a woman giving birth to a ten-pound baby boy whom she would name Mike—possibly after one of the officers who assisted in the delivery, Michael Cadlin.

Stories at the top of that page covered construction of the expected $40 million, twenty-three-story Palmer House hotel and cash offered for Democratic votes to support current Illinois Governor Len Small—who had been acquitted of embezzling millions of dollars while he was state treasurer. Small would win reelection, despite a *Tribune* editorial declaring him the "worst governor the state ever had."

We don't know which *Chicago Tribune* reporter wrote the first story following Kalstedt's murder in the Annan apartment. There's no byline, or credit, given. Yet it captures the confusion, or downright deception, the murderess created to hide her guilt.

With her lover's body slumped against a wall in her bedroom, Beulah told police at least two versions of the events that led to Kalstedt's murder—but not before Albert Annan tried to shoulder the blame by telling police he killed Kalstedt himself. They weren't buying it.

Beulah's first story: She killed Kalstedt to save her honor.

"He came into my apartment this afternoon and made himself at home," she said. "Although I scarcely knew him, he tried to make me love him. I told him I would shoot. He kept coming anyway, and I-I did shoot him."

Investigators, who had brought Beulah into the Hyde Park police station for questioning, weren't making any progress. So they took her back to the apartment

Beulah confesses to police at the Hyde Park station that she shot her lover, Kalstedt, earlier that day, April 3, 1924.

Beulah told police in the Hyde Park station at least two versions of the events that led her to fatally shoot Kalstedt on April 3, 1924.

and started asking detailed questions: What about the blood on the phonograph? What about the wine and gin bottles and empty glasses? Why was Kalstedt shot through the back?

Her second, more sober attempt: She was angry Kalstedt was leaving her.

"I'd been fooling around with Harry for two months," she said. "This morning, as soon as my husband left for work, Harry called me up. I told him I wouldn't be home, but he came over anyway.

"We sat in the flat for quite a time, drinking. Then I said in a joking way that I was going to quit him. He said he was through with me and began to put on his coat. When I saw that he meant what he said, my mind went in a whirl and I shot him. Then I started playing the record. I was nervous, you see."

Kalstedt

MEET THE DECEASED: HARRY KALSTEDT

The Hempstead, Texas, native, who was twenty-six years old when he was shot and killed, moved to Chicago when he was young. Kalstedt, five older siblings and his widowed Swedish immigrant mother were living in the city's Fifth Ward, according to the 1910 census.

He and girlfriend Lydia Lindgren settled in her hometown of Cambridge, Minnesota, forty miles north of Minneapolis. They had a child, Harriet, in 1916. The couple was married on April 14, 1917. Another daughter, Eleanor, would follow in 1918.

According to his draft registration card for World War I, Kalstedt moved back to Chicago and was living there as of August 1918. The Kalstedts later divorced.

Kalstedt met Beulah Annan while both worked at the same laundromat, Tennant's Model Laundry, before their fatal April 3, 1924, rendezvous.

INQUEST

In court, Beulah—wearing a fawn-colored dress and stockings with black shoes, dark brown coat and brown Georgette hat—elaborated on the details that led to Kalstedt's arrival at her apartment. She told the coroner's jury he called to say he would pick up some wine, then swung by her place to get the money with which to purchase it. About an hour into their two-quart (or was it a gallon?) wine tasting, Beulah began to tease her lover about his time served for a statutory offense in his home state of Minnesota. In response, Kalstedt told Beulah she was "no good."

Her lawyer, the Irish-born W.W. O'Brien, who several years later would survive a hail of bullets intended for his client and North Side gang leader Hymie Weiss, concocted another version of events.

"Both went for the gun!" O'Brien said.

Beulah reached it first. Kalstedt then turned and reached for his coat and hat but didn't make it that far. Why?

"Darned good reason: I shot him," Beulah answered.

When questioned on the stand, Albert Annan acknowledged the gun belonged to him and recalled finding the body of a man he did not know.

He was more forthcoming with police the night of the incident, saying, "I've been a sucker, that's all! Simply a meal ticket. I've worked, 10, 12, 14 hours a day and took home every cent of my money. We'd bought our furniture for the little apartment on time and it was all paid off but a hundred dollars. I thought she was happy. I didn't know. . . ."

Upon being charged with Kalstedt's murder and facing the possibility of the death penalty, Beulah "powdered her nose, took the money her husband had borrowed, and went back to jail to await developments."

AWAITING TRIAL

Albert Annan immediately returned to work, gathering what money he could to pay for his wife's defense. "Tell her I'll stick—that's all—that I'll stick," he told reporters. Beulah, meanwhile, lamented the restrictions of cellblock living: "(T)hey won't even let you have cold cream and powder!"

Reporters were given extraordinary access to women awaiting trial in the Cook County Jail—especially those charged with murder and

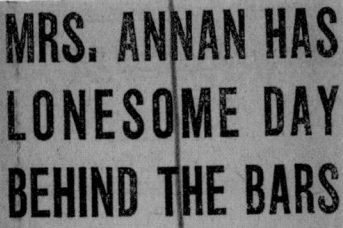

MRS. ANNAN HAS LONESOME DAY BEHIND THE BARS

Mrs. Beulah Annan's second day in the county jail, where she waits indictment for the murder of her sweetheart, Harry Kalstedt, was a trifle monotonous.

"Sunday's bad enough any place, but here——" and Chicago's prettiest woman "killer" shrugged her shoulders in disgust. She misses the conveniences of home—they won't even let you have cold cream and powder! And they tuned in the radio for a sacred concert instead of Hawaiian fox trots.

Thinks of Bonds.

And the uncertainty's growing tiresome. Will the grand jury indict her this week? Will she get bond? Will her father, John Sheriff, Kentucky farmer, furnish the money? For she hasn't heard from him since the arrest, nor from her mother, Mrs. Mary Neal, who moved from 4919 Lake Park avenue Saturday night and left no address because she didn't want to be "bothered."

But the husband, Albert Annan, who knew nothing of the "other man" till he found the dead body in his apartment, is "standing by." Yesterday afternoon he bundled up some clothes —a black crêpe dress and a checkered flannel—and took them down to the

Chicago Tribune, April 7, 1924

TRIBUNE: APRIL 6, 192

BEULAH ANNAN
SOBS REGRET FOR
LIFE SHE TOOK

Lives Through Crime Again
as She Awaits Trial.

BY MAURINE WATKINS.

"Of course I'm sorry! I'd give m
life to have Harry Kolstedt aliv
again! And I never said I was glad
Why, I couldn't. Why——" and tear
filled the eyes of Mrs. Beulah Ma
Annan, the "prettiest murderess,
held to the grand jury for shootin
her sweetheart in a drunken quarre
at her apartment on Thursday.
    Thursday night, a mad, hysteric
frenzy, when she babbled conflictin
accounts of the murder. Friday,
daze that left her cold and unmove
at the inquest. But yesterday after
noon in the county jail, where sh
awaits indictment for murder, sh
began to realize what it means to kil
    And the musics' changed, too. "Hub

Chicago Tribune, April 6, 1924

Top photo, from left: Albert Annan, his wife, Beulah, and attorney William Scott Stewart appear during the coroner's inquest, shortly after Beulah admitted to killing Kalstedt.

Bottom photo: Annan testifies at the coroner's inquest on April 4, 1924, in Chicago. Beulah, who admitted to murdering Kalstedt, did not testify, but her confession was read into the record. Afterward, her husband raised money for her legal defense.

In 1924, while facing murder charges for the death of her lover, Beulah plays cards at Cook County Jail.

living on a floor deemed Murderess Row. Here, outside of court, inmates could plead their case with the scribes, hoping for front-page write-ups. With nothing but time on their hands, the women were rivals for headlines.

It was here Maurine Watkins interviewed Beulah, who disputed how the April 3 murder had been reported in the newspapers.

"They say I killed him rather than have him leave me. Why, I was the one who was going to quit him. You see, I realized that we wouldn't go on, that we could never really be anything to each other. I never loved him as much as I did my hubby—and besides, he had nothing to offer me, no inducement to make me leave Albert."

Beulah's actions didn't deter admirers, who sent her flowers and meals, including one comprised of a juicy steak, French-fried potatoes and cucumber salad. As family members visited (excluding her father, who refused to travel to Chicago), Beulah grew more determined in proclaiming the shooting was justified.

"My defense will be that if I had not shot him I would now be dead," she said after a family visit.

Though a speedy trial was promised by the court—to get "all murder cases cleaned up before the summer vacation period begins"—Beulah's case was continued several times. Tired of waiting, Beulah made an announcement a little more than a month following her arrest: She told the court she was expecting a baby.

Her timing was ingenious. The court had a "four-term" rule, meaning Beulah's case could not be continued for more than four terms of court without her consent. If her case was brought to trial before fall, then her pregnancy could be considered by the jury. Even if she were found guilty, then an execution would be delayed until after the child was born—assuming Beulah was actually pregnant.

A poll of women on Murderess Row, taken for a May 9, 1924, *Chicago Tribune* story by Maurine Watkins about Beulah's fate, was clear: All believed she would escape death.

"A woman never swung in Illinois," one said triumphantly.

"A jury isn't blind and a pretty woman's never been convicted in Cook County," said another.

DEMAND NOOSE FOR 'PRETTIEST' WOMAN SLAYER

Mrs. Annan Held on Murder Charge.

BY MAURINE WATKINS.

(Pictures on back page)

Beulah May Annan, the 23 year old wife who shot "the other man" Thursday afternoon to the tune of her husband's phonograph, was held to the grand jury yesterday afternoon by a coroner's jury, which charged her with the murder of Harry Kolstedt. Assistant State's Attorneys Bert Cronson, Roy Wood, and William McLaughlin are preparing to rush the case to an early trial, at which they will ask the death penalty.

Thursday afternoon Mrs. Annan played "Hula Lou" on the phonograph while the wooer she had shot during a drunken quarrel lay dying in her bedroom at 817 East 46th street. And yesterday afternoon the chapel organ at Boydston's undertaking parlors played "Nearer, My God to Thee" for an old soldier's funeral, while she waited for the inquest to start.

Changes Her Story.

Thursday night at the Hyde Park station she insisted that Kolstedt's ad-

Chicago Tribune, April 5, 1924

Beulah's beauty became an object of prime consideration while attorneys were choosing a jury May 22, 1924, to try her for murder. The *Tribune* reported, "A nod of her pretty bobbed head: four bachelors were accepted as jurors. A pouting 'No' (from Beulah): peremptory rejection by her attorney, William Scott Stewart." The *Tribune* also reported, "The state dismissed those who said they weren't sure the effects a pretty woman might have on them."

TRIAL

The twelve jury members were chosen on May 22, 1924, and Beulah's trial was ready to proceed. Almost as many were excused from the trial for telling the court they believed her guilty.

"Too damned many women gettin' away with murder!" growled one of them.

One was let go for saying she should be acquitted.

"Kalstedt got what was coming to him—the fool! In a married woman's apartment," he said.

In a blow to Beulah's defense, the judge admitted all of Beulah's supposed confessions. The one where she said she killed Kalstedt to defend her honor. The one where she admitted to shooting him in the back as he turned to leave her. And the one where her attorney said it was both lovers who reached for the gun.

Would the jury believe any of them?

Beulah talks with her attorneys, Stewart, left, and W.W. O'Brien, during her murder trial in 1924.

Beulah—described by Maurine as pale, not quite as pretty and wearing a new brown, satin crepe dress with fur piece thrown over one arm—reiterated for the jury that she was the first to grab the gun and shot Kalstedt dead.

O'Brien portrayed his client as a career woman, a modest housewife ambushed by "bum" Kalstedt on her afternoon off from work. She knew he was desperate for booze and gave him a dollar in hopes he would go away for good, but he returned and she was fearful. She took a drink to satisfy Kalstedt, then turned on the phonograph to drown out the man's loud, drunken voice. Kalstedt threatened Beulah, boasting about serving time for "having his way with a woman," O'Brien said. Just when she went for the phone to call her husband at work, that's when Beulah noticed Kalstedt eyeing the revolver on the bed. She grabbed it, turned around, and that's how he was shot in the back.

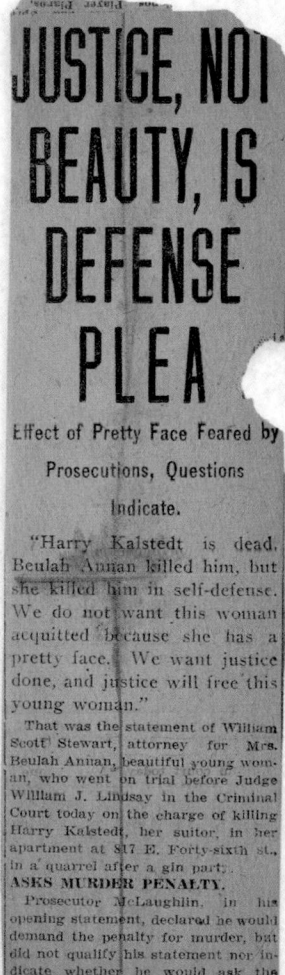

JUSTICE, NOT BEAUTY, IS DEFENSE PLEA

Effect of Pretty Face Feared by Prosecutions, Questions Indicate.

"Harry Kalstedt is dead. Beulah Annan killed him, but she killed him in self-defense. We do not want this woman acquitted because she has a pretty face. We want justice done, and justice will free this young woman."

That was the statement of William Scott Stewart, attorney for Mrs. Beulah Annan, beautiful young woman, who went on trial before Judge William J. Lindsay in the Criminal Court today on the charge of killing Harry Kalstedt, her suitor, in her apartment at 817 E. Forty-sixth st., in a quarrel after a gin party.

ASKS MURDER PENALTY.

Prosecutor McLaughlin, in his opening statement, declared he would demand the penalty for murder, but did not qualify his statement nor indicate whether he would ask the death penalty.

An unknown Chicago publication May 22, 1924

Beulah sits on the witness stand May 24, 1924, the day she was acquitted.

VERDICT

After Beulah took the stand one more time in a new, navy twill dress adorned with a crystal necklace, Maurine wrote, "(S)he made her debut as an actress. And the jury laughingly nominated the youngest of their sheiks as a Rudolf for the titian haired sheba."

Beulah closed her eyes, then told the jury, "I told him of my—delicate condition. But he refused to believe me—and boasted that another woman had fooled him that way, and that he had done time in the penitentiary for her. . . . 'You'll never send me back!'"

On cross-examination, Assistant State's Attorney William F. McLaughlin based his main argument on the witness' credibility or lack thereof: "You have seen that face, gentlemen. It's probable that she hadn't had many men tell her to 'go to hell,' and that was why she went for the gun!"

McLaughlin was right, the jury had seen her face. Her beautiful, sad face.

In under two hours, they decided Beulah's fate: On their third ballot, all twelve men agreed Beulah was not guilty. All twelve would pose for a photo with her and her husband before leaving the courtroom.

Beulah, center, is all smiles as she thanks the jury after her acquittal with her husband, Annan, on her right and attorney Stewart on her left, on May 24, 1924.

'I LOVED HARRY,' HE FOOLED ME, I KILLED HIM'

Kolstedt and Woman Quarreled Over His Past Life and Slaying Followed.

'HE WOULD HAVE SHOT ME'

'I Slid Into the Bedroom and Got the Gun First, Whirled and Fired.'

BY LEOLA ALLARD.

Beulah May Annan sank into a chair in her county jail cell last night, dropped her red head into her small hands and sobbed out her first direct story of how and why she killed Harry Kolstedt.

The iron nerve that had kept her comparatively calm all day in the face of a murder charge and the last stimulating effect of her red wine intoxication had gone.

She was just a pretty bundle of femininity—the prettiest, by all odds, ever held in the county jail on a slaying charge.

Fell in Love With Harry.

"I'm just a fool," and she wrung her hands, that had been powdering her nose all day in jail and at the coroner's inquest. "I'd been married to Albert four years. I haven't any excuse except that Harry came int...

Chicago Herald and Examiner, April 5, 1924

SELF-DEFENSE PLEA GAINS HER FREEDOM

Thanks Each Member After Verdict.

BY MAURINE WATKINS.

Beulah Annan, whose pursuit of wine, men, and jazz music was interrupted by her glibness with the trigger finger, was given freedom last night by her "beauty proof" jury.

The jury retired from Judge Lindsay's court at 8:30 and at 10:20 brought in the verdict "Not guilty" on the third ballot, acquitting her of the murder of her admirer, Harry Kalstedt, in her apartment, 817 East 46th street, on April 3. The fair defendant thanked the jury all around, assisted by her faithful husband, Al.

"O, I can't thank you!" she said, flashing a glance at each one as she pressed his hand. "You don't know, you can't know—but I felt sure that you would——" Her appealing glance ...d the sentence.

...band Nearly Overcome.

..., who has stood by her ...ight he found the man

Chicago Tribune, May 25, 1924

CROWD CHEERS, BEULAH SMILES AT VERDICT

Mrs. Annan Freed in Slaying of Harry Kalstedt After 1 Hour and 55 Minutes Debate.

HUSBAND RUSHES TO SIDE

Spectators Ignore Judge's Orders for Silence, and Are Rebuked; Woman Greets Jury.

Mrs. Beulah Annan, called "Chicago's most beautiful slayer," was found not guilty last night by the jury which tried her on the charge of murdering Harry Kalstedt.

The jury, which was locked up at 8:25 p. m., announced that it was ready with the verdict at 10:20 o'clock—one hour and fifty-five minutes after retiring.

It was understood that the first ballot taken stood ten for acquittal and two for conviction.

The two who voted at first against the beautiful defendant, according to reports from the jury room, quickly and graciously yielded to the urgings of the ten who desired to give the woman her freedom.

Applause From Crowd.

Disregarding Judge William Lindsay's warning, issued just before the verdict was announced, the mass of men and women jammed in the courtroom broke into applause and hurrahs as the words "not guilty" were uttered.

Beulah accepted the verdict with

Chicago Herald and Examiner, May 25, 1924

"Beulah Annan, whose pursuit of wine, men and jazz music was interrupted by her glibness with the trigger finger, was given freedom last night by her 'beauty proof' jury."

—MAURINE WATKINS, CHICAGO TRIBUNE, MAY 25, 1924

Beulah, left, hugs her mother, Mary Neel, just after Beulah's acquittal on May 24, 1924.

AFTERMATH

Beulah was free. She packed her belongings and left the jail with her husband, Albert, by her side. Three months later, he filed for divorce, leading Beulah to exclaim to the *Tribune*, "I'm through with men. I will never marry again."

BEAUTIFUL BEULAH   AGAIN TO COURT   SUES HUSBAND WHO DEFENDED HER

SHE KILLED ANOTHER MAN—BUT HE STUCK BY HER LOYALLY.

HIS LOVE WAS WELCOME— THEN

ALBERT'S TOO SLOW FOR ME

"TOO SLOW."
Beulah Marie Annan after she had been freed of a murder charge, declared her husband was "too slow for her."

SPURNS FAITHFUL MATE.
While a phonograph ground out the refrain, "Hula Lu, the Girl Who Never Could Be True," Harry Kalstedt was shot and killed by Beulah in her apartment.

MUSIC AND MUCH MOONSHINE.
On the witness stand Beulah admitted killing Kalstedt, declaring she begged him to leave before her husband returned, but that the "other man" said: "To h—l with your husband," and that they "took another drink," and that a quarrel followed.

"OLD FASHIONED-HOME BODY."
Now that the two years' limit is up, the woman who declared that the faithful husband "was too slow for her, doesn't like to go out evenings for a good time. He is just an old-fashioned home-body," is seeking a divorce in order that she may have a good time.

*Chicago Evening American,
June 15, 1926*

Facing page: Three months after the trial, Beulah and the husband who stuck by her side, Annan, divorced. In 1927, Beulah married her third husband, Edward Harlib (shown here), but they would divorce four months later.

Beulah was again front-page news on January 18, 1927. She was to be married that same day. Her third husband: Edward Harlib, former boxer and current parking garage owner. They had met six months prior at a party and were heading to Crown Point, Indiana, a border-city haven for quickie, no-wait weddings. His family was against the marriage—his brother claimed Harlib was still married to his first wife—but Harlib proceeded with the couple's plans. He had already purchased a new home for his bride in Barrington and intended to settle there upon returning from a honeymoon in Los Angeles.

Reporters asked Beulah if she had heard of the new play "Chicago," whose main character, Roxie Hart, resembled her. She said she had and was anxious to see it.

Beulah's third marriage ended in divorce fewer than four months later.

Under the fictitious name Dorothy Stevens, Beulah, not yet thirty, entered the Chicago Fresh Air Hospital for treatment of peritoneal tuberculosis. She died of the disease at 3:05 p.m. March 10, 1928, but not before she reconciled with her long estranged father, John Sheriff. Her mother, Mary, accompanied her body back to Kentucky for burial.

The simple funeral held at Mount Pleasant Cumberland Presbyterian Church in Utica, Kentucky, was attended by her parents and all three former husbands.

Ironically, Maurine Watkins used Beulah's life as inspiration not just for the role of Roxie Hart in "Chicago," but also for a short story she published shortly before the Kentucky-born slayer's death titled "Butterfly Goes Home." It relates the death of a girl whose experiences were similar to those of Beulah and her burial in the tiny town from whence she came.

The death certificate for Dorothy Stevens, a pseudonym used by Beulah when she entered the Chicago Fresh Air Hospital, shows she died of tuberculosis on March 10, 1928. Her death certificate says she was twenty-five years old, but there's no way to confirm her age since her birth certificate is missing from Kentucky vital records.

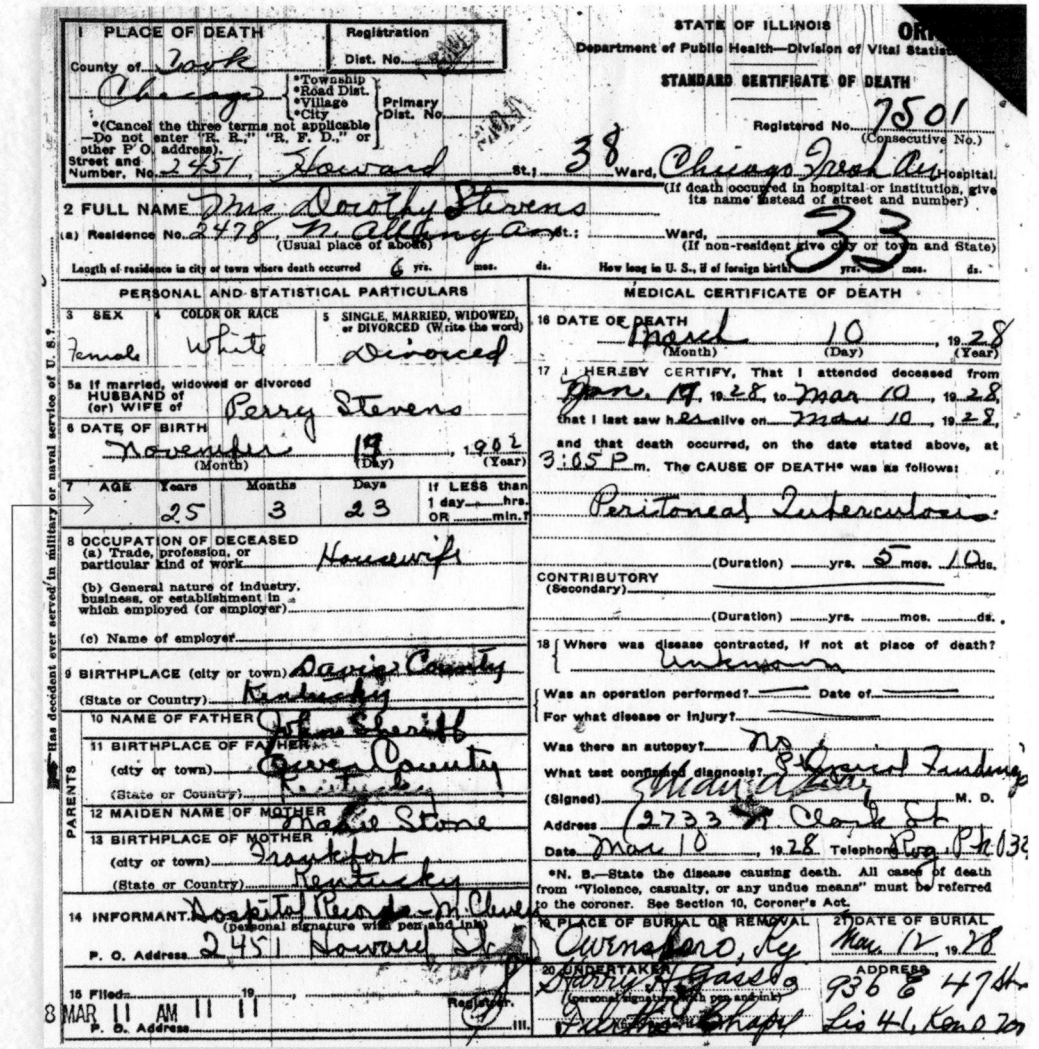

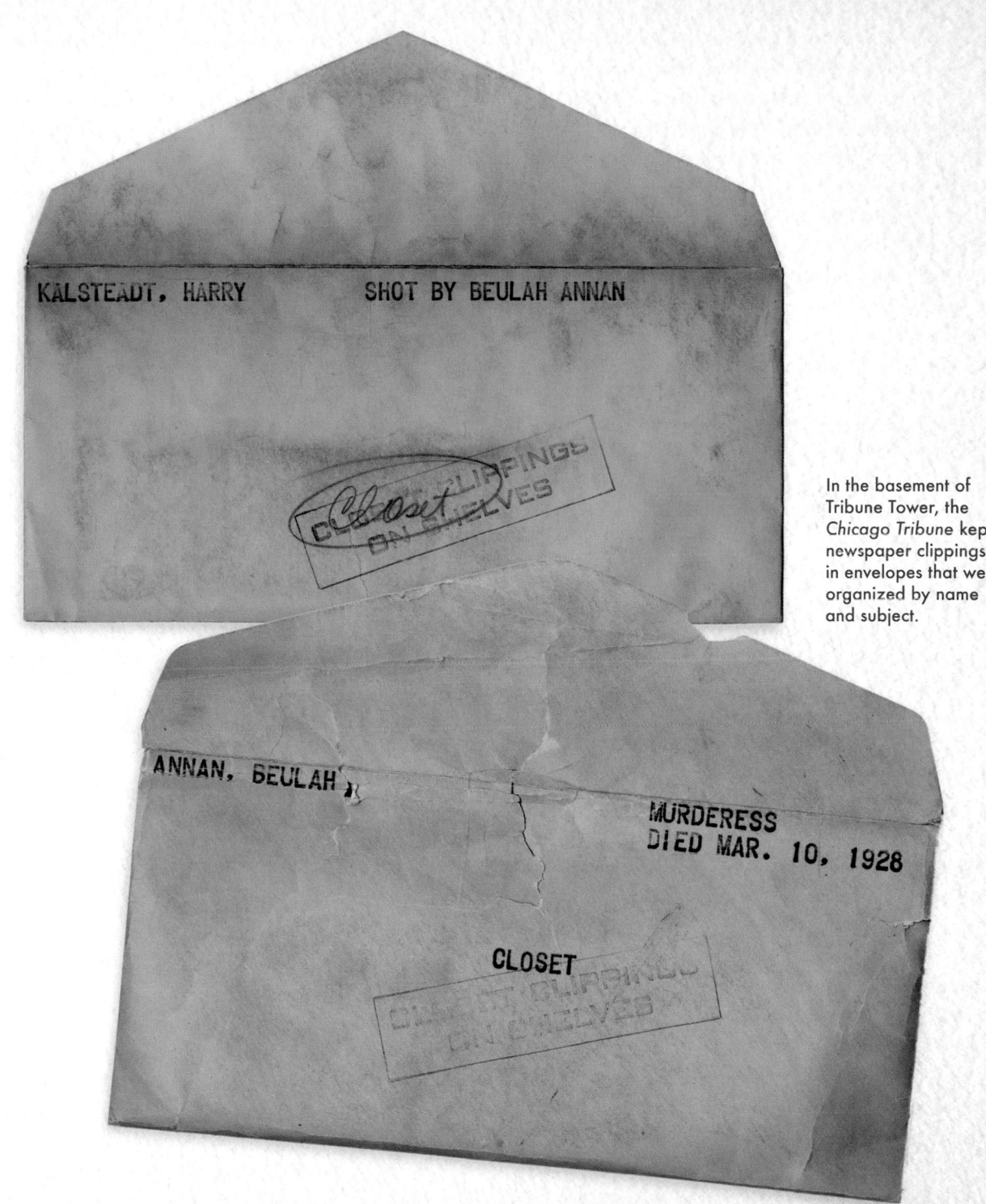

In the basement of Tribune Tower, the *Chicago Tribune* kept newspaper clippings in envelopes that were organized by name and subject.

NAMING ROXIE HART

How do you choose a name for the fictional murderess who's based on the real "prettiest woman ever accused of murder in Chicago?" For Maurine Watkins, the inspiration probably came from an earlier blockbuster trial that took place in her hometown when she was still in high school.

The young female witness? Roxie Hart.

On October 24, 1913, Crawfordsville, Indiana, farmer Walter Runyan shot friend and hired farmhand Artie Stull to death before turning himself in to local authorities. Runyan had hired Stull, a 1911 graduate of Crawfordsville High School, to help him raise money to attend the University of Notre Dame.

Why would two close friends end up in a fight to the death? "Gossip and scandal ran a race all through the trial," the *Indianapolis News* would later report.

"Clandestine correspondence" was at the heart of the case, which went to trial on January 13, 1914. Edith Runyan, the defendant's wife, admitted to passing fourteen letters to the younger Stull. In a letter from Stull to Edith Runyan, he mentioned his illegitimate birth and threatened to "throttle the damned, low-down son of a gun who ever mentioned it to him." The defense's position was Stull was in love with Edith Runyan and wanted to kill her husband, his good friend, who he believed knew of his origin story and began spreading it around town.

Walter Runyan told Stull that he and his wife's cousin, Roxie Hart, were secretly corresponding. Hart wrote a letter to herself in care of Walter Runyan, who then steamed it open, read it and sealed it up again before writing to Hart to say it was "awful sweet." The prosecution maintained Stull was killed by Walter Runyan to keep the affair secret.

Meanwhile, friends and neighbors were enlisted to carry these letters back and forth between recipients. This in a town where witnesses testified that "steaming open letters, reading them and sending them on their way" was not unusual, and whenever a telephone on a line rang, "every subscriber on the line listened to the conversation going on."

The five-week trial was so well attended—mostly by women, according to the *Princeton Clarion News*—that overflow seating for five hundred people was set up on a lower level of the courthouse. Robbers took advantage of homes vacant during the day, including the house owned by the defendant.

In an effort to clear her own name, Hart traveled from her home in Centralia, Illinois, more than three hours away, to testify during the trial.

During her almost two days on the witness stand, Hart said she visited the Runyan home several times and admitted to flirting with Walter Runyan, but she insisted nothing improper took place. Hart also said Walter Runyan would often put his arms around her, and hug and kiss her—even in his wife's presence. "None of us thought anything of it. It was just Walter's way," Hart said.

Walter Runyan took the witness stand in his defense, stating, "I never violated her chastity and our relations were never of a criminal nature."

After deliberating for just thirty-five minutes, the twelve-man jury returned a not guilty verdict for Walter Runyan.

Indianapolis News, January 29, 1914

Called the most stylish woman on Murderess Row, Belva Gaertner poses for a cameraman in an undated photo.

CHAPTER THREE

BELVA GAERTNER

"Too drunk to remember shooting gentleman-friend found dead in her motor-car in front of her apartment."

—*CHICAGO TRIBUNE*, OCTOBER 16, 1927

J UST ONE DAY AFTER a coroner's jury recommended she be held without bail, forty-year-old Belva Gaertner ruminated on the events that landed her in Cook County Jail: "Of course, it's too bad for Walter's wife, but husbands always cause women trouble." The dazzling, fashionable "divorcee of frequent newspaper notoriety" would know: She had been married or partnered with a man since she was sixteen years old and had a litany of last names— Pccpo, Oberbeck and, finally, Gaertner—to prove it.

For three months, automobile salesman Walter Law, a married man with a toddler son at home, and Belva spent their nights together visiting Chicago night-clubs and drinking illegal liquor. Their last rendezvous—in the early morning of March 12, 1924—ended in murder. Two police officers would discover Law's body slumped over the steering wheel of Belva's Nash sedan, a gift from her ex-husband, in front of her South Side apartment. He was found near a bottle of gin with a gunshot wound to the head—delivered by Belva's pistol, also a gift from her ex-husband. Of that night Belva said, "(G)in and guns—either one is bad enough, but together they get you into a dickens of a mess, don't they."

Whereas Beulah Annan had once professed she'd give her own life to have her lover be alive again, Belva told a reporter no sweetheart is worth killing. "I liked him and he loved me—but no woman can love a man enough to kill him. They aren't worth it, because there are always plenty more."

Belva was a wannabe cabaret performer, a polished, unapologetic woman who inspired the Velma Kelly character in Maurine Watkins' "Chicago."

A photographer captures an intimate portrait of Belva in her cell at Cook County Jail in 1924 as she awaits trial for the murder of Walter Law.

BIOGRAPHICAL DETAILS

Though no birth certificate exists, other records indicate Belva Eleanora Boosinger was born to farmer and Civil War veteran Charles Boosinger and his wife, Mary Jane, on September 14, 1884, in Litchfield, Illinois, which is about an hour south of Springfield and an hour northeast of St. Louis. At the time, the town was known for its railroad junctions and steam-powered mill, which was capable of producing up to two thousand barrels of flour a day. Later, it would become a tourist destination along U.S. Route 66.

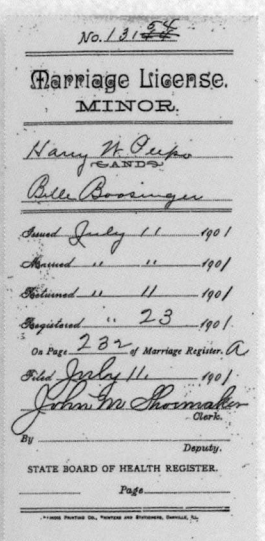

Belva and a younger sister, Malinda, were placed in the Illinois Soldiers' Orphans' Home in Normal, about two hours north of Litchfield, for several months in 1900 until their mother came to retrieve them. Their father died in 1889.

Seventeen-year-old Belva married for the first time in 1901. Her husband was twenty-four-year-old Iowa native Harry W. Peepo, who worked as a railroad machinist. They didn't stay together long, however, as he moved to Bloomington, Illinois, and married again in 1905.

In September 1905, Belva married Ernest Oberbeck in Portland, Oregon, though she later told a judge during her 1917 divorce that she couldn't recall the exact date. "I forget just the day. He took the certificate and hid it every time and would not let me have it," she told the Superior Court of Cook County in Chancery. Neither can the state of Oregon; there's no record of the marriage in the state archives.

Belva claimed Oberbeck abandoned her in September 1909, shortly after they moved to Chicago. "I always done the housework and had his meals and did the washing and the ironing," she said, according to court records. Yet she didn't request any alimony as part of the dissolution of the marriage—but maybe that's because she knew he had no money. "I was angry because he would not work and would gamble what little money he would get."

In Crown Point, Indiana, on June 4, 1917, a month after her divorce from Oberbeck, Belva married William Gaertner, a native of Magdeburg, Germany, who became a naturalized U.S. citizen and ran a successful scientific instrument manufacturing business that is still in operation today. The two—whose ages were separated by at least two decades—bonded over a mutual love for horseback riding.

This third marriage would land Belva in the public spotlight for the first time. At the time, Illinois law prohibited a divorced person from remarrying within

MARRIAGE LICENSE

THE PEOPLE
OF THE STATE OF ILLINOIS,
MONTGOMERY COUNTY.

To any person legally authorized to solemnize Marriage Greeting

Marriage may be celebrated

Between Mr. _Harry W. Peepo_ of _Cedar Rapids_ in the County of _Lynn_ and State of _Iowa_ of the age of _twenty-four_ years and Miss _Belle Boosinger_ of _Litchfield_ in the County of _Montgomery_ and State of _Illinois_ of the age of _seventeen_ years the mother of the said _Belle Boosinger_ having given assent to said Marriage.

Witness _John M. Shoemaker_ County Clerk and the seal of said County at his Office in _Hillsboro_ in said County this _11th_ day of _July_ A.D. 1901 _John M. Shoemaker_ County Clerk.

By _Louis E. Oberle_ Deputy County Clerk

State of Illinois } ss. I _M. J. McKinney_ a _Leo Judge_ hereby certify that Mr. _Harry Peepo_ and Miss _Belle Boosinger_ were united in Marriage by me at _Hillsboro_ in the County of _Montgomery_ and State of Illinois on the _11_ day of _July_ A.D. 1901

M. J. McKinney

Illinois Printing Co. Danville, Ill.

one year of the divorce decree—or two years if they had committed adultery. Those who violated the law faced up to three years in prison, and their new marriage would be voided. The law was also used by unhappy spouses seeking a quick annulment.

That's exactly what Gaertner did on August 3, 1917. Belva immediately filed a petition requesting alimony, which presented a question not tackled previously in Illinois courts—could a marriage in violation of the Illinois statute forbidding remarriage within the year entitle a woman to alimony?

The marriage license for Belva Boosinger (her maiden name), who also went by Belle Boosinger, shows her husband, Harry W. Peepo, was twenty-four years old and Belle was seventeen at the time of her first marriage. The two married on July 11, 1901, in Illinois.

STATE OF ILLINOIS   )
) SS
COUNTY OF COOK   )

                          IN THE SUPERIOR COURT OF COOK COUNTY
                                  IN CHANCERY

BELLE   OBERBECK   )
)
     vs   ) NO. 327,058.
)
ERNEST OBERBECK   )

CHARGE -- Desertion.
SERVICE -- Publication.
DEFAULT.

C E R T I F I C A T E O F E V I D E N C E.

        BE IT REMEMBERED AND CERTIFIED that, on the trial of

the above cause, upon the Bill of Complaint, before His

Honor, JUDGE FOELL, one of the Judges of said Court, on the

21st day of April, A.D. 1917, the same being one of the

regular days of the April Term thereof, the defendant having

been duly served and failed to appear, the complainant in-

troduced the following testimony, to-wit:

APPEARANCES:

CARL A. WALDRON, Esq.,
    solicitor for Complainant;

No one appearing on behalf of
   the Defendant.

Belva's second marriage, to Ernest Oberbeck, resulted in divorce, according to Cook County divorce records from April 21, 1917. Belva's testimony says her husband abandoned her, and the record shows Oberbeck was absent during the divorce proceedings.

BELLE OBERBECK

the complainant, called as a witness in her own behalf,

having been first duly sworn, testified as follows:

DIRECT EXAMINATION
By Mr Waldron:

Q What is your name?   A Belle Oberbeck.

Q Where do you live?   A 626 Oakwood Blvd., Chicago,

Illinois.

Q How long have you lived in the city of Chicago and State

of Illinois prior to the filing of this bill?

A About one year, about seven years prior, I was thinking

at the time he left.

Q How long have you lived in the city of Chicago?

A Eight years.

Q Prior to the filing of this bill?   A Yes.

Q You are the wife of Ernest Oberbeck, the defendant named

in this bill?   A Yes.

Q When were you married to him?

A In 1905 in Portland, Oregon, in the month of September.

THE COURT: Q The day?   A I forget just the day. He

took the certificate and hid it every time and would not let

me have it.

MR WALDRON: Q How long did you continue to live with

Mr Oberbeck?   A About four years.

The Cook County divorce records for Belle (Belva) and her second husband, Oberbeck, circa April 21, 1917. Belva claimed desertion, and her testimony is shown in court documents.

RIDING TO A FALL

Bridle Path Leads to Altar and Thence to Court, Where Counter Suit Will Test Remarriage Law.

SEP 16 1917

SCIENTIST AND SINGER TO TEST REMARRIAGE LAW

Former Wants Annulment and Latter Wants Alimony.

It has remained for a gentle, studious scientist and a rollicking cabaret singer to test the legal question of whether a marriage in violation of the Illinois statute forbidding remarriage within the year entitled the woman to alimony.

The gentle scientist is William Gaertner, 55 years old, a manufacturer of scientific instruments, of 5345 Lake Park avenue. The cabaret singer is his wife, under one of those quick Indiana marriages. Formerly she was Belle Brown on the stage and Mrs. Belle Oberbeck in real life.

Scientist Files Suit.

On Aug. 3 Mr. Gaertner filed a bill for an annulment of his marriage which took place on June 4. The former Mrs. Oberbeck had been divorced from her first husband on April 27. Mr. Gaertner alleged a violation of the Illinois statute forbidding remarriage within the year. The matter came up before Judge Foy yesterday and was continued until Tuesday, when it will be heard by Judge Joseph Fitch.

In the meantime Mrs. Gaertner a petition asking alimony. Her attorney declare that inasmuch as the m of the illegality of the marriage not been established their client itled to alimony. This is de r. Gaertner's attorneys, who inasmuch as under the l effect n marriage there ony.

MR. AND MRS. WILLIAM GA

Chicago Tribune, September 16, 1917

Instead of challenging the law, the couple ended up waiting and marrying again—this time legally—in Cook County on August 15, 1918. They stayed together almost two more years before Gaertner filed suit for divorce, making headlines yet again with the pair's troubles. This time, each spouse hired private investigators—sixteen altogether—to spy on the other. The *Tribune* reported that detectives hired by Gaertner to track Belva "followed as was Mary by her little lamb. The eight sleuths accompany her to the theaters, the shopping district, the telephone, even to the mailbox."

Divorced—again—on May 7, 1920, Belva was no longer a kept woman. "You see, my divorce left me with $3,000, my car, my furniture and a billiard table—that was the table from which Mr. Gaertner took the balls and hid them when I insisted on playing with my detectives who were watching his detectives who were watching me."

Belva earned another headline for her new career: taxi driver. "Well, I just can't take orders from anyone. Therefore I can't hold a job. I must be my own boss," she said. "But I shall not drive at night and I won't make trips into the suburbs. There are too many holdup men."

"Well, I just can't take orders from anyone. Therefore I can't hold a job. I must be my own boss."

—BELVA GAERTNER, *CHICAGO TRIBUNE*, JULY 10, 1920

Belva as she appeared during her venture as a taxicab driver in 1920.

"I don't know. I was drunk."

—BELVA GAERTNER, *CHICAGO TRIBUNE*, MARCH 12, 1924

THE INCIDENT

At 1 a.m. March 12, 1924, two policemen were walking on Forrestville Avenue when they observed a woman entering a Nash sedan in which a man was seated. Shortly thereafter, they heard three gunshots. Hurrying toward the car, the officers discovered the woman was gone but the man, later identified as Walter Law, was dead. Police used the vehicle's license plate to track the woman to her nearby apartment, where she paced the floor while wearing a bathrobe—her blood-drenched karakul coat, green velvet dress and silver slippers lay piled on the floor. She denied knowing anything about Law's death.

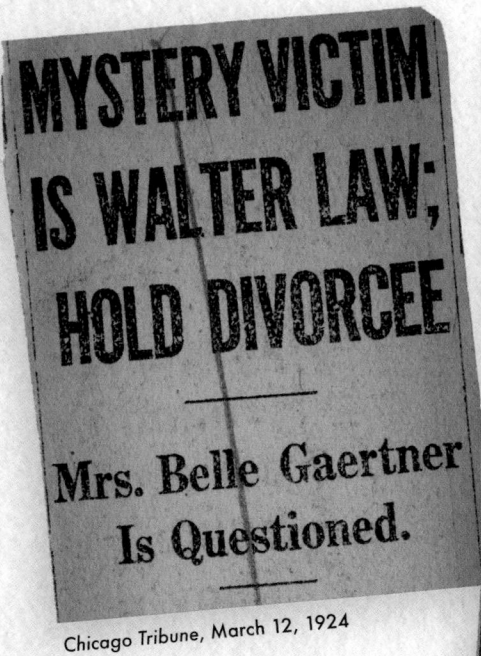

MYSTERY VICTIM IS WALTER LAW; HOLD DIVORCEE

Mrs. Belle Gaertner Is Questioned.

Chicago Tribune, March 12, 1924

(Picture on back page.)

Mrs. Belle Brown Overbeck Gaertner, a handsome divorcée of numerous experiences with divorce publicity, was arrested at an early hour this morning after the police had found the dead body of Walter R. Law, an automobile salesman, in her automobile.

Law had been shot through the head. His body was found slumped down at the steering wheel of Mrs. Gaertner's Nash sedan, a short distance from the entrance to Mrs. Gaertner's home, 4809 Forrestville avenue. On the floor of the automobile was found an automatic pistol from which three shots had been fired, and a bottle of gin.

Police Hear Shots.

The discovery of the shooting was made by Policemen David Fitzgerald and Morris Quinn of the Fiftieth street station. They were walking in Forrestville avenue soon after 1 o'clock. They saw a woman enter a sedan in which a man was seated. The two policemen went on to the corner of 50th street to pull the police call box. While they were at the box they heard three shots.

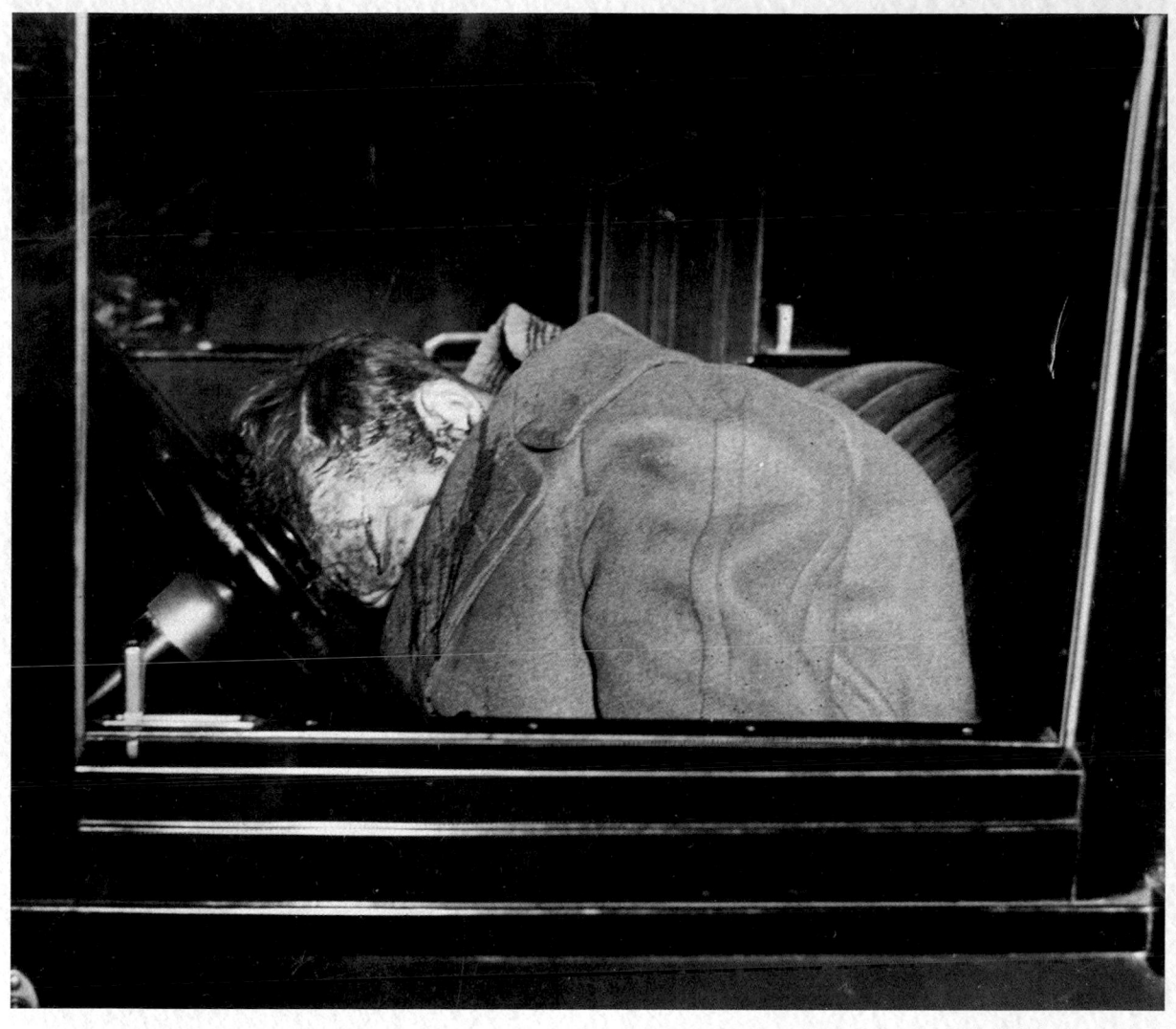

"We were sitting there talking. Mr. Law said something about holdup men and said he was afraid of them. I don't know what happened next. I remember that I saw blood on his face. I was frightened. He didn't say anything and I didn't hear any shots. I just got out of the car and ran away," Belva told them.

"Mystery Victim Is Walter Law; Hold Divorcee" read the headline on the *Chicago Tribune*'s front page on March 12, 1924. It appeared next to a story about two men unleashing a stench bomb into a barbershop operated by female, nonunion barbers. Like Belva, these suspects would also be captured by nearby police.

On March 12, 1924, Law was found with a gunshot wound to the head next to a bottle of gin outside Belva's apartment in Chicago in a car that she owned.

MEET THE DECEASED: WALTER LAW

Walter Law, a Chicago native who was twenty-nine when he was killed, was the youngest of five children born to Harry and Sarah Law. He registered for the World War I draft at age twenty-three and listed his occupation then as chauffeur for the Winton Motor Carriage Co.

Law married Freda Orton on March 7, 1919, and they had a child, Walter Law Jr., on February 11, 1921.

Belva met Law when she purchased an automobile through his car dealership. They then began to meet up weekly—sometimes more often— to go out drinking.

Paul E. Goodwin, a friend and co-worker of Law, told a coroner's jury that Law feared for his life when he was with Belva. "Walter told me Monday that he planned to take out more life insurance, because Mrs. Gaertner threatened to kill him," he testified. "Three weeks before he told me she locked him in her flat with her and threatened to stab him with a knife, unless he stayed there."

Walter Law is buried in Oak Woods Cemetery on Chicago's South Side.

FACING TRUE BILL

Mrs. Belva Gaertner and Walter R. Law, for whose death she is said to have been indicted.

Chicago Herald and Examiner, May 23, 1924

INQUEST

On March 21, 1924, Belva was charged with Law's murder, and the grand jury refused to set bond for her release. The assistant state's attorney presented evidence alleging she shot Law to death while the pair sat in her auto in front of her home. Belva's defense was unique: Could a woman who claims to have been drunk and can't remember if she killed a man be found guilty of the crime?

Sergeant William Sullivan and Lieutenant Joe Dubach question Belva after Law was found dead in her car parked outside her apartment on March 12, 1924.

Belva, center, listens during the coroner's inquest for the death of Law, held at the South Wabash Avenue station on March 12, 1924. The *Tribune* described her attire as a "brown sport dress, a plain black coat with a fur collar and a brown sport hat. Seven diamond rings and a wristwatch."

AWAITING TRIAL

If her religious faith and confidence in her own innocence weren't enough, then Belva knew she would be acquitted of Law's murder if she had the right jury of liberal men. "Now, that coroner's jury that held me for murder? That was bum. They were narrow minded old birds—bet they never heard a jazz band in their lives. Now, if I'm tried, I want worldly men, broad minded men, men who know what it is to get out a bit. Why, no one like that would convict me."

Another reason for her confidence: Her legal bills were paid by her ex-husband, Gaertner, whose business was then manufacturing oxygen regulators for the U.S. armed forces. Gaertner hired three attorneys to defend Belva and hoped for a reconciliation just as soon as the messy matter of her trial was concluded.

TRIAL

Chicago Tribune reporter Maurine Watkins covered Belva's trial, which began with jury selection on June 3, 1924, describing the accused murderess as "a perfect lady" as she patiently watched four men selected to determine her fate: "'Class'—that was Belva. For she lived up to her reputation as 'the most stylish' of Murderess' Row: a blue twill suit bound with black braid, and white lacy frill down the front; patent leather slippers with shimmering French heels, chiffon gun metal hose. And a hat—ah, that hat! Helmet-shaped with a silver buckle and cockade of ribbon, with one streamer tied jauntily—coquettishly—bewitchingly under her chin."

Even Assistant State's Attorney Samuel Hamilton took notice of Belva's hat, asking a prospective juror if he'd be persuaded by it to find her not guilty. The juror staunchly answered, "no," and solemnly agreed that "sex" should have no part in his verdict. It's unclear whether he was chosen to sit on the jury for Belva's trial.

Belva's trial began June 4, 1924, with the defendant, "Calm and poised—but her slim, French-heeled shoes beat the floor, twitched nervously and crossed and re-crossed themselves." The prosecution presented its opening statement, but the defense waived its right. So the questioning of witnesses began.

Dr. Joseph Springer, coroner's physician, noted there were no powder burns near the gunshot to Law's right temple. Had there been residue present, Dr.

Facing page: Still wearing her sport dress, Belva poses for a photographer in her cell at Cook County Jail in 1924 as she awaits trial for Law's murder.

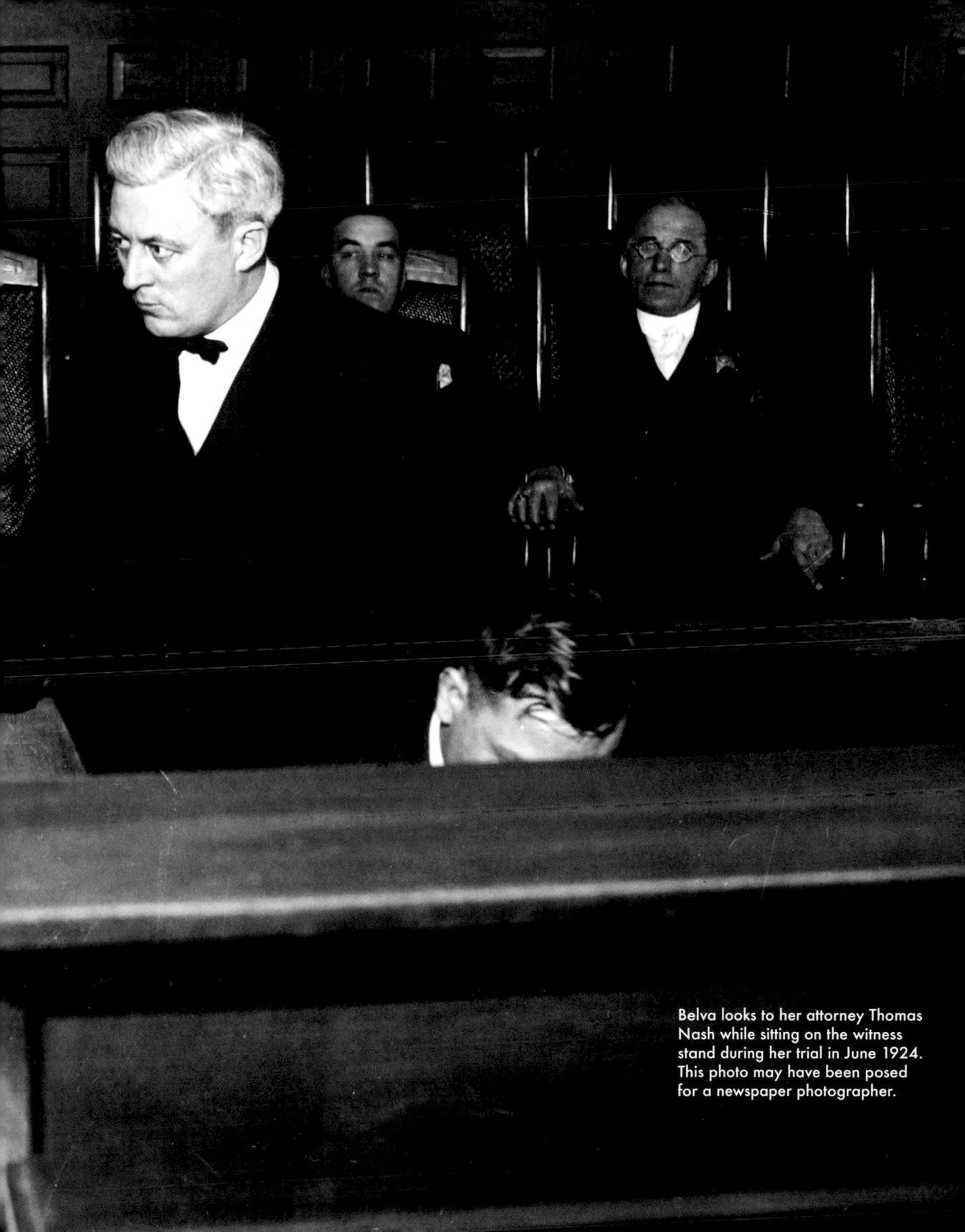

Belva looks to her attorney Thomas Nash while sitting on the witness stand during her trial in June 1924. This photo may have been posed for a newspaper photographer.

NO SWEETHEART WORTH KILLING— MRS. GAERTNER

Belva Hopes for Jury of "Liberal" Men.

No sweetheart in the world is worth killing—especially when you've had a flock of them—and the world knows it. That is one of the musings of Mrs. Belva Gaertner in her county jail cell and it is why—so she says—a "broad minded" jury is all that is needed to free her of the charge of murdering Walter Law.

The latest alleged lady murderess of Cook county, in whose car young Law was found shot to death as a finale to three months of wild gin parties with Belva while his wife sat at home unsuspecting, isn't a bit worried over the case.

"There Are Plenty More."

"Why, it's silly to say I murdered Walter," she said during a lengthy discourse on love, gin, guns, sweeties, wives, and husbands. "I liked him and he loved me—but no woman can love a man enough to kill him. They aren't worth it, because there are

Chicago Tribune, March 14, 1924

MRS. GAERTNER HAS "CLASS" AS SHE FACES JURY

Demure but with an "Air" at Murder Trial.

BY MAURINE WATKINS.
(Picture on back page.)

Belva Gaertner, charged with the murder of Walter Law, was a "perfect lady" yesterday in Judge Lindsay's court as she faced four of the jurors who will decide whether she really did shoot the young auto salesman, found dead in her sedan March 12.

For the lady herself was so "dead drunk" after a night of gin and jazz at the Gingham Inn that she doesn't remember!

And another woman studied the jurors, a sweet-faced woman in heavy mourning; Mrs. Walter Law, who did not know Belva existed till they met at the slain man's inquest, and of the two she seemed more concerned.

Twice a Divorcee.

Cabaret dancer and twice divorcee, Mrs. Gaertner was as demure as a convent girl— yesterday!—with brown eyes dreamily cast downward. Her lid were closed in a not-quite-smile, contour of her cheek was unbroken lines, and rejuvenating rouge m her well on the dangerous side of

Chicago Tribune, June 4, 1924

'FULL OF GIN' AND CANNOT REMEMBER, HER PLEA

Accused Slayer of Walter Law Asserts That Whole Affair Is a Nightmare.

Her brain was so befuddled from drinking gin that she can remember nothing about the events of the early hours of March 12, when she is accused of having shot to death Walter Law, automobile salesman, married and the father of a 2-year-old son, says Mrs. Belva Gaertner.

It's all a nightmare to Mrs. Belva Gaertner, the gin party that had its beginning at the Gingham Cafe and was climaxed in the slaying of Walter Law, automobile salesman, who was married and the father of a 2-year-old son. It happened in the early hours of March 12.

That it was a nightmare is to be the gist of her story from the witness said. she said yesterday in the county jail. Her trial comes up this morning.

"I can't believe it happened," she continued vaguely, her brown eyes following the vagaries of an Easter sunbeam. "All I can say is that I don't remember, and I will be speaking the truth."

KEEPS HER POISE.

Religion and her guiltlessness, according to Mrs. Gaertner, are responsible for her calm poise in the face of the ordeal she cannot hope to evade.

Chicago American, April 21, 1924

"Her sultry eyes never lost their dreaminess as policemen described the dead body slumped over the wheel of the Nash sedan—the matted hair around the wound, the blood that dripped in pools—and her revolver and 'fifth' of gin lying on the floor. Her sensuous mouth kept its soft curves as they told of finding her in her apartment."

—CHICAGO TRIBUNE, JUNE 5, 1924

Springer said, Law might have taken his own life. Defense attorney Michael Ahern picked this theory apart during cross-examination.

Next on the witness stand were the two police officers who discovered Law's body then went to Belva's residence to question her. As they testified, the *Chicago Tribune* reporter noted Belva's appearance: "Her sultry eyes never lost their dreaminess as policemen described the dead body slumped over the wheel of the Nash sedan—the matted hair around the wound, the blood that dripped in pools—and her revolver and 'fifth' of gin lying on the floor. Her sensuous mouth kept its soft curves as they told of finding her in her apartment."

Both the doctor and police officers testified Belva was sober when she was questioned early that same morning about the incident. In a statement, an employee of the Gingham Inn, which the couple visited before navigating the Nash sedan to the driveway outside Belva's apartment, said the establishment "is matched in dryness only by the Sahara; no liquor is sold there, no liquor is brought there, no liquor is displayed there on table, floor, or under cover."

"You're saying that to protect the place where you're employed!" flared the counsel for the defense.

How did the gun end up in Belva's vehicle? A police sergeant who questioned her that night revealed she grabbed it before leaving with Law, "for fear of a hold-up, and put it into the pocket of the car."

With that, the first day of testimony concluded. The *Tribune* reported that Belva "fastened her 'choker,' gathered up her white kid gloves as court was adjourned and was swept out."

Chicago Tribune, June 6, 1924

Belva and her attorneys Michael Ahern, on her left, and Nash, on her right, smile following the jury's verdict of not guilty.

Facing page: Belva on the day the jury acquitted her of murder in June 1924.

VERDICT

On adjudication day, June 5, 1924, Belva dressed accordingly—and the *Tribune* continued its fashion log: "(Belva) wore a new dress—cafe au lait, braided in black, with bell shaped sleeves and deep cuffs—that clung in soft folds to her body. And the cloche hat of a deeper brown matched her eyes and the mink 'choker' softened the lines of her throat. Only her hands with their rosily tinted nails showed her age—and nervousness, as she played with her gloves and fur while the state attempted early in the day again to prove she was 'not too drunk to remember.' "

After almost seven hours of deliberation and eight ballots, the jury's verdict was in: not guilty.

As Maurine Watkins described the scene, "Mrs. Gaertner lost the emotionless poise she maintained throughout the trial, burst into hysterical laughter, threw her arms around her attorneys and thanked the jury, 'O, I'm so happy!' she exclaimed over and over. 'So happy! And I want to hurry out now and get some air!' "

A woman saved from the gallows by her insistence that she couldn't remember how a man died was now ready to dismiss from her memory the experience of being tried for his murder. What would she do next? "I'm going to rewed William, go to Europe and forget," Belva told reporters.

From court, Belva went to her former cell on Murderess Row to gather her elaborate wardrobe then headed to the home of her sister, Malinda. Freda, Law's widow, also retreated to the comfort of her sister's arms after the verdict was read. She apparently fainted then recovered to tell reporters, "There's no justice in Illinois! No justice! Walter paid—why shouldn't she?"

Assistant State's Attorney Harry Pritzker could only summon a three-word reaction to the verdict: "Women—just women!"

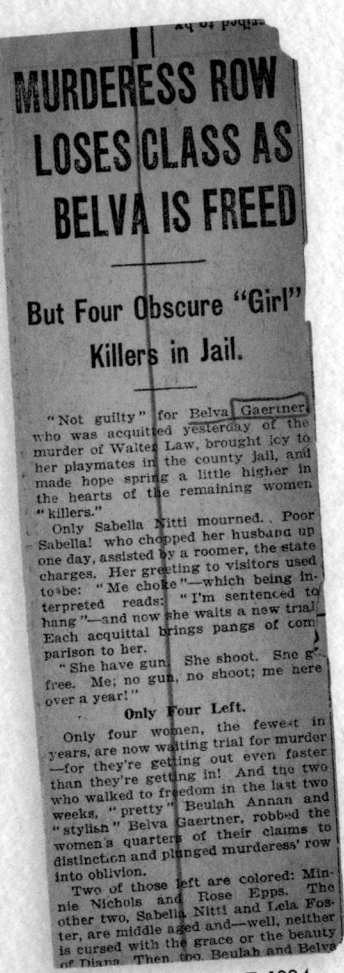

MURDERESS ROW LOSES CLASS AS BELVA IS FREED

But Four Obscure "Girl" Killers in Jail.

"Not guilty" for Belva Gaertner, who was acquitted yesterday of the murder of Walter Law, brought icy to her playmates in the county jail, and made hope spring a little higher in the hearts of the remaining women "killers."

Only Sabella Nitti mourned. Poor Sabella! who chopped her husband up one day, assisted by a roomer, the state charges. Her greeting to visitors used to be: "Me choke"—which being interpreted reads: "I'm sentenced to hang"—and now she waits a new trial. Each acquittal brings pangs of comparison to her.

"She have gun, She shoot. She go free. Me; no gun, no shoot; me here over a year!"

Only Four Left.

Only four women, the fewest in years, are now waiting trial for murder—for they're getting out even faster than they're getting in! And the two who walked to freedom in the last two weeks, "pretty" Beulah Annan and "stylish" Belva Gaertner, robbed the women's quarters of their claims to distinction and plunged murderess' row into oblivion.

Two of those left are colored: Minnie Nichols and Rose Epps. The other two, Sabella Nitti and Lela Foster, are middle aged and—well, neither is cursed with the grace or the beauty of Diana. Then, too, Beulah and Belva

Chicago Tribune, June 7, 1924

VICTIMS— Mrs. Walter Law, widow of the slain automobile salesman, and her son, Walter Jr. This photo was taken at the time of the tragedy two years ago.

Chicago Herald and Examiner, August 15, 1926

"There's no justice in Illinois! No justice! Walter paid— why shouldn't she?"

—FREDA LAW, CHICAGO TRIBUNE, JUNE 6, 1924

Belva poses for a news camera circa 1926, a few years after she was acquitted of murder. The *Tribune* reported on her remarriage to William Gaertner and eventual divorce from the wealthy businessman.

AFTERMATH

Though Belva would describe her trial as a "terrible strain," the *Chicago Tribune* called her three-month stay in jail a "rest cure." Several of her fellow inmates lamented her departure from Murderess Row. The *Tribune* wrote, " 'The place ain't the same without her,' they mourn for she was the best dancer, the best card player among them. She also was a source of income for a few, paying them to wash and iron her clothes."

Gaertner and Belva did remarry for a third time on May 2, 1925. They would continue to break up and make up while traveling together to exotic destinations, including Puerto Rico and Cuba. But in July 1926, Gaertner filed for divorce again, alleging Belva tried to kill him, to which she responded, "I don't just remember what it was we quarreled about— nothing much. It wasn't unusual for him to get angry at me and refuse to speak for weeks at a time." In a *Tribune* story published a month later about the divorce, Belva vowed to get her share: "Yes, of course I shall ask for plenty of alimony."

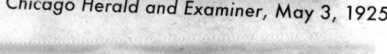

Chicago Herald and Examiner, May 3, 1925

A postcard published in the *Chicago Tribune* on March 13, 1924, shows Belva and her husband, Gaertner.

Yet, Gaertner stuck with Belva—even after she continued to make headlines. He remained her husband after she was held by police under suspicion of driving while intoxicated on November 2, 1926, and then requested a jury trial. He remained married to Belva when she reported thieves stole a carton of cigarettes—and nothing else—from her home while she was out of town in April 1927.

When Gaertner died at his home on December 3, 1948, at eighty-four, he left the bulk of his estate—valued at $25,000, more than $261,000 in today's dollars—to Belva. In an unusual move, he also placed the operation of his business for a period of twenty-one years in the trust of the University of Chicago, which ensured jobs for his veteran employees. He's buried in Mount Greenwood Cemetery in Chicago.

In the 1950s, Belva moved to the Los Angeles area to live near her younger sister, Malinda. She died on May 14, 1965, at Methodist Hospital in Arcadia, California, of cardiovascular disease. She was eighty. Her ashes are interred, next to her sister's, at Mountain View Cemetery and Mausoleum in Altadena, California.

Facing page: The death certificate for Belva shows she died of cardiovascular disease on May 14, 1965, in California.

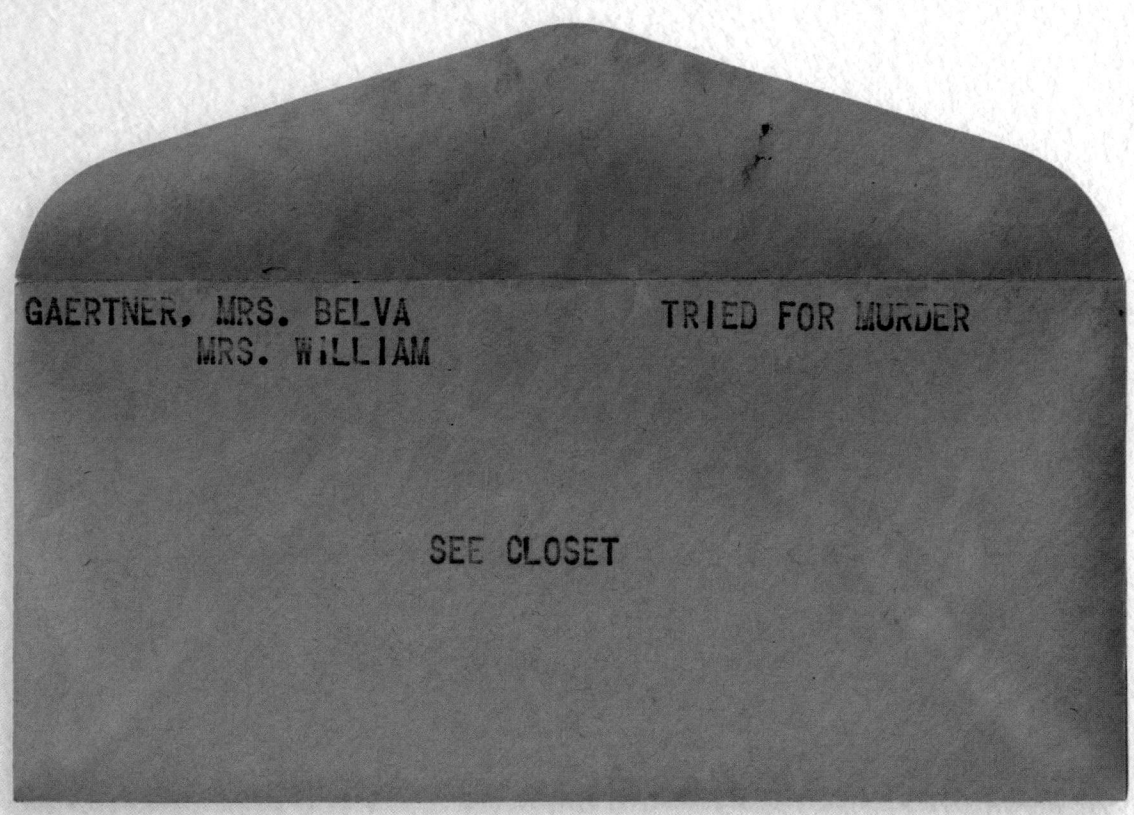

Katherine "Kitty Malm" Baluk is photographed after turning herself in to police and confessing her involvement in the death of Edward Lehmann, circa 1923.

CHAPTER FOUR

KATHERINE KITTY MALM' BALUK

"Packed a gat where most girls
harbor their love-letters . . .
a life-timer at Joliet."

—*CHICAGO TRIBUNE*, OCTOBER 16, 1927

Though portrayed in "Chicago" briefly as the brash Go-To-Hell Kitty—stealing the spotlight away from a freshly acquitted Roxie Hart—the real-life story of Katherine Baluk is one of melancholy.

Unlike Beulah Annan—the inspiration for Roxie Hart, who abandoned her young son to pursue a more gratifying life for herself—nineteen-year-old Katherine defied her circumstances to provide a better life for her beloved two-year-old daughter. Estranged from a husband who she claimed verbally abused her, the young, poor, uneducated immigrant entrusted few others with her daughter's care. "The only one in this whole damn world I'd let take care of her is my mother. She'd be good to her," Beulah told the *Chicago Tribune* after she was convicted in March 1927. "But I'd never want my mother to tell the baby who her mother was. Not a word."

Katherine had good reason to shield her daughter from her exploits: The company she kept was criminal. After taking up with convicted murderer Otto Malm, who called her "Sweetheart," the two attempted to break into a sweater factory on the night of November 4, 1923, in today's Lakeview neighborhood. They were startled, however, by two men who cruised up in a vehicle, bathed them in beams from their flashlights and demanded to know what they were doing. Shots rang out, wounding both men—one slightly, the other critically—and Katherine, too. The lovers, who referred to each other as husband and wife, dashed away from the scene and into a nearby getaway car.

If not for her desire to see her young daughter again, Katherine could have escaped Chicago forever. She returned, however, to confess her involvement, hoping to see her child. One day after a warrant was issued for her arrest, Katherine walked into the Hudson Avenue police station and said, "Do you want me? I'm Mrs. Malm. I wanted to see my baby."

But her partner in crime was first to confess—telling the court they both fired that night, but that it was a bullet from Katherine's gun that killed one of the men.

Reporters labeled Katherine "Tiger Girl" and "Tiger Woman" as she waved off Malm's confession: "Men, they're brave as the devil, but they can't hold out the way a woman can. Now me, they could beat the hell out of me and I wouldn't of squealed." Yet, beneath the tough exterior were signs of desperation. She claimed to be on a hunger strike, attempted suicide and fainted frequently during her trial.

Her biggest fear was not to be found guilty of the crime but to be sentenced to hang for it. Life imprisonment would not only give Katherine years to build an appeal and pursue her education but also provide opportunities for her mother and daughter to visit.

Katherine was found guilty following a blockbuster trial and sentenced to life in prison. It was a relief. She later said, "I thought for sure they would give me the rope. And when they didn't, I was so surprised I just went all to pieces."

Katherine was portrayed as a tiger in the courtroom, but once incarcerated, she became a kitten. Her commitment to bettering herself was so profound that the prosecutor from her trial became the biggest proponent for her clemency. But there's no happy ending to this story: Katherine died at twenty-eight of a sudden illness, snuffing out her attempt to rewrite her legacy.

A postcard shows
Katherine at age 18.

BIOGRAPHICAL DETAILS

Katherine Walter was born to parents Henry and Margaret in Hungary on July 26, 1904. In 1911, she and her mother traveled to the United States in the steerage of a boat. Katherine's father died when she was just thirteen, leaving her to take care of four younger brothers and sisters. Katherine would later tell the *Tribune*, "We came to Chicago and I went to school until I was in the fifth grade. My mother said there was no need for girls to go to high school—just spend a lot of money on them and then they get married—but fine for the boys. Still, I ain't blamin' my mother for she had no money. So I went to work in a machine factory with her."

At work, Katherine met another immigrant, Max Baluk. Originally from Grodno, Russia, he was at least twenty years her senior and served as a private in the U.S. Army during World War I. Katherine and Max were married on February 7, 1921, but not happily. "Then I learned what rotten names a bad man can call his wife," Katherine later told a reporter.

The bright spot in the marriage was the June 29, 1921, birth of a daughter, also named Katherine but affectionately called "Tootsie." Katherine was floored by her love for the child, though she didn't express it in a civilized way: "'God, I could kill a woman who'd rather have a dog than a kid." Katherine left her husband and sent her baby girl to her mother's house, paying $15 a week for her care.

Otto Malm, who had previously been convicted and sent to prison for committing murder, called girlfriend Katherine "Sweetheart."

During the late summer of 1923, Katherine asked Otto Malm to pose as her husband for half an hour "and smash the face of a dirty man down the street who's tryin' to steal my kid." Malm was a convicted felon who served time in the Pontiac Correctional Center for the February 24, 1915, murder of August Jantzen, who was shot when he stumbled into a grocery store while Malm and several young friends tried to rob it. Malm was paroled in 1917, then returned to the reformatory in 1918 after violating his parole. He was paroled again in 1922.

Katherine and Malm traveled to Crown Point, Indiana, on October 23, 1923, and obtained a marriage license, but it was invalidated because she was still married to Baluk. The duo's partnership was not legal, nor were their extracurricular activities.

"Get Bockelman. He's the man who shot me." —EDWARD LEHMANN, NOVEMBER 4, 1923

A note on spelling: State of Illinois and Cook County clerk records spell the victim's name Edward **Lehmann**. Newspaper clippings, family and court documents, and other records spell his name Edward **Lehman**. The spelling from the official county clerk records has been used here.

THE INCIDENT

In the early morning hours of November 4, 1923, Malm took Katherine to the Delson Manufacturing knitting works, in today's Lakeview neighborhood. He was attempting to break in when they were confronted by a night watchman, Albert Stemwedel, and another man, Edward Lehmann. Malm fired several shots. After Katherine was grazed in the head by a bullet from Malm's gun, the couple retreated to a waiting getaway car. Stemwedel was shot in the right arm. Lehmann was taken to Alexian Brothers Hospital, where he told a detective, "Get Bockelman. He's the man who shot me." He died a few minutes later.

AWAITING TRIAL

Twenty-eight-year-old Walter Bockelman was arrested November 5, 1923, though he claimed he was in a craps game on the West Side at the time of the shooting—and a policeman also involved in the game could corroborate his alibi. Confusing matters, someone else confessed to involvement in Lehmann's murder. Ethel Beck, described as "a 19 year old waitress with six aliases, an unknown Greek husband and three service stripes in the night court," said she and Bockelman committed the crime.

Police captured Malm while he was involved in committing yet another robbery. Malm confessed on November 23, 1923, to slaying Lehmann: "I never heard of Bockelman in my life and I never heard of that Beck girl. I never met either one of them. They had no more to do with that job than a rabbit. My wife and I pulled it."

Beck immediately recanted her confession, but both she and Bockelman were still held by police. Malm said he and Katherine both fired guns, but "right now I

From left: Katherine, Ethel Beck, Walter Bockelman and Malm were all held by police for the murder of Lehmann on December 1, 1923. Both Katherine and Beck, who had never met, confessed to taking part in the robbery, but Beck was found innocent. Beck accused Bockelman, seated next to her, of being her partner in crime in the robbery attempt, but he denied her charges and was also found innocent. Malm confessed his part in the murder but fingered Katherine, saying it was the bullet from her gun that killed Lehmann. Standing behind the quartet are bailiff Fred Strassheim, left, and Assistant State's Attorney John Sbarbaro.

MEET THE DECEASED: EDWARD LEHMANN

Lehmann, circa 1923

The Chicago native, who had been working as a chauffeur, was contemplating a career change. That's why he was accompanying night watch company owner Albert Stemwedel on November 4, 1923.

Lehmann was the son of Paul and Margaret Lehmann, who were German immigrants. He was born June 18, 1904, and had an older sister.

Just nineteen years old, Lehmann was single and living in the Lakeview neighborhood at the time of his death.

Baffled by conflicting confessions, police took Katherine to the scene of the crime, where she reenacted the robbery attempt on November 28, 1923. Policewoman Theresa Johnson stands nearby, left, along with Assistant State's Attorney Sbarbaro, Katherine and Captain John Martin, right.

MOTHER-LOVE TRAP SET FOR WOLF WOMAN

"They'll Not Take Her Alive," Says Malm, Who Told of Her Killing 2.

WAITED DEPUTY WITH GUN

Presence of Little Sister Keeps Her From Shooting; Tesmer Death Laid to Her.

The strangest enigma ever confronting the police department, Katherine Williams Malm—wolf woman and devoted mother; two-fisted, two-gun queen of criminals, and tender hearted, clinging vine wife—hides somewhere in the Chicago underworld today, the key figure in the murders of Edward Lehman November 4 and Richard C. Tesmer last June.

The trail of the girl-wife, whose honeymoon was a series of robberies to obtain her trousseau and to furnish the newlywed nest at 1531 N. La Salle st., has been crossed twice in the last two

Unidentified Chicago newspaper, circa November 1923

A warrant was issued for Katherine's arrest, and the police had a hunch she might come home to see her daughter, Tootsie. She quickly turned herself in to the police but insisted she didn't pull the trigger.

'BAIT' FOR MOTHER

Catherine Baluk, baby of Katy Malm, sought as an accomplice of her husband in the Lehman slaying, is being watched by police in the belief that mother love will triumph over fear of apprehension, and that the woman sought will visit the child. Photo of Catherine by Chicago Evening American staff photographer.

Chicago American, November 27, 1923

think it was a bullet from her gun that killed Lehmann." The getaway car driver, Eric Noren, was also arrested. He pleaded guilty.

Police, who believed Katherine might come home to see Tootsie, kept surveillance on the home of Katherine's mother. A warrant was issued for Katherine's arrest on November 26, 1923.

Katherine, who successfully eluded police and hid in Indianapolis with plans to continue on to New York City, missed her daughter. She turned herself in to police the next day. Katherine, described as "pretty, handsomely garbed, her raven hair bobbed," confessed her involvement in a series of robberies but said it was Malm who shot and killed Lehmann. She didn't have a gun. "I'll tell you what I did, but not what I didn't do," she said.

Katherine is questioned by Martin, left, and Sbarbaro in 1923.

In an effort to sort out who should be charged with Lehmann's murder, Beck, Bockelman, Katherine and Malm were brought together by authorities on November 28, 1923. "The men looked enough alike to be brothers. The girls were strikingly dissimilar," the *Chicago Tribune* reported on November 29, 1923. "Katherine, with her straight black hair was sullen because the officers would not let her 'talk to Otto alone' and Ethel, with her corn-colored bobbed hair appeared nonchalant and indifferent." Later, all four were indicted for Lehmann's murder.

The stress wore on Katherine. She sobbed while speculating on what could happen to her daughter: "There ain't nobody can ever be as good to her as me. God help me to kill her if they ever try to take her away from me."

On November 30, 1923, a matron in charge of the women's section of the West Chicago Avenue police station found Katherine hanging by her bedsheet. "Why didn't you let me alone?" Katherine demanded. "It won't do you any good to save me. I'll end it the next time."

At the conclusion of a preliminary hearing—in which Bockelman and Beck asserted their innocence—Malm stepped forward and announced, "I want to plead guilty to the charge." Bockelman and Beck were exonerated.

Katherine alone stood trial.

Rival Girl 'Killers' Analyzed by Expert

Dr. Neymann Finds Mrs. Malm Has All Traits of the Cavewoman; Ethel Beck Found to Be "a Weakling."

The confessions of two women, each claiming to have been a party to a cold-blooded murder and each having enacted the crime at the scene, have so puzzled authorities they have decided to let the grand jury decide which shall be held for murder.

In view of the fact that the girls are exactly opposite types, The Herald and Examiner asked Dr. Clarence A. Neymann, associate professor of Psychiatry at Northwestern University and former head of the Cook County Hospital, to visit the girls and make an analysis of their traits to find out which is the criminal.

This is the story of that visit.

BY LEOLA ALLARD.

"No ethical conception of life. She would have been a howling success three million years B. C., but today she is an absolute misfit!"

Dr. Neymann had just talked with Katherine Malm, at the West Chicago av. station. She dragged herself out of her cell, and sat dejected and with heavy eyes, telling him her story.

"What would you say if I said you were crazy?" he asked the girl.

"I'd want more than one doctor to say it before I'd be convinced. You would have to prove it, and you would have hard sledding."

Dr. Neymann agreed with her.

"You Mustn't Get Caught."

"What do you think of a man who robs people for a living?" he asked the girl, who tells of the robberies planned in her home night after night by Otto Malm and his pals, and in which she took an active part.

Shrugging her shoulders and shaking the ashes from her cigaret, the girl said:

"It is all right if you get away with it. It's when you get caught that it matters."

"But suppose," said Dr. Neymann, "that you have $10 with which to buy your baby milk and crackers and some one steals it from you."

"I'd call him a sneak," growled this primitive woman, who would be a leader in a tribe in the days when men and women lived in caves.

"That," said Dr. Neymann, "shows that the woman harks back to the period when society was not organized. The cave man period when men and women depended upon physical strength to meet any situation. It was every one for himself, and the only bond there was was the bond of family."

"Why did you confess to this murder?" he asked.

"Because I wanted to see my baby."

"I should think," said Dr. Neymann, "that you would have fled to Mexico?"

"You do, do you; well, how would I get my baby to flee? You don't think I'd go without her?"

"But you are sending this man to the gallows by confessing."

"He squealed first. I knew then I couldn't save him anyway. He hanged himself. That being the

Mrs. Katherine Walters (above) and Ethel Beck

ered too.

"was asked about the crime and the confession it was perfectly normal."

Ethel told of a man named Kline, who, when she was released from Lawndale Hospital, said he would help her and give her a "lift."

"Why did you go through the whole crime and show them how it was committed?" Ethel was asked.

Had to Go the Whole Way.

"Well, they said I did it," was her reply. "If I was goin' to get away with it I had to go through with that part of it."

There is no resentment in Ethel Beck. Life hasn't given her much and she expects exactly nothing. She has a foster mother who promises to send her to her mother's home in the country near Rockford. Yes, she will go and she will stay, and in fact she will do anything she is told.

Only one thing breaks Ethel Beck. It is conversation relative to her morals.

"A high-grade moron. She will do . . . anybody tells her," said . . . mann.

Chicago Herald and Examiner, November 30, 1923

Malm Criminal Type, Character Expert Says

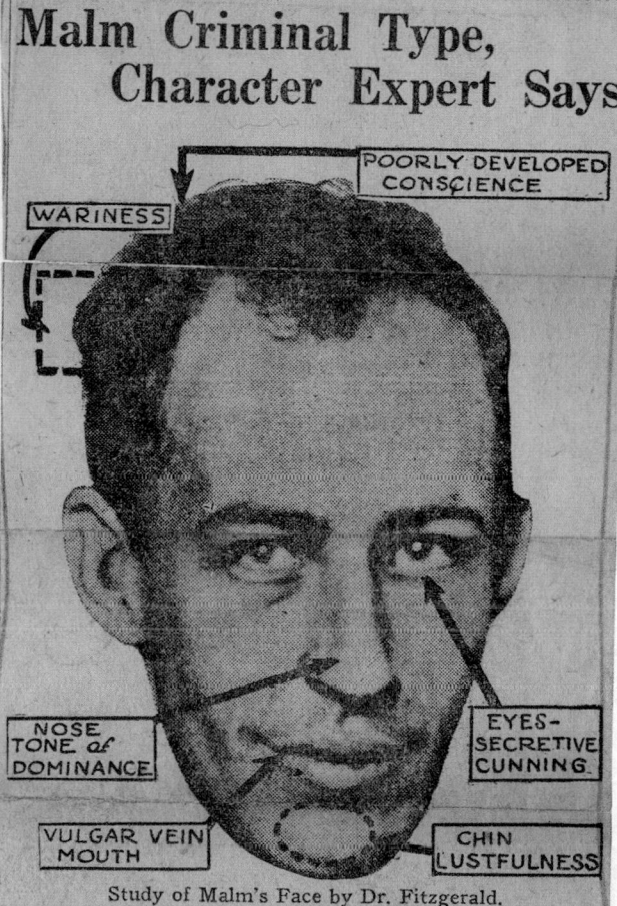

POORLY DEVELOPED CONSCIENCE

WARINESS

NOSE TONE of DOMINANCE

EYES— SECRETIVE CUNNING

VULGAR VEIN MOUTH

CHIN LUSTFULNESS

Study of Malm's Face by Dr. Fitzgerald.

Dr. J. M. Fitzgerald, nationally known character analyst and vocational counselor, yesterday studied at close range the mentalities of Otto Malm and Walter Bockelman. In the past thirty years Dr. Fitzgerald has examined the skulls and minds of hundreds of criminals and his conclusions have been considered of highest value by fellow scientists. After chatting with Malm and Bockelman, strangers to each other, but both held for the murder of Edward Lehman, Dr. Fitzgerald wrote the following reports:

Chicago Herald and Examiner, December 1, 1923

'WOLF WOMAN' ON TRIAL FOR KILLING

Pleads Not Guilty After Husband and Chauffeur Admit Slaying; Other Cases Dropped.

[Photos on Picture Page.]

Dressed in somber black and carrying a prayerbook kept well in sight, Katherine Baluk Malm, "the wolf woman," was placed on trial for murder yesterday while her 2-year-old daughter, "Tootsie," romped about the courtroom before Judge Walter P. Steffen.

Four other defendants, indicted with her for the slaying of Edward Lehman, 18-year-old night watchman, were eliminated from the trial shortly after the opening of court. The state nolle prossed cases against Walter Bockelman and Alvina Timm, alias Ethel Beck, and they were freed.

Husband Pleads Guilty.

Otto Malm, supposed husband of Katherine, and Eric Noren, who drove the car in which they went to the scene of the murder, pleaded guilty, the former after a dramatic catechism by Judge Steffen.

Mrs. Malm, in a clear voice, responded to the judge's question with:

"Not guilty!"

Noren, admitted he drove the car, said he was not guilty of murder and at first declined to plead that way, but when the questioning of veniremen started he interrupted to enter his plea of guilty, which was accepted.

Mrs. Malm seemed utterly undisturbed and unworried. In fact she had no occasion for uneasiness.

"I've got about as much chance for the rope," was the way she put it, "as Otto Malm has for angel

Facing page:
Katherine hugs her daughter, Tootsie, on December 23, 1923. "There ain't nobody can ever be as good to her as me," Katherine said.

Chicago Herald and Examiner, February 19, 1924

"Men are quitters. They're long on talk, but, Lord, when it comes to the showdown, they're yellow."

TRIAL

As prospective jurors were asked on February 18, 1924, if they would be willing to give the death penalty to "this woman, even if she has a child." Katherine projected confidence to the reporters. "Say, I have about as much chance of getting the rope as Malm has of getting angel wings when he croaks," she said.

She pulled out a small Bible, paging through it as men were chosen to determine her fate. She said, "I know it almost by heart, for I was brought up in the Catholic church, you know, even though I am really a Lutheran." It would take five days to complete jury selection—no word on how many books of the Bible she revisited in this timespan.

Katherine's daughter, Tootsie, was also in court for the first day of jury selection, "a plump youngster, well rounded out with leggings and a puffy blue coat and hat." When she saw the back of her mother's head, she jerked the all-day sucker out of her mouth and shouted: "There's mommie. I want to go to mommie." But a bailiff instructed her grandmother that it was against the law for Tootsie to communicate with her mother.

The twelve jurors who decided Katherine's fate pose for a photograph in 1924. The *Tribune* reported, "Each of the jurors went on record during his examination as having 'no conscientious scruples against the infliction of the death penalty, even though the defendant be a woman.' "

Just as confident in the trial's outcome was Assistant State's Attorney Harry Pritzker, who would go on later the same year to prosecute another suspected murderess, Belva Gaertner: "Mrs. Malm is the hardest woman ever to walk into a courtroom. The evidence will show that she fired the shots that killed Lehmann. We will ask that she receive the heaviest penalty the state can inflict." Pritzker, who was the great-uncle to Illinois Governor J.B. Pritzker, said he planned to seek the death penalty for Katherine.

Formerly described as "pretty," *Chicago Tribune* reporters from that day forward bestowed a new moniker upon Katherine: "Tiger Girl" or "Tiger Woman." They would continue to use animalistic terms for her as the trial progressed. On February 25, 1924, the *Chicago Tribune* described her screaming and snarling at a jail guard who offered her a slice of cherry pie—only being "calmed when Warden Wesley Westbrook gave her a piece of peach pie."

Facing page: Katherine reads from a prayer book as the jury is selected for her murder trial on February 18, 1924.

Chicago Herald and Examiner, November 28, 1923

On February 21, 1924, the first day of Katherine's trial, the state introduced a surprise witness—Blanche King, who stayed in the same boardinghouse in Indianapolis as the defendant. King testified that Katherine carried two guns, nicknamed Big Bertha and Little Betsy, with her everywhere, except "when she was eating, when she was sleeping and one other time." King also claimed Katherine boasted about "doing a job at a sweater joint" and pulling a gun on a doctor, forcing him to dress her wound. King's testimony prompted Katherine to faint—twice.

On cross-examination, one of Katherine's attorneys said a bank book—crediting $600 to Tootsie—was missing. King was supposed to bring it to Chicago.

Two days later, Malm's getaway driver, Eric Noren—who had already pleaded guilty to his involvement in the crime—said Katherine said "she'd go along" when Malm proposed breaking into the Delson plant. Then, Stemwedel, the surviving night watchman, declared that at no time the night of the robbery attempt did he see a woman on the premises.

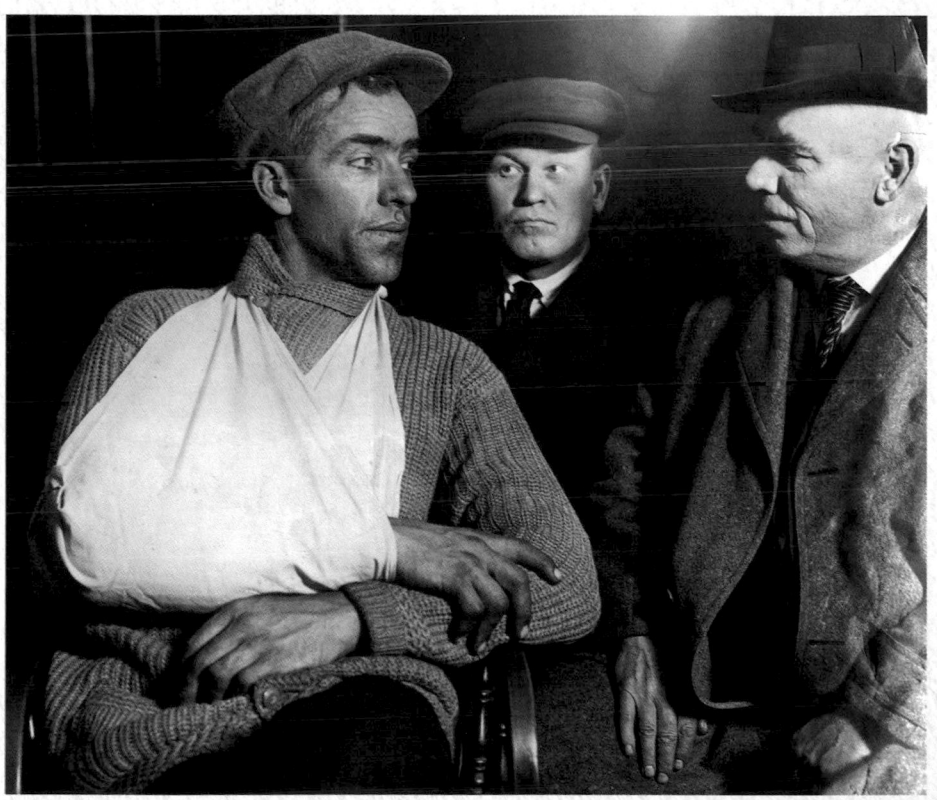

Night watchman Albert Stemwedel, left, who was injured during the attempted robbery, said he never saw a woman that night.

Facing page: Katherine's mother, Margaret Walter, brought granddaugher Tootsie (shown holding a sucker) to the courthouse to see Katherine during the murder trial.

On February 25, 1924, Katherine took the stand in her own defense, confessing she was with Malm at the time Lehmann was slain. This honesty surprised prosecutors, who had expected her to produce an alibi in an attempt to fight the murder charges. "But I didn't know they planned a robbery when I started out with Otto and Eric for a joy ride," Katherine said. "Otto tried to shoot me, too, because he feared I would tell that he had killed Lehmann."

She also confirmed many of King's assertions but refuted ever carrying a gun—let alone two. "No, sir. I never carried or fired a gun in my life."

Facing page:
Katherine took the stand in her own defense during the murder trial, saying she had never carried a gun.

Chicago Herald and Examiner, February 24, 1924

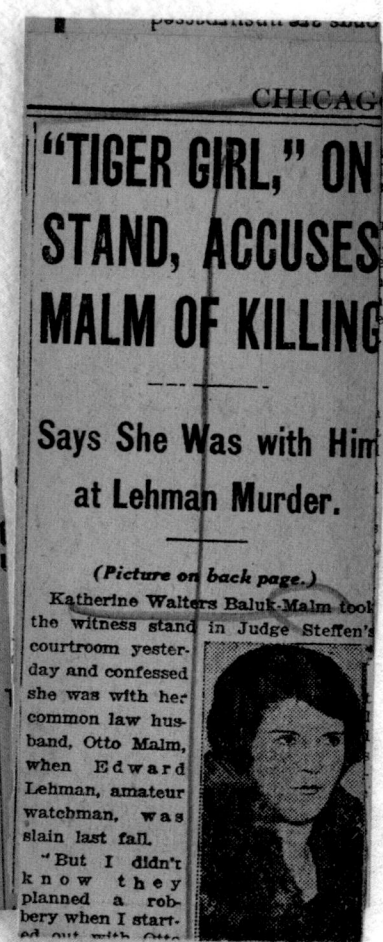

Chicago Tribune, February 26, 1924.

"She waved her arms and shook her black bobbed hair, moaning in a loud voice to the bailiffs gathered about her, 'Keep away. I don't want to see anybody.' Then she fainted."

—*CHICAGO TRIBUNE*, FEBRUARY 27, 1924

A composite image shows Katherine when she was found guilty of Lehmann's murder in 1924.

VERDICT

After the jury deliberated for an hour and twenty minutes, Katherine was found guilty on February 26, 1924.

The punishment of life in prison was reached after the jury's efforts to send her to the gallows failed. Its members believed that though Malm fired the shots, Katherine was "as guilty under the law as he."

After the verdict was read, Katherine flew into rage. The *Tribune* reported, "She waved her arms and shook her black bobbed hair, moaning in a loud voice to the bailiffs gathered about her, 'Keep away. I don't want to see anybody.' Then she fainted."

The courtroom was thrown into disorder. A "great crowd of court fans moved forward to where she lay on the floor. Bailiffs darted here and there while Judge Walter Steffen rapped for order."

Then, deputy sheriffs lifted Katherine from the floor and placed her on a chair. They carried the chair to the prisoners' elevator, then down to the bridge of the jail. She fainted again in her cell.

When it was announced that she had been given a life term in prison, Katherine fainted into the arms of a deputy. Her attorney McCarthy (not pictured) was thunderstruck.

KITTY MALM AND HUSBAND GIVEN LIFE IN PRISON

She Takes Sentence with Apparent Calm.

Katherine Baluk Malm and her common law husband, Otto Malm, were sentenced to Joliet penitentiary for life yesterday for the murder of Edward Lehman. Eric Norine, another defendant, was sent to prison for fourteen years. Judge Walter P. Steffen delivered the sentences.

Mrs. Malm was sentenced after Judge Steffen overruled a motion of Attorney Jay J. McCarthy for a new trial. Malm was sentenced after he entered a plea of guilty to the killing. Norine also pleaded guilty.

In Good Spirits.

Mrs. Malm showed little emotion at the ruling of the court. She appeared in better spirits than at any time since she was arrested, and reiterated that she really expected to be hanged and was so happy when the jury said life imprisonment that she fainted.

Assistant State's Attorneys Harry Pritzker and Robert E. McMillan argued against the motion for a new trial for Mrs. Malm.

Chicago Tribune, March 9, 1924

An emotional Katherine clutches her daughter, Tootsie, while her attorney McCarthy looks on.

KATHERINE GLAD TO ESCAPE ROPE

Overcome With Joy, Not Horror, When Verdict Was Read, Says "Wolf Girl."

Joy, not horror, sent Katherine Baluk Malm reeling to the floor of Judge Steffen's courtroom Tuesday night upon learning that a jury had just sentenced her to life imprisonment for the killing of Eddie Lehmann.

Rocking back and forth in her chair in the hospital section of the women's quarters in the county jail yesterday, she repeated over and over how overwhelmed she was at the jury's leniency.

Expected Death Penalty.

"Everybody had gone so against me that I was sure they were going to give me the rope," she said.

"When I found it was just life, gee, everything went bloo-ey.

"But I'm sure sorry I passed out. My motto has always been 'Take what's coming with a smile.' And I had planned to thank that jury no matter what they done to me. Then that funny feeling came and——"

It is that "smile" which Cook County's latest lifer is turning on

Chicago Herald and Examiner, February 28, 1924

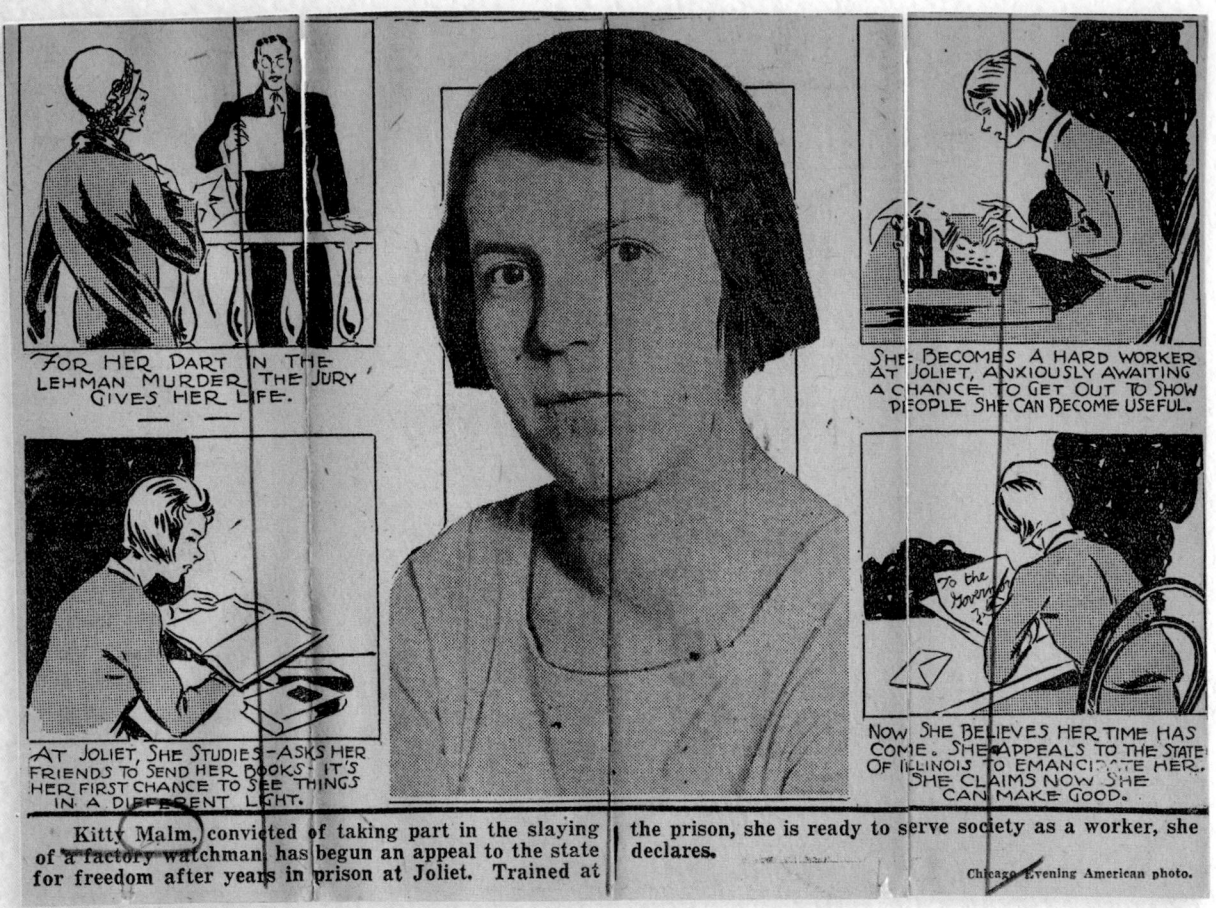

Chicago American, August 20, 1929

"I thought for sure they would give me the rope. And when they didn't, I was so surprised I just went all to pieces."

—KATHERINE BALUK, *CHICAGO TRIBUNE*, FEBRUARY 28, 1924

AFTERMATH

The day after her trial, Katherine told a reporter she fainted because "You see, everything at the trial seemed to go against me. I thought for sure they would give me the rope. And when they didn't, I was so surprised I just went all to pieces."

She also pledged to be a "Tiger Girl" no more: "You'll not find me making any trouble if they put me under lock and key. This rough stuff doesn't get you anything, anyway. If I have to go to prison for a long stretch, I'm going to behave myself and maybe they will let me out sooner."

Katherine pointed to this hardened persona created by reporters as being to her benefit during the appeals process: "My attorney says he is going to take my case up to the Supreme Court. They beat me in the trial because of the things the papers said about me being a 'Tiger Girl' and carrying a gun, but I won't have to go up against that bunk in the higher court."

Both Malm and Katherine were sentenced to life imprisonment on March 8, 1924. She reiterated to the court that she was happy she wouldn't be hanged. "This woman's rights were fully protected," Pritzker said. "She is lucky, in my estimation, in that she is not now facing the gallows. If the defendant had been a man it is safe to say the jury would have voted the death penalty. She went out to kill and now it is the duty of the court to see that the wages of murder are paid her."

On March 12, 1924, her real husband, Max Baluk, sued Katherine for divorce.

Malm killed another man while incarcerated at Joliet Correctional Center on July 18, 1925, and added another life term to his stay in Joliet.

Katherine entered prison in Joliet on May 29, 1924. She became a proficient stenographer, studied typewriting and shorthand, and worked as a clerk in the prison's office. She sought a pardon three times, the latest in 1932. Archdeacon of Chicago Winfred Ziegler came to her defense, saying Katherine wrote him a letter that was thankful for her incarceration: "If I had not been caught, I would be dead now, the way I was living." Lehmann's parents protested any pardon attempt, writing to then-Illinois Governor Louis Emmerson to say, "She got life in prison. Why not give it to her? . . . The victim, the late Edward Lehmann, was our only son that she murdered. Governor Emmerson you may have a son of your own. What would you do if this great disaster fell upon him?"

Years after prosecuting her, Pritzker became her fiercest advocate, working on

'TIGER WOMAN' ASKS LIBERTY

With the public brand of murderess and "tiger woman," Katherine Baluk, known as "Kitty Malm," went to Joliet penitentiary on May 29, 1924, to stay for "the rest of her natural life."

Tomorrow the case of Kitty Malm comes up before the board of pardons and paroles, and pleading for a parole for Kitty will be Harry N. Pritzker, the assistant state's attorney whose prosecution put her in prison, and Bishop George Craig Stewart, head of the Episcopal diocese of Chicago.

"I feel," said Mr. Pritzker, "that the girl received an extremely harsh sentence. After all, she didn't kill any one. Her common-law husband, Otto Malm, shot and killed a watchman, Edward Lehman, during a holdup in 1923, in which she was participating."

Bishop Stewart has forwarded a recommendation for clemency.

Chicago Herald and Examiner, October 10, 1932.

Katherine applied for parole in 1929. It was denied.

October Term, 19 29

9185 Jones

No. 6004

Application for ~~Commutation~~ or Parole of

Katherine Baluk

Convicted of

Murder

at the March Term,

19 24, of the Criminal Court of

Cook County, and sentenced to the Illinois State Penty

at Joliet

for Life

Filed August 13 , 19 29

N. L. Keeler Clerk

Brother

Margaret Walter Petitioner

C/o John R. Horan, 10 N. Clark St.,
Attorney for Petitioner Chicago

Judge NOTIFIED Stmt.

Atty. NOTIFIED Stmt

Pub. FILED EXECUTIVE DEPARTMENT.

JUL 31 1933

(SEE INSIDE)

Edward J. Hughes
SEC'Y OF STATE

STATE'S ATTORNEY PROTEST Aug. 19-1929

PROTEST

COMPLAINING WITNESS

3536 N. Ashland Ave.,
Chicago, Ill.
June 2, 1932.

Governor Emmerson
Springfield, Ill.

Dear Sir:-

In regard to the freeing of the "Wolf Girl" Kitty Malm.
Please look into this matter before you free her. She didn't get
what's coming to her. She got life in prison. Why not give it to
her? She killed and letting her out she's steal and kill again

If we let all the killers out of prison so easy we will
never stop this business of murdering our citizens. This Kitty Malm
was up to you before for her freedom but it wasn't granted to her.
Please stick to it and keep her in prison where she belongs. The
victim the late Edward Lehman was our only son that she murdered.
Governor Emmerson you may have a son of your own what would you do if
this great disaster fell upon him.

This Harry U. Pritzler assistant States Attorney must be
insane to try to have her pardoned after he wanted to give her the
rope. Trusting you we remain

Yourstruly,

(Signed) Mr. Mrs. P. Lehman

3536 No. Ashland Ave.,

Chicago, Illinois.

PROTEST

COMPLAINING WITNESS

Lehmann's parents
wrote a letter pro-
testing a pardon for
Katherine in 1932.

KITTY MALM IS NOW GENTLE AND HAPPY

Kitty Malm, tiger woman of yesteryear, and convicted man killer, who boasted that she "packed two guns and would rather shoot it out with a copper than be caught," today is a sweet, demure, docile, accurate and accomplished stenographer.

And she could, if she but had the notion, leave unlocked prison doors behind her.

But Kitty wouldn't.

The transition from a woman who thirsted for blood and thrilled at robbery with a gun to a woman who loves obedience for its own reward, who works diligently because therein she finds solace, and who smiles throughout the day because her smiles are reflected and make her happier, has taken place behind the cold, stark walls of the women's penitentiary at Joliet.

The champion of Kitty Malm is Mrs. Elmer Ruline, superintendent, in whose office today Kitty is a trusty and a stenographer, and, as Mrs. Ruline puts it, "an exceptionally efficient young clerk."

"EXCEPTIONAL GIRL."

"Kitty could walk from this office ...

Chicago American, date unknown

PRISON TAMES 'TIGER WOMAN'

Petruchio tamed his kate with tongue lashing, but the Joliet penitentiary has tamed Kitty Malm, erstwhile "tiger woman" and convicted man killer, with a typewriter.

She's known now as the model prisoner. She's a "trusty," and every day she's at her steno's desk in hte office of Mrs. Elmer Ruline, superintendent. "An exceptionally efficient young lady," says Mrs. Ruline.

Kitty began serving her life sentence May 29, 1924, for the murder of Edward Lehtmann, night watchman, killed when kittey and her husband, Otto, attempted to rob a knitting factory. She was sullen and morose then, boasting her hate of society and the law. Now—

"If there were more girls in prison like Kitty Malm," says Mrs. Ruline, "we would need no locks. She has endeared herself to all of us by her sweetnes sand charm. She radiates happiness."

Prudence Penny is a nationally known authority on home and household economics. Her column is a daily feature of The Herald and Examiner.

Chicago Herald and Examiner, November 3, 1927

> "The newspapers, in their sense for news, often give titles not warranted. They called her 'Tiger Girl' and the 'Panther Girl,' and all kinds of animal names. But the girl today is no more of a Tiger Girl than any girl who had the same kind of training she has had."

—PROSECUTOR HARRY PRITZKER

behalf of her release. Records show he traveled to Springfield, Illinois, on October 11, 1932, to speak to members of the pardon board, telling them, "This is only one out of a thousand cases I tried while state's attorney on which I feel there is justification for appearing before you gentlemen."

After previously portraying Katherine as the "hardest woman ever to walk into a courtroom," Pritzker admitted she might not have been "as bad as I made her out to be." More likely, she was a product of her environment: "She was raised in practical poverty and had no education of any kind, no home training and by the time she was fifteen she was married to some person who did not amount to anything, and at sixteen was the mother of this child."

Still, he pointed out, "I am not trying to create the impression this girl was lily-white." He said Katherine readily confessed her involvement in the crime while testifying during the trial and that "on cross examination, she convicted herself. She was not trying to conceal anything."

Pritzker told the pardon board he "offered her fourteen years if she would plead guilty. I believe she was ill advised. At no time did I believe she had proper legal advice. But I was a new assistant state's attorney and it was my duty to prosecute." He also admitted he had no evidence she was carrying a gun the night of the attempted break-in at the Delson plant.

Pritzker believed sensationalism also swayed the jury to convict Katherine: "The newspapers, in their sense for news, often give titles not warranted. They called her 'Tiger Girl' and the 'Panther Girl,' and all kinds of animal names. But the girl today is no more of a Tiger Girl than any girl who had the same kind of training she has had."

The following institution record of Katherine Baluk
was received in this office under date of October 10, 1932:

"1924
August 24 - Talking at cell door
November 20 - Talking at cell door without
              permission
November 23 - Passing food from back kitch-
              en
1925
January 1 - Talking in cell house
January 25 - Talking in lower hall after
             bell rang
January 24 - Very impudent
January 3 - Talking in cell house
August 13 - Talking with another inmate
            in her cell
December 27 - Whispering during services
1926
April 18 - Impudent to matron
May 7 - Bad conduct at table
May 16 - Talking in cell house
May 22 - Insolence
May 25 - Talking in cell house
May 28 - Holding mirror out of cell
         door
June 14 - Insolence
July 31 - Swearing at an officer
September 13 - In another inmate's cell
               without permission
November 9 - Bad conduct in dining room
November 29 - Insolence
1927
January 19 - Talking in cell house
January 20 - Talking with girl behind
             her at table
February 22 - Talking across cell house
March 21 - Talking at cell door without
           permission
April 2 - Talking across cell house
April 23 - Talking at cell door without
           permission
May 12 - Talking aloud from cell
May 12 - Talking across cell house
June - Talking in the morning
June - Talking across cell house
June - Talking and very noisy in
       cell house
September 12 - Stopped at doors on balcony
               to talk
October 20 - Going into cell without
             permission
1928
January 23 - Talking at cell door
January 25 - In cell talking with an-
             other inmate
February 22 - Talking at cell door
March 24 - Sitting on floor reading

REJECTS PLEA OF KITTY MALM

Mrs. Katherine Baluk, alias Kitty Malm, known as the "Tiger Girl," who is serving a life sentence for the murder of Edward Lehman in 1923, was refused clemency yesterday by Governor Louis L. Emmerson.

The governor's action was made in accordance with recommendation of the state board of pardon and parole.

Mrs. Baluk has been in the penitentiary at Joliet since her conviction on March 8, 1924, for the murder of Lehman during the robbery of a factory warehouse.

Dr. F. R. Lillie Named U. of C. Biology Dean

Appointment of Dr. Frank R. Lillie as dean of biological sciences at the University of Chicago was announced yesterday. He succeeds Dr. Richard Schammon, who will become dean of medical sciences at the University of Minnesota. Dr. Lillie was a member of the university's original faculty in 1892.

Chicago Herald and Examiner,
May 15, 1931

A list of Katherine's transgressions while she was imprisoned in Joliet was given to the pardon board in 1932.

Following the trial, Pritzker said he met with Katherine and told her: "You go to the institution to which sentenced and make something of yourself. Get in there, study and work hard and if you do that I will appear before the board and I am sure they will give you consideration. She did and I am here."

Before he was excused, Pritzker left the pardon board with this thought: "Any further incarceration will harden the girl to the point where she will be hopeless and will say, 'Well, what is the difference?'"

Katherine's pardon request was denied on December 19, 1932. In its statement to the governor, the pardon board included a list of forty-four instances from 1924 to 1928 in which Katherine was reprimanded. These offenses included talking or whispering at her cell door, in the hall or with another inmate; holding a mirror out of her cell door; swearing at an officer or other bad conduct; going into a cell without permission; and general disobedience and insolence.

She fell ill within a week. Her mother and daughter, then twelve years old, were admitted to her bedside in the prison's infirmary. Katherine died of the flu and bronchopneumonia at Joliet Correctional Center on December 27, 1932, and is buried in Forest Home Cemetery in Forest Park, Illinois.

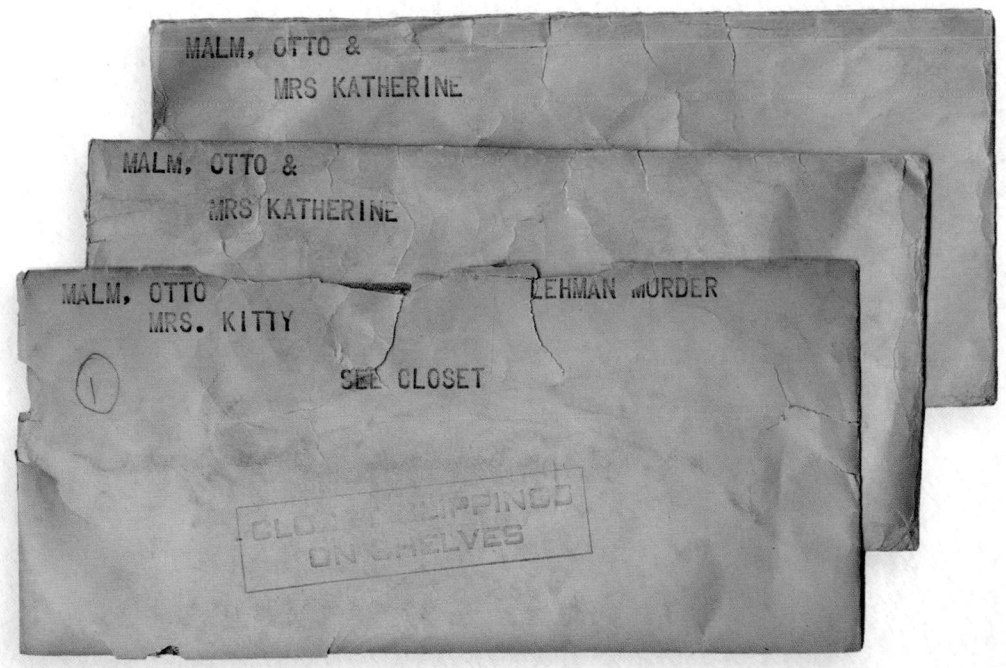

'TIGER WOMAN' DIES IN PRISON; HOPES BLASTED

Kitty Malm Sinks Fast After Promised 'New Chance' Is Denied; Taken by Stratagem

Kitty Malm, "the tiger woman," died yesterday in prison at Joliet, and the record will say pneumonia was the cause.

But whether that was the only cause is a question likely to be much debated by those who were interested in the girl, and perhaps it never will be answered.

Certainly a staggering disappointment came to her only last week, when her plea for parole, a plea supplemented by social workers and even by the lawyer who had sent her to prison, was rejected.

GIVES UP IN DESPAIR.

When she didn't get it, or even a promise of it for some future time, she "let go." It was early Monday morning that the prison doctor was called to see her. And a day later she was dead.

Chicago Herald and Examiner,
December 28, 1932

Facing page: Katherine at Cook County Jail in 1924. Katherine, who sought a pardon three times, died shortly after her last pardon was denied in 1932.

Kitty Malm Dies in Prison

KITTY MALM

The Parole Board only last week refused to parole Kitty Malm, "the tiger woman," serving a life sentence at Joliet for murder.

Chicago American, December 27, 1932

Sabella Nitti in
Cook County Jail
in 1923.

CHAPTER FIVE

ISABELLA NITTI

"The farm lady who achieved fame
as instant as Byron's when she was
heralded as the first woman in the
county to receive the death sentence."
— *CHICAGO TRIBUNE*, OCTOBER 16, 1927

Wʜᴇɴ ᴀ ᴊᴜʀʏ ꜱᴇɴᴛᴇɴᴄᴇᴅ Sabella Nitti to death—she was the first woman, a mother at that, to face the rope in Cook County—Sabella didn't cry, scream or faint. Instead, she "ran stubby fingers, where the dirt was ingrained into broken nails, into her matted hair. She shifted her stocky legs and smoothed out the dark blue skirt, made full and short for work in the field."

On that day, July 9, 1923, Sabella had no idea her fate had been sealed by twelve men who took twelve ballots to agree that she should hang for the mysterious disappearance of Francesco "Frank" Nitti, her truck-farmer spouse. She was found guilty, along with farmhand-turned-husband Peter Crudelle, of bludgeoning Nitti to death and then dumping his body in either the Des Plaines River or the Chicago Sanitary and Ship Canal, near their small plot of land in Stickney, Illinois.

In fact, Sabella hadn't understood any of the court proceedings. An Italian immigrant, Sabella could not read, write or speak any English. Her distinctive Bari dialect was difficult for other Italians to understand. Her attorney, Eugene Moran, couldn't find a competent translator, with one session devolving into "Three frantic interpreters sweat(ing) over the dialectic mes-alliance of Italian peasant jargon and academic Genoese phrases."

SABELLA NITTI

one of the defendants herein, called as a witness on her own behalf, having been first duly sworn through an interpreter who was also duly sworn, interpreted the questions so propounded from the English language into the Italian language and the answers thereto from the Italian laugnage into the English language, testified as follows:

DIRECT EXAMINATIon

By Mr. Moran:

411   MR MORAN: Now, this witness does not even speak pigeon English, she does not even understand me, so I will have to call on the interpreter.

Q What is your name ? A Sabella Nitti.

285

Sabella's attorney Eugene Moran describes her as not speaking or understanding English, not even "pigeon English."

Facing page: Sabella's daughters, Philomena, six, and Mary, four, visit her in Cook County Jail in 1923. During the trial, the children stayed with neighbors in Stickney, Illinois.

"If this is all that woman suffrage has brought the women of this country then it's a disgrace to us and more of a disgrace to the men of the country."

—LEONORA Z. MEDER, *CHICAGO TRIBUNE*, JULY 11, 1923

Sabella was mocked mercilessly by reporters—especially by the *Chicago Tribune*'s Genevieve Forbes. Sabella's appearance, social status and inability to communicate were all topics of ridicule. After the guilty verdict was read, Forbes pulled no punches, saying the jury gave "the death penalty to the dumb, crouching animal-like Italian peasant." Even worse, no one was willing or capable of explaining the decision to Sabella until the following day.

Assistant State's Attorney Michael Romano boasted, "The verdict has made husband killing no longer the safest sport on the continent. It was a cold blooded murder, horrible and she was treated like a cold blooded murderess. That was just."

The court was so distracted by the language barrier and the incompetence of Sabella's attorney that no one involved in the trial questioned the evidence. An execution date was soon set for October 12—Columbus Day—to which Sabella responded, "They chokes me? They chokes me?"

Public outcry soon followed, as people questioned whether Sabella should be put to death—especially since her land and livelihood had already been taken. Leonora Z. Meder, attorney and officer of the Society for the Abolition of Capital Punishment, said, "If this is all that woman suffrage has brought the women of this country then it's a disgrace to us and more of a disgrace to the men of the country."

A team of attorneys of Italian ancestry stepped forward to fight on Sabella's behalf, including a young, astute lawyer named Helen Cirese, who had experienced discrimination herself within the legal community.

It would take an Illinois Supreme Court opinion to bring justice to Sabella. Unlike the Hunyak character based on the Italian immigrant in the musical "Chicago," Sabella would live to see her name cleared and go on to live a long, happy life—maybe the most inspiring ending of all women housed on Cook County's Murderess Row.

U. S. DEPARTMENT OF LABOR
BUREAU OF NATURALIZATION

No. **1D 21913**

CERTIFICATE OF ARRIVAL

I HEREBY CERTIFY that the Immigration records of the Department of Labor show that the alien named below arrived at the port, on the date, and in the manner shown, and was lawfully admitted to the United States of America for permanent residence.

Port of entry: New York, NY
Name: Travaglio, Isabella
Date: August 10, 1916
Manner of arrival: SS Dante Alighieri

I FURTHER CERTIFY that this certificate of arrival is issued under authority of, and in conformity with, the provisions of the Act of June 29, 1906, as amended, solely for the use of the alien herein named and only for naturalization purposes.

IN WITNESS WHEREOF, this Certificate of Arrival is issued

May 2, 1930

BY DIRECTION OF THE SECRETARY OF LABOR.

Raymond F. Crist
Commissioner of Naturalization.

Form 160   U S GOVERNMENT PRINTING OFFICE: 1929   14—2624

Sabella immigrated to the United States on August 10, 1916, to meet her husband, Frank, who was already living in America.

BIOGRAPHICAL DETAILS

Isabella Maria Travaglio was born on March 14, 1879, in Southern Italy, outside Bari. She arrived in New York City aboard the SS Dante Alighieri on August 10, 1916, with sons Michele ("Michael") and Pasquale ("Charles"). Her husband, Francesco Nitti, had immigrated to the United States three years earlier with the couple's oldest son, Vincenzo ("James").

Nitti shared his name with a gangster nicknamed "The Enforcer" and a former Italian prime minister, but he was neither. He lived a relatively humble life: His family settled on a small leased plot of land just outside Chicago, where they grew vegetables and crops to be sold at market. Soon, two daughters would join the family: Philomena ("Theresa") in 1917 and Maria ("Mary") in 1919.

Neighbors and acquaintances said Nitti had a temper and was known to quarrel frequently with almost every member of his household. He had come to blows

The Nittis' farmhouse near Stickney, a Chicago suburb.

with them on more than one occasion. The latest altercation occurred on July 15, 1922, as recalled by a farm employee. Nitti's middle son, Michael, asked his father for $500. Nitti refused, and a fight ensued. Michael beat his father so severely that his features were almost unrecognizable. Nitti then stood up, held his stomach and cried, "You have got me."

THE INCIDENT

Sabella's husband was last seen alive on July 29, 1922. Accounts differed among family and friends as to what the fifty-five-year-old man was doing just before he disappeared: playing cards, tending to his oat fields or sleeping under a wagon on his property.

One neighbor, Mike Travaglio, testified he last saw Nitti at a market on Randolph Street selling vegetables about 7 a.m. that day. Shortly before Nitti's disappearance, a man named John Cieslak saw Nitti driving along a public road, his face bruised and swollen. Nitti told him his "bum son" did it.

Sabella later testified her husband told her around 9 p.m. July 29, 1922, he was going outside to check on the family's oat field and for her to take the children and go to bed. Another Nitti employee, Mike Desanto, said he visited with the man later that night, before leaving around 11 p.m. in Nitti's one-horse wagon.

Early the next morning, Sabella said she arose to find her husband not inside their home or on their property. She went to the home of Louis Kral, Stickney's police magistrate, and complained of the disappearance of her husband and asked for help. Kral, instead, referred her to Charles Eisele, Stickney's chief of police.

Eisele said in his affidavit that around 5 a.m. July 30, 1922, Sabella and another woman came to his house and made a great fuss about Nitti not returning home that night and asked him to help in their search. Several hours later, Eisele and another police officer, along with Sabella's youngest son, Charles, spent the entire morning looking for him. When Eisele reported later that day that he could not find her husband, Sabella wept.

When Desanto returned the wagon to the Nitti farm that morning, he was told Nitti was missing. Also missing was Michael Nitti, the couple's middle son, who had argued about money with his father two weeks prior. Michael Nitti stayed away from the family farm for the next week.

The *Chicago Tribune* did not report on the farmer's disappearance that summer. In "Ugly Prey: An Innocent Woman and the Death Sentence That Scandalized Jazz Age Chicago," author Emily LeBeau Lucchesi fills in the gaps. Lucchesi's research reveals that Cook County Deputy Sheriff Paul Dasso took an interest in the case and visited the Nitti farm often.

In 1897, Dasso—a Democrat whose political experience consisted of membership

GILBERT

Chief Deputy Henry
C.W. Laubenheimer
and the Coast Guard
search for the body
of Sabella's husband,
Frank, in 1922. They
believed his body
would be found in
Stickney. Sabella's
son Charles is fourth
from left.

in the Cook County Democratic Marching Club—was appointed assistant superintendent of the city's Bridewell prison by Mayor Carter Harrison Jr. He resigned the position several years later, admitting only to using "harsh language" against a prison guard. But charges of cruelty used against the boys in his charge—including the use of a leather-covered paddle for spankings and imprisonment in a darkened cell with only bread and water for nourishment—were more likely the reason for his exit.

Though Dasso spoke Italian, he could not communicate with Sabella in a way she could understand. Crudelle, the farmhand, would step in to translate.

After weeks with no leads in his missing person investigation, Dasso drummed up charges of adultery and fornication against Sabella and Crudelle, who was bunking in the Nitti shack while working on their farm. They were taken into custody on September 14, 1922. Unable to post bond, the couple remained in jail and awaited a hearing in front of a local magistrate. Two of Sabella's sons—James and Michael—implicated their mother and her boarder in their father's disappearance.

James, Sabella's oldest son, used his mother's incarceration as an opportunity to apply for letters of administration of his father's estate. Though James had been living in Wisconsin and had not seen his father for almost a year prior to his disappearance, he was quick to cash in on his father's property. Records show he began selling off pieces of his father's estate on September 17, 1922.

Around the same time, the assistant state's attorney and James' attorney, W.W. Witty, conducted an inquiry into Nitti's disappearance. This included interviewing Sabella's oldest daughter, Theresa. The child told the men she had seen her father's body slung on a wagon and dragged to the Des Plaines River, where it was thrown in.

As authorities searched the Des Plaines River for Nitti's body, Dasso attempted to interview the youngest son, Charles, about his father's disappearance. Charles refused at first, asking to speak with his brother Michael. Then, as the *Chicago Tribune* reported, "Michael Nitti's appearance loosened Charles' tongue."

Charles told the men: "Father, Peter (Crudelle) and mother played cards that night. Father went out in the yard and Peter followed. He hit father on the head with a sledgehammer. Then he got some rope, tied it around the hands and feet, put pop in a wagon and hauled him to the river." Yet Charles refused to reveal the location where he claimed to have witnessed his father's body tossed into the river.

When questioned further, Charles said Crudelle forced him to help with the disposal of his father's body. As a result of this disclosure, Crudelle was booked for Nitti's murder. Sabella was charged as an accessory before and after the fact, though Charles

STATE OF ILLINOIS   } SS.
COUNTY OF COOK   )

IN THE PROBATE COURT OF COOK COUNTY.

In re: Estate of   )
Frank Nitti, alleged)
to be deceased.   )

Appraisement.

1 black horse (male).......$40.00	1 frame house $50.00
1 gray horse (mare)........ 50.00	1 plow.............. 1.50
1 brown horse (mare)....... 40.00	1 cultivator........ 2.00
1 light brown horse(male)...30.00	1 old horse........ 10.00
1 colt aged 5 months....... 15.00	1 ice box.......... 2.00
1 single set harness........ 5.00	1 range............ 3.00
1 double " " 7.00	2 seeding machines 3.00
2 plows.$6.50 ea.......... 13.00	2 kerosene cans 1.00
2 cultivators $5.00 ea..... 10.00	19 bage oats..exhausted
1 binder.................. 50.00	1 corder........... 25.00
1 light market wagon....... 30.00	$569.10
1 large wagon............. 25.00	
2 small farm wagons, $7.50ea14.00	
1 hay mower............... 40.00	
1 hay rack................ 5.00	
1 wash tub................ .20	
3 sheets $ .15 ea......... .45	
6 pillow slips $ .10........ .60	
1 comforter............... .50	Amounts received from sale
2 comforters..$.50 .... 1.00	of farm products:
1 feather bed............. 2.00	1922, Sept.17.....$12.50
2 bed steads $1.00 ea...... 2.00	" 20...... 11.75
1 sewing machine.......... 3.00	" 23...... 9.50
4 dining room chairs .25... 1.00	" 25...... 12.00
1 kitchen range........... 2.00	" 28 /// .. 13.50
1 kitchen table........... .50	" 30...... 7.65
1 doz. spoons and forks..... .60	Oct. 1..... 11.00
1 buggy.................. 1.00	" 3..... 12.00
2 dressers $2.00 ea....... 4.00	" 5..... 10.00
1 wardrobe .... .75	" 7..... 23.00
52 windows.$1.50 ea........ 78.00	" 9..... 12.50
	" 11..... 9.75
	" 13..... 11.50
	" 15..... 12.75
	" 17..... 10.50
	" 19..... 10.00
	" 21..... 12.00
	" 23..... 12.75
	" 25..... 12.45
	" 25..... 8.00
	$235.10
	569.10
	$804.20

The appraisement of Frank Nitti's estate, completed while Sabella was in jail, showed that her son James had started selling off assets from the estate—about $235 worth.

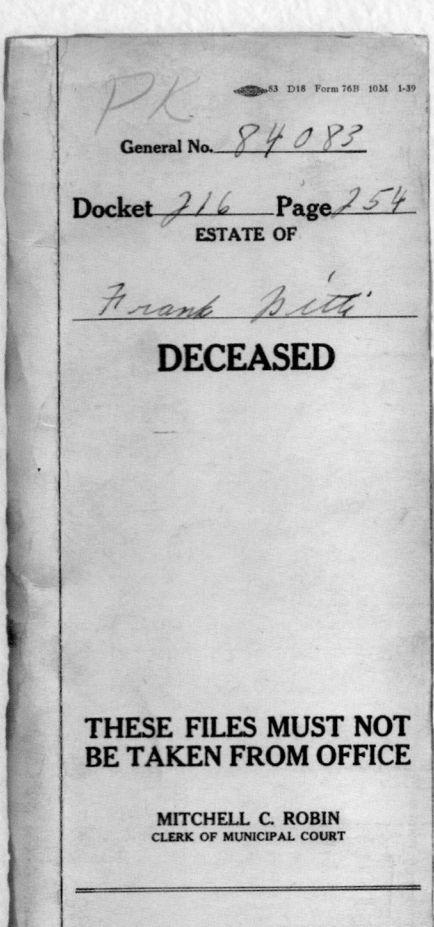

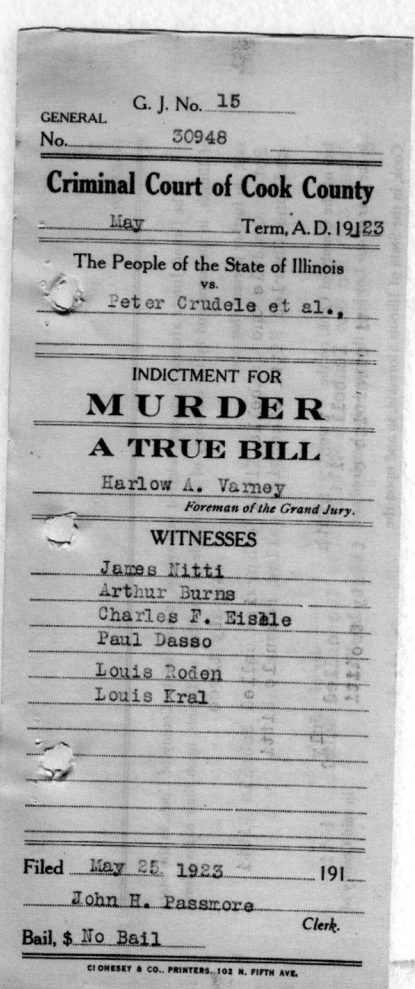

The cover for the estate file of Nitti, circa 1923.

Peter Crudelle and Sabella were held without bail after being charged with Nitti's murder on May 25, 1923, according to this indictment. One of the witnesses is listed as James Nitti, Sabella's oldest son.

MEET THE DECEASED: FRANCESCO NITTI

No definitive proof links the body found in 1923 in the Stickney catch basin with Francesco Nitti. Yet a gravemarker in Mount Carmel Cemetery in Hillside serves as a memorial. It reads:

In honor of our grandfather Frank Nitti, July 23, 1871–July 29, 1922

At the time of his supposed death, Nitti was estimated to possess an estate that included one frame house ($50 value), five horses and a colt ($185 value), one large wagon ($25), one wash tub (20 cents), one plow ($1.50) and two seeding machines ($3). Not on the list: a sledgehammer.

said his mother knew nothing of the murder until told about it by Crudelle. Later he told investigators his mother held Nitti's arms down while Crudelle bludgeoned him.

When a state's attorney asked Sabella if she killed her husband, she said, "Whatever Charlie said, that is true."

Police stopped looking for Nitti's body on September 27, 1922. One deputy sheriff believed the body floated through the locks at Lockport.

James Nitti testified before Judge Henry Horner in the Probate Court of Cook County on October 20, 1922, to demonstrate he could legally inherit his father's property. He claimed his father had died July 29, 1922. He also provided the names of six heirs. With his mother still incarcerated, James was named administrator of Nitti's estate. About a month later, Sabella's attorney announced he would file a petition asking the court to turn over the estate's assets to Sabella.

With no body and no evidence to support adultery charges, Sabella and Crudelle were released from jail on December 6, 1922. A week later, the court ordered James to return his father's estate to his mother. Records show James had already sold $235 (more than $3,500 in today's dollars) in items. This left just under $570 of appraised goods—including horses, wagons, farming implements and housewares—in the estate. In January, the probate court awarded Sabella about $800 (almost $12,000 in today's dollars) with the option to ask for a future increase.

Possibly fearing another adultery arrest, Sabella and Crudelle were married on March 7, 1923. They lived in Cicero.

And then, a decomposed body was found in a storm drain near the Nittis' Stickney property on May 9, 1923, almost one year after Francesco Nitti's disappearance. Sabella, Crudelle and Sabella's son Charles were charged with his murder.

AWAITING TRIAL

The body was unrecognizable. Without dental records or modern DNA testing, identifying the body was a challenge. From the waistline up, it was just a skeleton. The coroner's physician offered little to go on: He said the body was of a man between twenty-three and fifty-five.

At an inquest on May 10, 1923, neighbor Mike Travaglio said he saw the body at that time and identified it as the body of Francesco Nitti "by means of a pair of shoes and ring." Nitti's aunt also identified the body by its gold ring, and two of her sons verified the identification.

MR SMITH: I object to it, there is no question.

THE COURT: I dont know what it is.

MR SMITH: Judge, he asked her the question, do you know where your husband is now.

THE COURT: All right; go on, the objection over-ruled. What is the answer ?

A He said you go to bed, I am going out to the oats and see that somebody does not put a match to it and burn it up.

MR MORAN: Q Did you and Peter Crudelle hit Frank Nitti on the head with this hammer and kill him on July 29th, 1922 ?

A If I had seen Pete Crudelle strike my husband on the head with that hammer, I would have killed Pete Crudelle beforehe would have killed my husband.

MR MORAN: That is all.

THECOURT: Strike it out.

MR MORAN: That is responsive to the question.

THE COURT: Strike it out.

MR SMITH: That is why I object.

418   THE COURT: Now, listen, if you dont understand it.

MR SMITH: No, but that calls for a yes or no answer and she said fourteen words.

392

Sabella strongly responds that she did not murder her husband while being questioned by her attorney during the 1923 trial.

TRIAL

On July 2, 1923, jury selection took place. The next day, the prosecution presented the waterlogged pair of shoes found in the storm drain as belonging to Nitti.

Chicago Tribune reporter Genevieve Forbes ridiculed Sabella's appearance in court, describing her as an "alleged husband-killer who acknowledges 39 years and possesses 46, according to her eldest son, who testified against her. A seamy faced, weather-beaten peasant, the senora, at home in a truck garden, and but little used to the refinement of even the stiff wooden chair in which she hunches restlessly."

No longer in charge of his father's estate, James testified on July 5, 1923, that his mother killed his father and pointed to where she was sitting in the courtroom: "Ma said to me, 'If you want to see your father he is in the corn field.' The corn field is beside the catch basin."

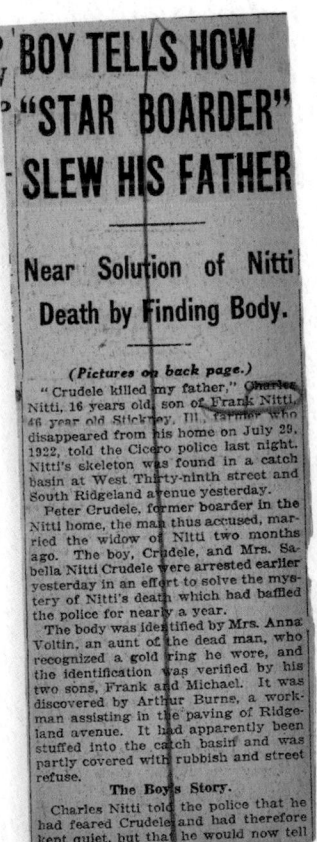

Chicago Tribune, May 10, 1923

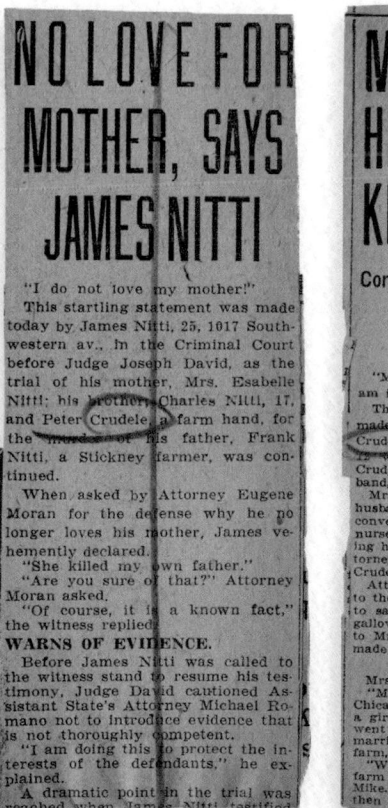

Chicago American, July 5, 1923

Chicago Journal, July 17, 1923

DIALECT JARGON 'MAKES 'EM DIZZY AT NITTI TRIAL

Even Interpreters Dazed by Babel of Tongues.

BY GENEVIEVE FORBES.

Justice spoke Italian in seven different dialects yesterday, as Judge Joseph David presided over a legal Tower of Babel in the prosecution of Mrs. Sabelle Nitti-Crudelle, her youngest son, Charles, and Peter Crudelle, her second husband, charged with the murder of Frank Nitti, who disappeared on July 29, 1922.

JUDGE DAVID.
[TRIBUNE Photo.]

Three frantic interpreters sweat over the dialectic mes-alliance of Italian peasant jargon, and academic Genoese phrases; a benchful of Neopolitan gentlemen were threatened with jail for laughing at their kinswoman, gesticulating from the witness stand; an infuriated judge called the linguistic battle a "disgrace"; an everlasting whirligig of Italian vowels, with gestures, and Chicago consonants, with yells. It was perpetual motion with everybody at a standstill.

Defendants Alone Understood.

And the most static of all were the trio of defendants, the only ones who really understood what the language lesson was all about.

First, there is Senora Sabelle, alleged husband-killer, who acknowledges 39 years, and possesses 46, according to her oldest son, who testified against her. A seamy faced, weatherbeaten peasant, the senora, at home

Chicago Tribune, July 7, 1923

Throughout the proceedings, interpreters attempted to communicate questions and answers to and from witnesses, including the defendants, with little success. And onlookers in the gallery, some of whom also had a limited understanding of English, tried to follow along. During the questioning of one female witness, Judge Joseph David became so frustrated with the language barrier he proclaimed, "Gentlemen, this is a disgrace. Tell that woman to answer the questions that are put to her. And bailiff, tell those people in the audience they'll go to jail if they laugh any more."

David was also frustrated by Moran, the defense attorney for Sabella and Crudelle. Throughout the trial, David questioned Moran's competence and understanding of even the simplest legal terms and rules. Consider this exchange, as recorded by the court:

JUDGE DAVID: You are asking a lot of questions here that are highly improper and detrimental to your client, that are not competent. . . . You must stop calling for hearsay testimony unless you insist on doing it, because such evidence is detrimental to your client and ought not to bring it out. I ought not tell you how to try your case.

ATTORNEY MORAN: Your Honor, I have got my case pretty well in hand.

JUDGE DAVID: This court cannot stand by and permit you constantly to ask questions that are detrimental to your clients. You must stop it.

Despite this frustration, however, David refused to declare a mistrial or appoint a new lawyer for the defense. Charges against Charles were dropped on July 7, 1923.

Crudelle, left, and Sabella are sentenced July 9, 1923, to die by hanging for the murder of Sabella's first husband, Nitti. At the time, Sabella didn't understand the English words that condemned her to death.

VERDICT

After deliberating almost two hours, the jury found Sabella and Crudelle guilty of Nitti's murder. Both were sentenced to hang. *Chicago Tribune* reporter Genevieve Forbes noted of Sabella, "She hadn't understood the words that made a national figure out of an obscure Italian woman."

Sabella's attorney Moran's reaction: "Verdicts seem to be inversely proportional to the charm of the woman defendant. In this list, the homelier the woman, the more severe the penalty."

From left: Sabella, her son Charles Nitti and her second husband, Crudelle, appear during the trial for the murder of Sabella's first husband, Nitti, circa 1923.

Joseph B. David   Judge of the Superior   Court
of Cook County, Illinois, and Ex-Officio Judge of the
Criminal Court of Cook County, Illinois.
        ROBERT E. CROWE, State's Attorney, PETER M. HOFFMAN,
Sheriff, and JOHN H. PASSMORE, Clerk.
        The following among other proceedings were had and
entered of record in said Court, which said proceedings
are in the words and figures following to-wit:

The People of the State of Illinois)
)
30948   VS   )   INDICTMENT FOR
)
Peter Crudele   )   MURDER:
)
   Isabella Nitti otherwise called   )
     Sabella Nitti   )

        This day come the said People by Robert E. Crowe,
State's Attorney and the said defendants as well in their own
proper persons as by their counsel also come.

        And also come the jurors of the jury aforesaid.

        And they hearing the arguments of Counsel and instructions
of the Court retire in charge of sworn officers to consider of
their verdict, and afterwards return into open Court and for their
verdict say.

        " We the jury find the defendant
        Peter Crudele GUILTY of Murder in
        manner and form as charged in the
        Indictment and we fix his punishment
        at death."

        The said defendant by his counsel now here demanded that
that the jury be polled and the Jurors of the Jury aforesaid
being separately called and demanded whether the above verdict
by him rendered was and is his verdict, each for himself
answering says, that the above verdict was and is his verdict.

        Whereupon it is ordered that the verdict be received
and entered of record which is done.

        " We the jury find the defendant
        Isabella Nitti otherwise called
        Sabella Nitti GUILTY of Murder in
        manner and form as charged in the
        Indictment and we fix her punish-
        ment at death."

        The said defendant by her counsel now here demanded that
the jury be polled and the jurors of the jury aforesaid being
separately called and demanded whether the above verdict by him

17

The jury finds
Crudelle and
Sabella guilty
of murder,
punishable by
death, in 1923.

MRS. NITTI TO
HANG WITH MAN
SHE WED AFTER
KILLING MATE

Jury Finds Her and Crudell
Guilty of Crime After Tw
Hours' Deliberation and Tal
ing a Total of Twelve Ballo

*Chicago Herald and Examiner,
July 10, 1923*

MRS. BUZZI IS SENTENCED

Man Sneers When Warrant Announcing Penalty Is Read in Judge David's Court; Woman Sobs Her Anguish in Jail

Two American women were sentenced yesterday to pay the supreme penalty for murder. Mrs. Anna Buzzi for the killing of Frederic Schneider, wealthy Bronx contractor, must go to the electric chair. Sabella Nitti Crudelle, the slayer of her husband, Frank Nitti, will go to the gallows.

Mrs. Sabella Nitti Crudelle and her "star boarder," whom she married after they had slain her husband, Frank Nitti, were both found guilty of mur-

A jury of twelve men found Sabella and Crudelle guilty of first-degree murder on July 9, 1923. Sabella was the first woman sentenced to hang in Chicago.

The signatures of the men who condemned Sabella to death in 1923.

AFTERMATH

The outrage in response to the ruling was immediate.

The wife of jury foreman Thomas Murtaugh reportedly threatened to leave him and return to her mother's home if Sabella were hanged.

Sabella's cellmates in Cook County Jail drafted a letter in her defense, blaming the *Chicago Tribune* for "stacking the cards against her because she wasn't a 'vamp,' but they wince at the adjectives 'dumb' and 'crouching' as used in the *Tribune's* description" of her.

The congregation of Olivet Institute protested Sabella's execution. Its pastor requested the Church Federation of Greater Chicago launch a crusade against all capital punishment and "especially in the case of this woman."

However, the *Chicago Tribune* supported the sentence. Under the headline "Discouraging Gunwomen," the newspaper's editorial board wrote: "The evidence was clear and decisive and the verdict logical and justified. The jury deserves nothing but credit. The fact that the woman in the case was ugly and repulsive is beside the point."

On July 12, 1923, "a number of prominent Italians organized . . . in an effort to prevent an Italian woman being the first woman in Illinois to be hanged." One of these new attorneys was Helen Cirese, a 1920 graduate of DePaul University's law school. She made headlines throughout the United States that year for having passed the Illinois bar examination at age twenty—the youngest woman to ever pass the test—but she was barred from practicing until she was twenty-one, per state law.

"The evidence was clear and decisive and the verdict logical and justified. The jury deserves nothing but credit. The fact that the woman in the case was ugly and repulsive is beside the point."

—*CHICAGO TRIBUNE*, FEBRUARY 21, 1924

OCT. 12 IS SET AS DATE TO HANG WOMAN SLAYER

Citizens Plead in Vain for Life of Mrs. Nitti.

Mrs. Sabelle Nitti Crudelle was yesterday sentenced to die on the gallows on Oct. 12—Columbus Day—for the murder of her husband, Frank Nitti Peter Crudelle, her present husband, for whose love she plotted the death of the father of her five children, was sentenced to die on the same day.

Judge Joseph B. David pronounced the sentences on the young man and the disheveled Italian peasant woman at the conclusion of lengthy arguments for a new trial by attorneys for the defense as well as representatives of local civic organizations.

"I feel that the evidence presented at the trial proved beyond all doubt that the defendants were guilty of a most atrocious murder and the jury was justified in returning a verdict of guilty," the court stated before pronouncing sentence.

Word "Dead" Startles Her.

Mrs. Nitti was present when the words setting the date of her death

Sentenced to Hang

Mrs. Sabelle Nitti Crudelle formally doomed to die on gallows on Oct. 12 by Judge David yesterday.

not believe the honorable court here will permit a mother to hang."

Chicago Tribune, July 15, 1923

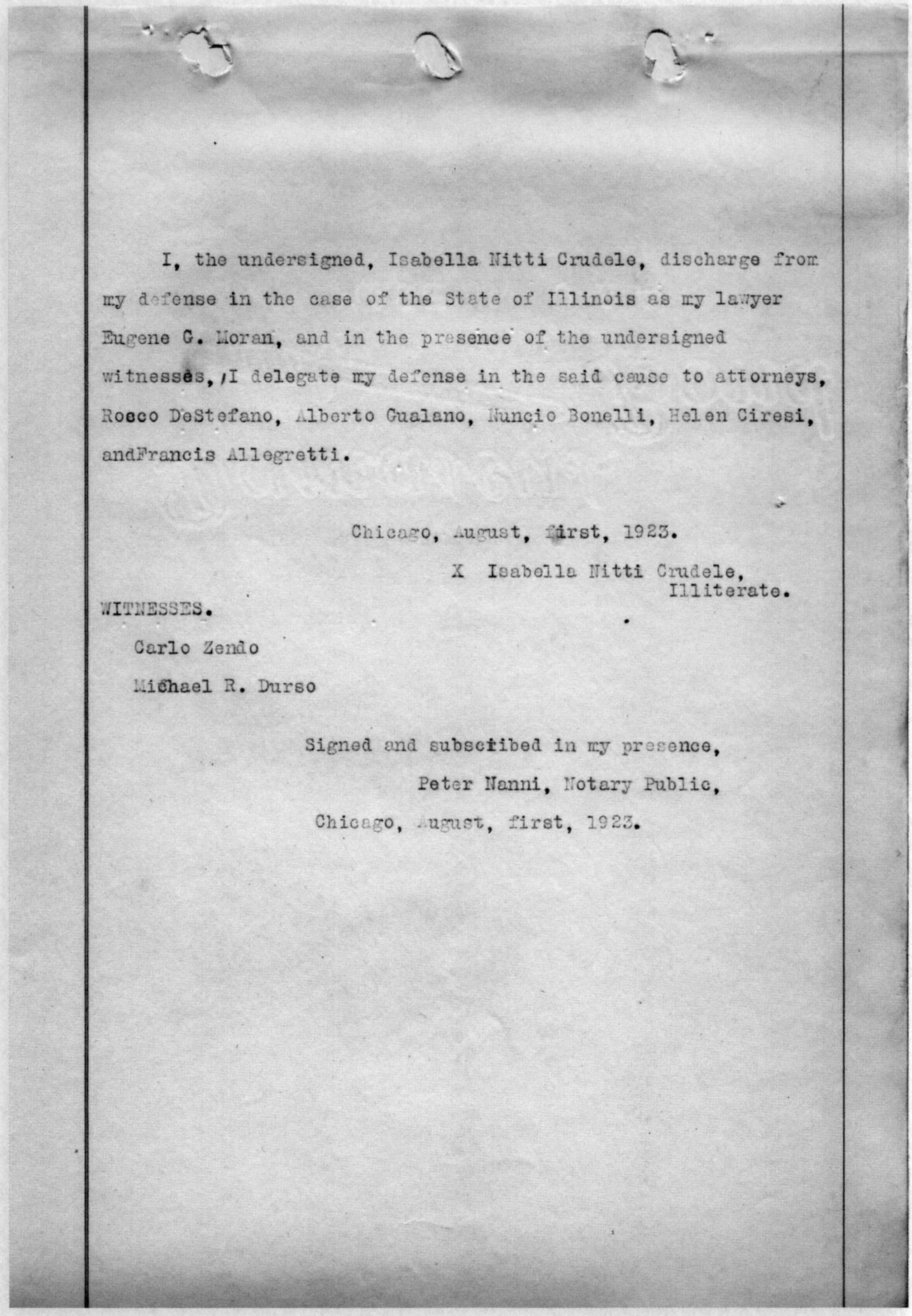

I, the undersigned, Isabella Nitti Crudele, discharge from my defense in the case of the State of Illinois as my lawyer Eugene C. Moran, and in the presence of the undersigned witnesses, I delegate my defense in the said cause to attorneys, Rocco DeStefano, Alberto Gualano, Nuncio Bonelli, Helen Ciresi, andFrancis Allegretti.

Chicago, August, first, 1923.

X   Isabella Nitti Crudele,
Illiterate.

WITNESSES.

Carlo Zendo

Michael R. Durso

Signed and subscribed in my presence,
Peter Nanni, Notary Public,
Chicago, August, first, 1923.

Sabella discharges Moran, the lawyer who represented her during her murder trial, in 1923. She acquired new representation and took her appeal to the Illinois Supreme Court.

Sabella, meanwhile, was despondent. As the public rallied on her behalf, she attempted suicide twice—once by trying to choke herself to death and later ramming her head against a wall.

After hearing arguments for a new trial on July 14, 1923, Judge David set the execution date for Sabella and Crudelle for October 12. An elderly man, identified as Judge McKenzie Cleland, arose from his seat toward the back of the courtroom and asked for permission to speak. When given the opportunity to do so, he said, "I am not here to argue on the guilt or innocence of this woman, but just to try and save her. Whatever be the facts she should not be hanged. She is a mother and a mother has never been hanged in the history of this country. I do not believe the honorable court here will permit a mother to hang."

David responded, "I will not listen to such stuff. I will not be swayed by any outside influence, whether it be public sentiment, society, civic organizations or the so-called howling mob. I took an oath of office to uphold the laws of our state. One of them is that a murderer may be hanged, whether man or woman, mother or father."

Another *Tribune* editorial under the headline "Racial Inequality" confirmed the newspaper's position—and took it a step further: "Those who seek to set aside this verdict seek to set aside the law and practice of this country. When they do so because of racial affiliations they prove themselves especially dangerous to American institutions. They are either Americans or Italians. If they are Americans, either by birth or naturalization, their duty must be to America before the blood of their fathers. . . . If their allegiance is primarily to their race—in this case, the Italian—they have no proper place in America. They should go back or be sent back to Italy."

Sabella yearned for her daughters and was concerned for their well-being. On July 28, 1923, her attorney filed a petition for the recovery of her two daughters, who were in the custody of neighbors James and Anna Volpe—both of whom testified against Sabella during her trial. During an impassioned custody hearing, Sabella clutched her four-year-old daughter, Mary, as she rose from the witness chair and shouted in Italian, "If I've got to stay in jail, they stay with me; if I got to die, they die with me."

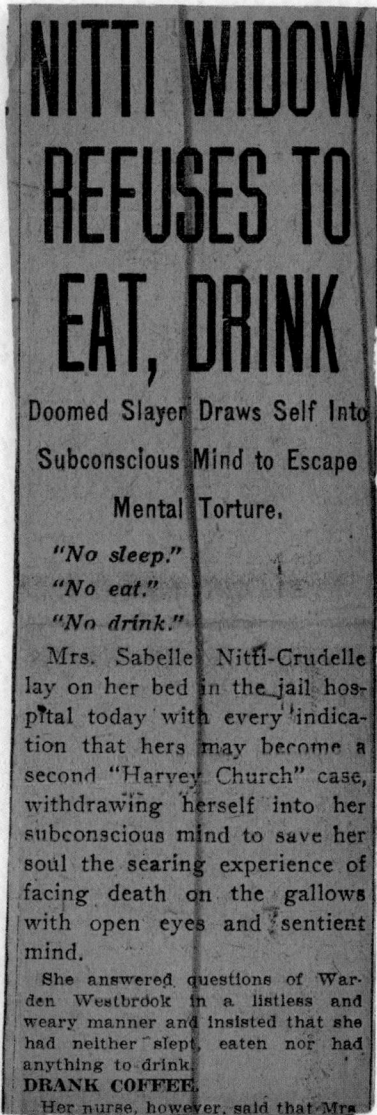

NITTI WIDOW REFUSES TO EAT, DRINK

Doomed Slayer Draws Self Into Subconscious Mind to Escape Mental Torture.

"No sleep."
"No eat."
"No drink."

Mrs. Sabelle Nitti-Crudelle lay on her bed in the jail hospital today with every indication that hers may become a second "Harvey Church" case, withdrawing herself into her subconscious mind to save her soul the searing experience of facing death on the gallows with open eyes and sentient mind.

She answered questions of Warden Westbrook in a listless and weary manner and insisted that she had neither slept, eaten nor had anything to drink.

DRANK COFFEE.

Her nurse, however, said that Mrs.

Chicago American, July 12, 1923

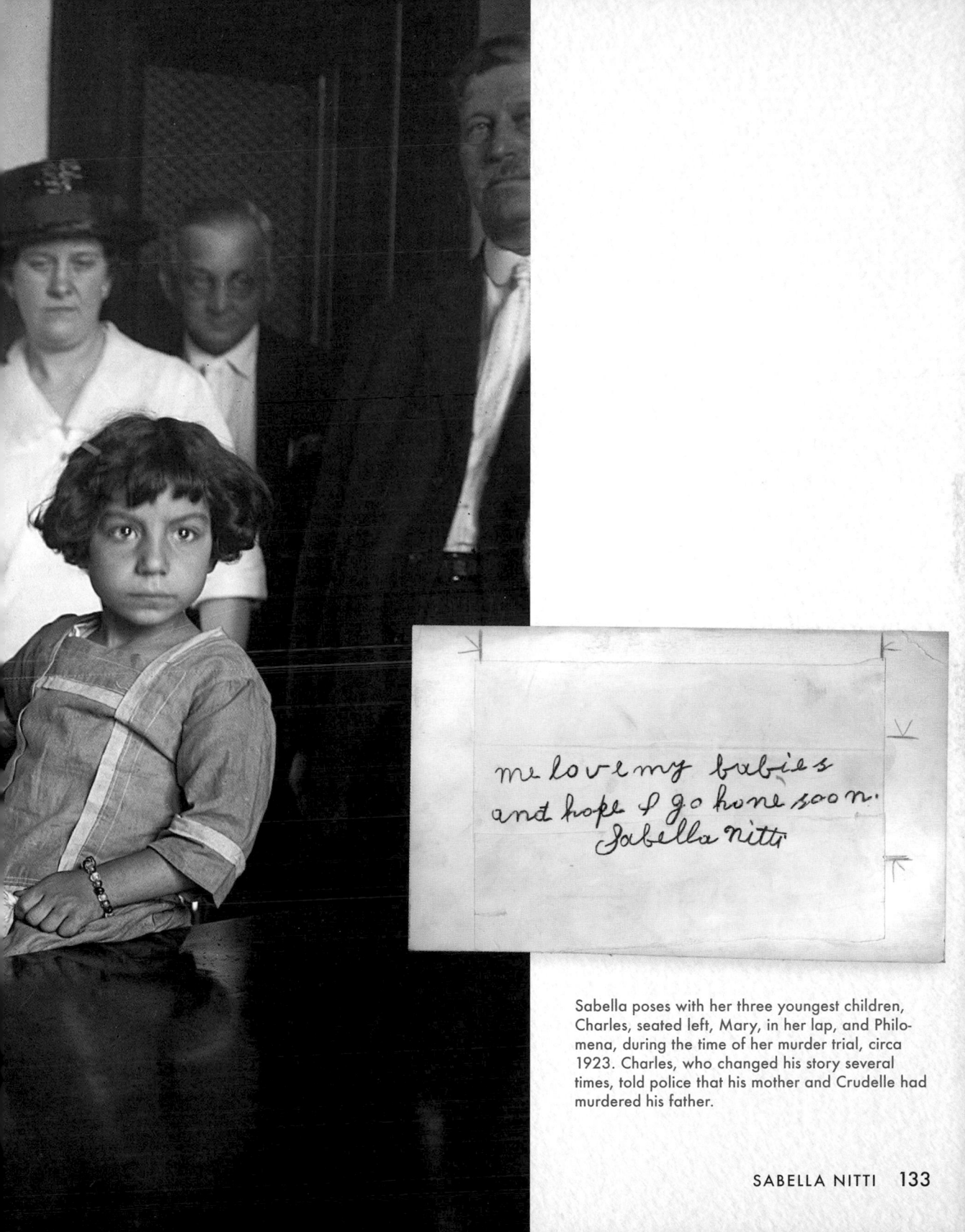

me love my babies
and hope I go home soon.
Sabella nitti

Sabella poses with her three youngest children, Charles, seated left, Mary, in her lap, and Philomena, during the time of her murder trial, circa 1923. Charles, who changed his story several times, told police that his mother and Crudelle had murdered his father.

Judge Joseph Sabath of Superior Court directed the children be removed from the Volpes' home and taken to St. Mary's Training School, now known as Maryville, in Des Plaines.

On August 1, 1923, Sabella sent a notarized letter to the court requesting her lawyer Eugene G. Moran be discharged. She delegated her defense to six lawyers, and on August 29, the new team argued that Moran was incompetent and that Sabella and Crudelle didn't get a fair hearing. But David denied a motion to vacate their death sentences and give them a new trial. "The motion is overruled and I feel that I am doing the right thing for the community and civilization by so doing."

There were "only two places left open to the corps of Italian lawyers for the defense—the state Supreme Court and Gov. (Len) Small." On September 25, 1923, Illinois Supreme Court Justice Orrin Carter stayed the execution of Sabella and Crudelle pending review. After a substantial defense fund for Sabella and Crudelle was raised by Chicago's Italian community, attorneys Rocco de Steffano and Thomas E. Swanson presented arguments before the Illinois Supreme Court in Springfield on December 15, 1923, seeking a reversal of their convictions.

Facing page and below: Sabella and Crudelle look despondent after a judge refused to vacate their death sentences in order to give them a new trial on August 28, 1923.

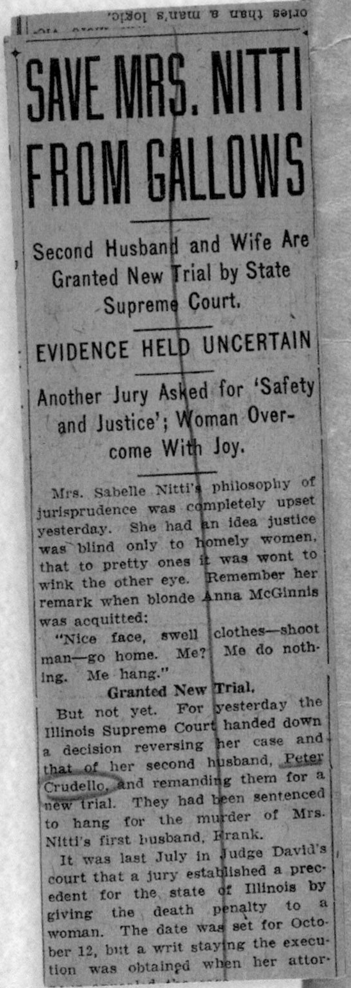

SAVE MRS. NITTI FROM GALLOWS

Second Husband and Wife Are Granted New Trial by State Supreme Court.

EVIDENCE HELD UNCERTAIN

Another Jury Asked for 'Safety and Justice'; Woman Overcome With Joy.

Mrs. Sabelle Nitti's philosophy of jurisprudence was completely upset yesterday. She had an idea justice was blind only to homely women, that to pretty ones it was wont to wink the other eye. Remember her remark when blonde Anna McGinnis was acquitted:

"Nice face, swell clothes—shoot man—go home. Me? Me do nothing. Me hang."

Granted New Trial.

But not yet. For yesterday the Illinois Supreme Court handed down a decision reversing her case and that of her second husband, Peter Crudello, and remanding them for a new trial. They had been sentenced to hang for the murder of Mrs. Nitti's first husband, Frank.

It was last July in Judge David's court that a jury established a precedent for the state of Illinois by giving the death penalty to a woman. The date was set for October 12, but a writ staying the execution was obtained when her attor-

Chicago Herald and Examiner, April 15, 1924

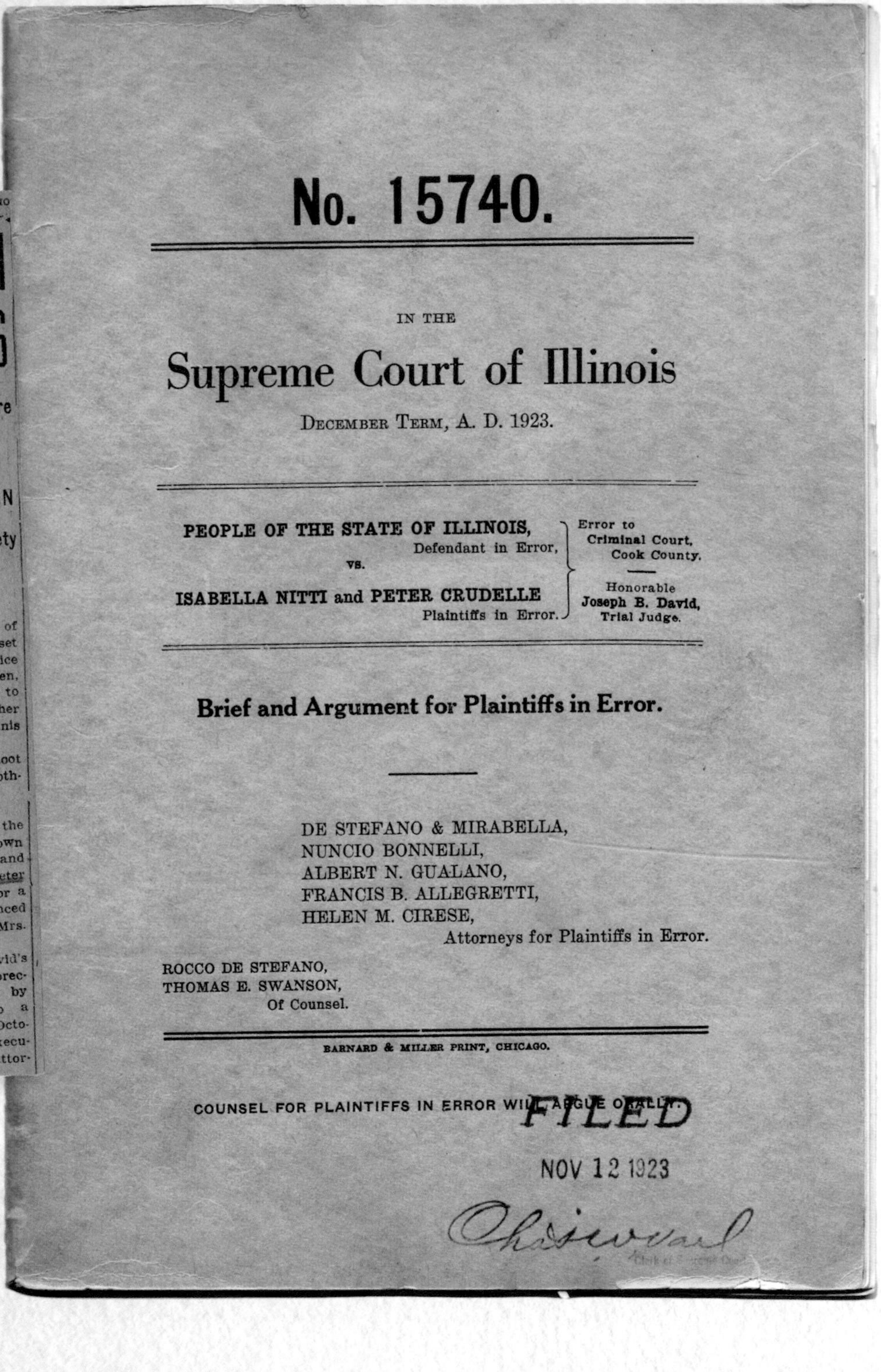

No. 15740.

IN THE

Supreme Court of Illinois

December Term, A. D. 1923.

PEOPLE OF THE STATE OF ILLINOIS,
Defendant in Error,

vs.

ISABELLA NITTI and PETER CRUDELLE
Plaintiffs in Error.

Error to Criminal Court, Cook County.

Honorable **Joseph B. David,** **Trial Judge.**

Brief and Argument for Plaintiffs in Error.

DE STEFANO & MIRABELLA,
NUNCIO BONNELLI,
ALBERT N. GUALANO,
FRANCIS B. ALLEGRETTI,
HELEN M. CIRESE,
Attorneys for Plaintiffs in Error.

ROCCO DE STEFANO,
THOMAS E. SWANSON,
Of Counsel.

BARNARD & MILLER PRINT, CHICAGO.

COUNSEL FOR PLAINTIFFS IN ERROR WILL ARGUE ORALLY.

FILED

NOV 12 1923

Sabella and Crudelle's new legal team argued before the Illinois Supreme Court to reverse their convictions.

Among the claims presented by her new legal team were:

Sabella was promised immunity by local law enforcement: After a body was discovered, Deputy Sheriff Dasso promised Sabella "inasmuch as she was a woman and the mother of children if she would make no denial of her guilt, the prosecution would be easy on her and that she would not have to stay in jail but would be discharged and allowed to return to her children." This deal for immunity was known to her attorney but not presented at trial, the new legal team maintained, "because of the gross incompetency and stupidity of her attorney."

Was Nitti really dead?: "There is no satisfactory proof that this body recovered from the catch basin was the body of Frank Nitti."

Charles' story didn't add up: Acquaintance Desanto took the Nittis' wagon home the night of July 29, 1922—the same night Charles said it was used to transport his father's body—but Desanto was not called to testify during the trial. Also, why would Charles assist investigators in searching for Nitti the morning after his father's disappearance if he had supposedly just hours earlier assisted in transporting his father's body from the property? Furthermore, Sabella's new legal team said after Charles was dismissed from the trial, "the court should have stricken (his story) from the record."

There was no evidence: "There is no circumstantial evidence directly connecting either of the defendants with the alleged murder."

Both Sabella and Crudelle would have fared better without an attorney: "(F)or in the face of repeated admonishings of the trial judge their counsel insisted in bringing out incompetent evidence that was calculated to convict them."

The trial judge failed to appoint competent counsel for the defense: "The learned trial judge knew as the trial progressed that the defendants were being sent to their doom. . . . He should have stopped the farce—no, not the farce, but the tragedy."

Before the dread sentence of death is finally passed upon this man and woman on evidence as uncertain and unsatisfactory as that on which this conviction stands, there ought to be a further investigation with competent counsel representing the accused. Safety and justice require that this cause be submitted to another jury. The judgments are reversed and the cause is remanded to the criminal court of Cook county.

Reversed and remanded.

The Illinois Supreme Court voided Sabella and Crudelle's murder convictions in February 1924. The ruling sent their case back to Cook County Criminal Court to be retried.

On April 14, 1924, Sabella and Crudelle were spared from the gallows by the Illinois Supreme Court. It took the court two hours to decide to reverse the verdict and send the case back for a rehearing.

Illinois Supreme Court Justice Floyd Thompson, in his opinion, agreed Sabella and Crudelle were failed by an incompetent lawyer and convicted solely upon the assumption they "confessed the killing by failing to deny their guilt when Charles implicated them by the story he told in their presence." Thompson also wrote that the incident between Nitti and his middle son, Michael, two weeks before the disappearance was enough to be admitted into evidence during the trial—but wasn't. He said Michael should have also been called as a witness during the trial, yet he wasn't.

Meanwhile, Cirese worked to soften Sabella's appearance. According to "Ugly Prey," Cirese encouraged Sabella to learn English and taught her mannerisms befitting a lady. With no new evidence to use to prosecute her, however, Sabella was released on bonds of $12,500 on June 16, 1924. For the first time in her life, she affixed her signature to an official document; she had been taught to write her name by several female prisoners in the county jail. Crudelle was released the next day.

me love my babies and hope I go home soon. Sabella Nitti

JAIL A SCHOOL TO MRS. NITTI

Learns to Write Daily Letters to Her Children While Awaiting a New Trial.

Sabella Nitti was in America ten years and could not read, write or speak English. "No time, always working," she explained. Then she got herself into trouble by killing her husband. She and her present husband, Pete Crudelle, were tried for the crime, convicted and sentenced to hang. It was while waiting for her fate, a prisoner in the Cook County jail, that Sabella learned what she might never have known without her imprisonment.

Writes Letters Daily.

Granted a new trial, filled with new hope that she will some day go home to her two babies, who are now in school, Sabella writes letters every day to the children and other relatives.

No one who has not undergone the difficulties that were Sabella's, because she didn't know the language of the country in which she lived, can appreciate how happy she is over her new education.

Warden Wesley Westbrook thinks

Chicago Herald and Examiner, May 20, 1924

WOMAN SLAYER LEARNS TO WRITE IN JAIL.—Though sentence of death for killing her husband hangs over her, Mrs. Sabella Nitti, of Chicago, is diligently studying in her cell. She writes daily letters to her children, hoping for freedom. (Int'l Newsreel.)

Courier News via International Newsreel, June 2, 1924

A smiling Sabella, right, who had previously been sentenced to hang, was released from Cook County Jail pending a new trial in 1924.

MRS. NITTI AND MATE WIN STAY OF DEATH

Mrs. Sabelle Nitti Crudelle will not hang on Columbus Day—October 12.

Neither will Peter Crudelle, her present husband, found guilty with her of the murder of her first husband, Frank Nitti.

Justice Carter of the Illinois Supreme Court today signed writs of supersedeas, staying execution until February, when the Supreme Court is to review the case.

The writs were obtained in the condemned couple's behalf by Attorney Thomas E. Swanson.

DE STEFANO AIDS CASE.

Attorney Rocco De Stefano was associated with Attorney Swanson in the hearing before Justice Carter today. The grounds upon which the writs were obtained, according to Attorney Swanson, were the introduction of incompetent evidence and failure to appoint competent counsel for the defense.

"My prayers have been answered! My prayers have been answered!" Mrs. Nitti cried when informed of Justice Carter's decision. "Oh, how I have prayed that some kind judge would not let them choke me! Thank God! God is good to me!"

SENTENCED JULY 14.

Mrs. Nitti Crudelle and Peter Crudelle were sentenced to death on July 14 last by Judge David in the Criminal Court after conviction by a jury. They are charged with having murdered Mrs. Nitti's husband, a farmer at Stickney, Ill., whom Mrs. Nitti is said to have held while Crudelle beat in his head with a hammer.

Nitti's body was found later, concealed in a catch basin at Thirty-ninth st. and Ridgeland av. Charles, 16, a son of Nitti, testified against his mother and Crudelle, who became his stepfather after Nitti's death.

Chicago American,
September 25, 1923

Sabella hugs her two youngest children, Mary and Philomena, on June 18, 1924, after her release from jail pending a new trial.

MRS. CRUDELLE, BACK ON NITTI FARM, REJOICES

She's Out on Bond to Await New Trial.

(Picture on b...

On a rainy afterno...
months ago, Mrs.
Crudelle fainted whe...
words of a Criminal...
tencing her to die on...
participation in the m...
band, Frank Nitti, o...
out near Stickney, I...

She almost fainted...
but with happiness,...
out of the front do...
jail bound once mo...
farm southwest of...

She's Only O...

She did not go fo...
it is true, merely...
pending a new hear...
Illinois Supreme...
cently set aside th...
the lower court or...
had not "received...
trial."

As she walked...
the arm of her a...
Stefano, she felt s...

Chicago Tribune,
June 17, 1924

LEAST STYLISH OF COURT LADIES ONLY HAPPY ONE

Mrs. Crudelle Is Glad to Get New Trial.

(Picture on back page.)

Beulah has been told she's beautiful.
Belva knows she's stylish.

Sabelle is neither—and she's happy.

These three women, each accused of
murder, all dressed for jury trials,
passed yesterday in sequence before
Judge William Lindsay in the Criminal court.

In each case, however, difficulties
arose in the way of an immediate
Easter Monday trial, and the women
returned to the woman's quarters at
the county jail.

Belva Feels Confident.

Mrs. Belva Gaertner is first. Her
memory still is too befuddled, she pro-
tests, to know who killed Walter R.
Law on the morning of March 12,
when, seated next to him in her motor

Chicago Tribune, April 22, 1924

Sabella smiles for a photo as she leaves Cook
County Jail after sixteen months on June 16, 1924.
With her are Margaret Bonelli, left of Sabella, who
helped her obtain a new trial, and Sabella's attorney, Rocco de Steffano, to the right of Sabella.

About six months later, murder charges against Sabella and Crudelle were dropped.

Later, the couple moved to a small farm in Maywood, but Crudelle didn't stick around for long. In September 1925, Sabella asked an assistant state's attorney to help her find him. She told the *Tribune*, "He left Monday for the market with a truckload of vegetables. He returned with the truck, but not with the $400 he should have got for the farm produce. It's all the money I have. Please help me find him." It's not clear whether the two ever met again.

Sabella married a third time, on November 2, 1940, to Giuseppe "Joseph" Campobasso. At sixty-two, she submitted paperwork to become a naturalized U.S. citizen; she received citizenship five years later.

Facing page: Isabella Campobasso, formerly Nitti, declares her intention to become a naturalized citizen of the United States on November 5, 1941.

In 1949, she moved to Los Angeles and lived there for eight years before dying of acute coronary syndrome on December 10, 1957. She was seventy-seven years old. The once despised farmworker was buried in Culver City's Holy Cross Cemetery, which is also the final resting site for actors John Candy, Jimmy Durante, Rita Hayworth, Bela Lugosi, Ricardo Montalban, crooner Bing Crosby and bandleader Lawrence Welk.

TRIPLICATE
(To be given to declarant
when originally issued; to be
made a part of the petition
for naturalization when petition is filed; and to be retained as part of the petition
in the records of the court)

UNITED STATES OF AMERICA

DECLARATION OF INTENTION
(Invalid for all purposes seven years after the date hereof)

No. 186187

UNITED STATES OF AMERICA
NORTHERN DISTRICT OF ILLINOIS } ss:

In the __DISTRICT__ Court
of __UNITED STATES__ at __CHICAGO__

(1) My full, true, and correct name is __ISABELLA CAMPOBASSO__
(Full, true name, without abbreviation, and any other name which has been used, must appear here)

(2) My present place of residence is __1322 S. Sawyer Ave__ my occupation is __Housewife__
(Number and street) (City or town) (County) (State)

(4) I am __62__ years old. (5) I was born on __March 14, 1879__, in __Triggiano, Italy__
(Month) (Day) (Year) (City or town) (County, district, province, or state) (Country)

(6) My personal description is as follows: Sex __female__, color __white__, complexion __fair/dark__ color of eyes __brown__
color of hair __brown__, height __5__ feet __—__ inches, weight __148__ pounds, visible distinctive marks __mole on right cheek__
race __White__, present nationality __Italian__

(7) I am __married__; the name of my wife or husband is __Joseph (2nd)__; we were married on __11-2-1940__
at __Chicago, Illinois__; he or she was born at __Triggiano, Italy__
(City or town) (State or country) (City or town) (County, district, province, or state) (Country)
on __Nov. 17, 1881__; and entered the United States at __New York__
(Month) (Day) (Year) (City or town) (State)
on __March 2, 1929__ for permanent residence in the United States, and now resides at __with me__
(Month) (Day) (Year) (City or town) (County and State)

(8) I have __five__ children; and the name, sex, date and place of birth, and present place of residence of each of said children who is living, are as follows:
__James, M., Sept. 14, 1900; Michael, M., Dec. 28, 1903; Charles, M.,__
__Nov. 15, 1906; Philomena, F., May 19, 1917; Mary, F., Aug. 15, 1919; first__
__three born in Italy, last two in Illinois; all reside in United States__

(9) My last place of foreign residence was __Triggiano, Italy__ (10) I emigrated to the United States from
(County, district, province, or state) (Country)
__Naples, Italy__ (11) My lawful entry for permanent residence in the United States was
(City or town) (Country)
at __New York__ under the name of __Travaglio Nitta, Isabella__
(City or town) (State)
on __Aug. 9, 1916__, on the __SS Dante Alighieri__
(Month) (Day) (Year) (Name of vessel or other means of conveyance)

(12) Since my lawful entry for permanent residence I have __not__ been absent from the United States, for a period or periods of 6 months or longer, as follows:

DEPARTED FROM THE UNITED STATES			RETURNED TO THE UNITED STATES		
PORT	DATE (Month, day, year)	VESSEL OR OTHER MEANS OF CONVEYANCE	PORT	DATE (Month, day, year)	VESSEL OR OTHER MEANS OF CONVEYANCE

(13) I have __not__ heretofore made declaration of intention: No. ____, on ____ at ____
(Month) (Day) (Year) (City or town)
____ in the ____
(County) (State) (Name of court)

(14) It is my intention in good faith to become a citizen of the United States and to reside permanently therein. (15) I will, before being admitted to citizenship, renounce absolutely and forever all allegiance and fidelity to any foreign prince, potentate, state, or sovereignty of whom or which at the time of admission to citizenship I may be a subject or citizen. (16) I am not an anarchist; nor a believer in the unlawful damage, injury, or destruction of property, or sabotage; nor a disbeliever in or opposed to organized government; nor a member of or affiliated with any organization or body of persons teaching disbelief in or opposition to organized government. (17) I certify that the photograph affixed to the duplicate and triplicate hereof is a likeness of me and was signed by me.
I do swear (affirm) that the statements I have made and the intentions I have expressed in this declaration of intention subscribed by me are true to the best of my knowledge and belief: SO HELP ME GOD.

Isabella Campobasso
(Original and true signature of declarant without abbreviation, also other name if used)

Subscribed and sworn to (affirmed) before me in the form of oath shown above in the office of the
Clerk of said Court, at __Chicago, Illinois__
this __5th__ day of __November__, anno Domini 19__41__ I hereby certify that
Certification No. __323316__ from the Commissioner of Immigration and Naturalization, showing the lawful entry for permanent residence of the declarant above named on the date stated in this declaration of intention, has been received by me, and that the photograph affixed to the duplicate and triplicate hereof is a likeness of the declarant.

[SEAL]

Isabella Campobasso

__HOYT KING__
Clerk of the __U.S. DISTRICT__ Court.
By ____ Deputy Clerk.

Form N-315
U.S. DEPARTMENT OF JUSTICE
IMMIGRATION AND NATURALIZATION SERVICE
(Edition of 1-13-41)

o16—19119   U.S. GOVERNMENT PRINTING OFFICE

HELEN CIRESE

Sabella's freedom would not have been possible without the assistance of Helen Cirese, a young, groundbreaking attorney. Born to an Italian immigrant family on December 1, 1899, Cirese thought she would become a reporter. At least that's what she told the editor-in-chief of her high school newspaper in Oak Park River Forest—a student by the name of Ernest Hemingway. But her plans changed when an older brother left Northwestern University to enlist during World War I. Proud of his patriotism, she decided to instead join the legal profession.

She studied law at DePaul University, where she served as class president and never completed a course with a grade lower than eighty-eight percent. Cirese was named a commencement speaker for the graduating class of sixty-five men and five women. In her address, titled "Youth and Loyalty," given on June 18, 1920, she said, "(T)he youth that went out to war did their work and did it well—having done it well once and under the unbearable conditions of war, cannot they be relied upon to shoulder the burdens under the favorable conditions of peace?"

That summer, Cirese became the youngest woman to pass the Illinois bar exam, ten months before her twenty-first birthday—making headlines nationwide. Twenty-one was the age required to be admitted to the bar at the time, so she was prevented from practicing law for another year.

While waiting to practice, Cirese fought for the rights of women to serve on juries. Her contention: "William the Conqueror has been dead a long time and that this is 1921, when women vote for president, and do other things that were not contemplated in 1006."

After pleading Sabella's case at age twenty-four, Cirese went on to handle seven murder cases within the next seven years. In July 1924, she was believed to be the first female attorney in Illinois to represent an alleged murderess. She helped acquit Lela Foster, a white woman, of the murder of her black husband.

Just five years out of law school but already a member of the U.S. Supreme Court bar, Cirese ran for justice of the peace in Oak Park as an

Facing page: Helen Cirese during the time of her candidacy for justice of the peace in Oak Park in April 1925.

> "I can't cook and I'm not interested in learning how.
> I escaped it growing up and I've avoided it since."
>
> —HELEN CIRESE, *CHICAGO TRIBUNE*, OCTOBER 10, 1930

independent with "no party affiliations or party promises." Her chances seemed promising: Six candidates were running for five positions. "A wisp of a girl, with a vivacious smile and dressed to the moment, Miss Cirese is making a vigorous campaign against what she terms a machine controlled ticket," according to the April 6, 1925, *Chicago Tribune*. She was, however, defeated by a two-to-one ratio.

Still, the accolades within the legal community continued to mount for Cirese. She was elected president of the Women's Bar Association of Illinois in 1930. But her role as a professional woman baffled those who believed a woman's place was in the home. In a *Chicago Tribune* story published on October 10, 1930, Cirese was asked if she liked to cook. She responded yes, but that she didn't have time to do it. "It's an awful thing to admit, I suppose," she said, "but I can't cook and I'm not interested in learning how. I escaped it growing up and I've avoided it since. When I was in school I was forced to learn to sew, but that's my only domestic art."

On March 28, 1931, she married in Indianapolis. The groom was Harry Hunnewell, a trust fund recipient from a wealthy Boston family who had been declared mentally incompetent two years prior. He filed for a quickie divorce in Reno, Nevada, on March 30, 1932, before escaping for the South Pacific. A judge tossed the divorce request, citing a residency requirement that Hunnewell didn't meet.

Hunnewell's extramarital affairs may have contributed to the demise of the marriage. In July 1933, Cirese told a Reno judge that she found Hunnewell intoxicated in the first-floor bedroom of the Beverly Hills home they shared; he was with another woman.

Cirese, seated middle, along with other members of the Women's Bar Association of Illinois, helped plan a statewide campaign for the right of women to serve on juries, circa 1930.

Returning to Chicago, Cirese was elected president of the National Women Lawyers' Association—the youngest ever—in July 1939. On her second attempt in 1945, Cirese was elected one of Oak Park's five justices of the peace. She served in that capacity until 1961. Cirese practiced law until she was eighty-two. She died in Florida on October 10, 1983.

ovie Revives
Chicago Girl
Writer's Play

"ROXIE HART."
...duced by 20th Century-Fox.
...rected by William A. Wellman.
...ed upon play "Chicago" by Maurine...
...kins.
...esented at the Chicago.
THE CAST.
...e Dart..............Ginger Rogers
...Flynn..............Adolphe Menjou
...er Howard........George Montgomery
...Callahan..........Lynne Overmont
...my Benham.........Nigel Bruce
...................Phil Silvers
...Norton...........Sara Allgood
...alley............William Frawley
...y Sunshine........Spring Byington
...rt Chapman........Ted North
...sa Watt...........Helene Reynolds
...a Hart............George Chandler
...les E. Murdock....Charles D. Brown
...in S. Harrison....Morris Ankrum
...e.................George Lessey
...................Iris Adrian
...ncer..............Milton Parsons

By Mae Tinee.
...od Morning!
...ne years ago Maurine Watkins
...used to work on THE TRIBUNE
...a very swell play called "C...
...and produced by Sam Har...
..."Roxie Hart" is its movie...

...s Watkins' heroine was a ci...
...ns..... A 1927 girl in wh...
...ran the excited and undis...
...blood of the gangster era...
...tory was based on fact.

...the picture opens a gray hai...
...aper man of 1942, who had be...
...blooded reporter in 1927, te...
...tory of Roxie over the bar...
...'Malley's saloon.
...e-out—and now it's 1927 and...
...e Chandler is frantically...
...g to the murder of a man w...
...een found dead in his flat...
...fellow was burglarizing, sa...
...dler. . . . Mrs. Chandler?
...town shopping — or someth...
...hat. . . . BUT it turns out t...
...Chandler was right there a...
...t particular moment is up...
...oof, keeping well out of sig...

...e corpse is identified as a the...
...agent with whom Roxie Cha...
...d been having more than bu...
...dealings. (You gather.) But, f...
...d story, the sort of reporters w...
...know anything about, persuad...
...o con...........gets killed t...
...ct he...............A famou...
...nal a........the case. . . .
...re wa........job sisters ge...
...and R........yearned fo...
...picture........e tha...
...sing........comes t...
...a ....while sh...
...s tri........co...
...d and now........s lavis...
...ttenti........Bertha
...What to do? Roxie thinks up...
...one. . . . Never mind what it...
...from here on the little woma...
...rly drowned in limelight.
...would have been right nice i...
...lirector had known just wh...
...d his epic. For the most pa...
...ie Hart" is right clever sat...
...I think a lighter touch migh...
...been employed.

Actress Phyllis Haver plays imprisoned murderess Roxie Hart in the silent film "Chicago," directed by Frank Urson in 1927.

CHAPTER SIX

'CHICAGO'

The women in these pages inspired one of the most iconic dramatic works to come out of the city of Chicago. Maurine Dallas Watkins wrote a play that later morphed into two films and a musical—one that continues to play on the stage today. *Chicago Tribune* critics Chris Jones and Michael Phillips consider these works and their place in American culture.

The publicity poster for the Bob Fosse musical production of "Chicago" from 1975.

'CHICAGO' ON STAGE

By Chris Jones

Did Maurine Dallas Watkins arrive from Indiana at the *Chicago Tribune* in 1924 with genuine plans to be a great *Tribune* reporter? Or was the crime-reporter persona merely a ruse to get to know some of Chicago's killer women so Maurine then could steal their stories and make her mark on Broadway?

Maybe it was both. More likely, it was the latter. Either way, we'll never know for sure. But we do know that Maurine became one of the most important dramatic writers the mean streets of Chicago ever produced.

She would become the author of a play, a play that became a musical that not only carried the name of this city for decades, but has for years played a crucial role in the international definition of the town Maurine called home. For as long as it served her needs.

Any Chicagoan who has traveled abroad is familiar with how it usually goes.

"Where are you from?"

"Chicago."

"Bang. Bang. Rat-a-tat-tat-tat."

THE THEATRE OF TODAY
EDITED BY GEORGE JEAN NATHAN

CHICAGO

MAURINE WATKINS

PUBLISHED BY ALFRED·A·KNOPF

Sure, you can blame Al Capone or John Dillinger or "The Untouchables." But the reputation of Chicago also has a lot to do with the popularity of "Chicago."

Walter Bobbie's revival of the Bob Fosse-styled crime musical has been performed eight times a week on Broadway since the fall of 1996, playing mostly to an audience of international tourists. It has been performed almost ten thousand times. And that doesn't include the long-running duplicate productions in London—which lasted for more than fifteen years—and on tour after tour across the world. And it's still going strong.

More than thirty million people all over the globe—most of whom never have clapped eyes on the real Chicago—have met Velma Kelly and Roxie Hart, thrilled to the lawyer Billy Flynn and the mysterious "sob sister" called Mary Sunshine. They've seen through "Mister Cellophane" and learned that when you're good to Mama, Mama most certainly is good to you. And as they've watched all of that old razzle-dazzle with their new best friends, they have felt like they have come to know a town they don't really know at all.

Or maybe they do. After all, what Maurine really did was to take her Page One stories for the *Tribune* and change a few of the names. Some of the crimes that she reported were beyond even the most theatrical of imaginations.

Within months, Maurine quit her job at the *Tribune* and headed to Yale University, where she studied with professor George Pierce Baker, perhaps the most influential playwright teacher in the history of America and a man widely credited with helping forge an American theater that was becoming less dependent on writers from abroad. Most of Baker's most famous students, though, were men—like Eugene O'Neill, Sidney Howard and Philip Barry. But he worked with two women who became prominent writers.

One was Hallie Flanagan. The other was Maurine Dallas Watkins.

Maurine started writing "Chicago," subtitled "A Satirical Comedy in Three Acts," as a project for Baker's class. The play opened on Broadway at the Music Box Theatre on December 30, 1926. The critic—and sometime correspondent for the *Tribune*—Burns Mantle would call the play "an overnight hit" in New York, where it ran all the way through the following May for a total of one hundred twenty-seven performances. In an era when theaters tended to turn over shows far more quickly, that was enough to be considered a substantial hit.

Read the play today and you'll be struck both by the accuracy of how Maurine depicted the way people in Chicago spoke and the specificity of her descriptive

Facing page: A 1927 first-edition printing of the play "Chicago," written by former *Chicago Tribune* reporter Maurine Watkins in 1926.

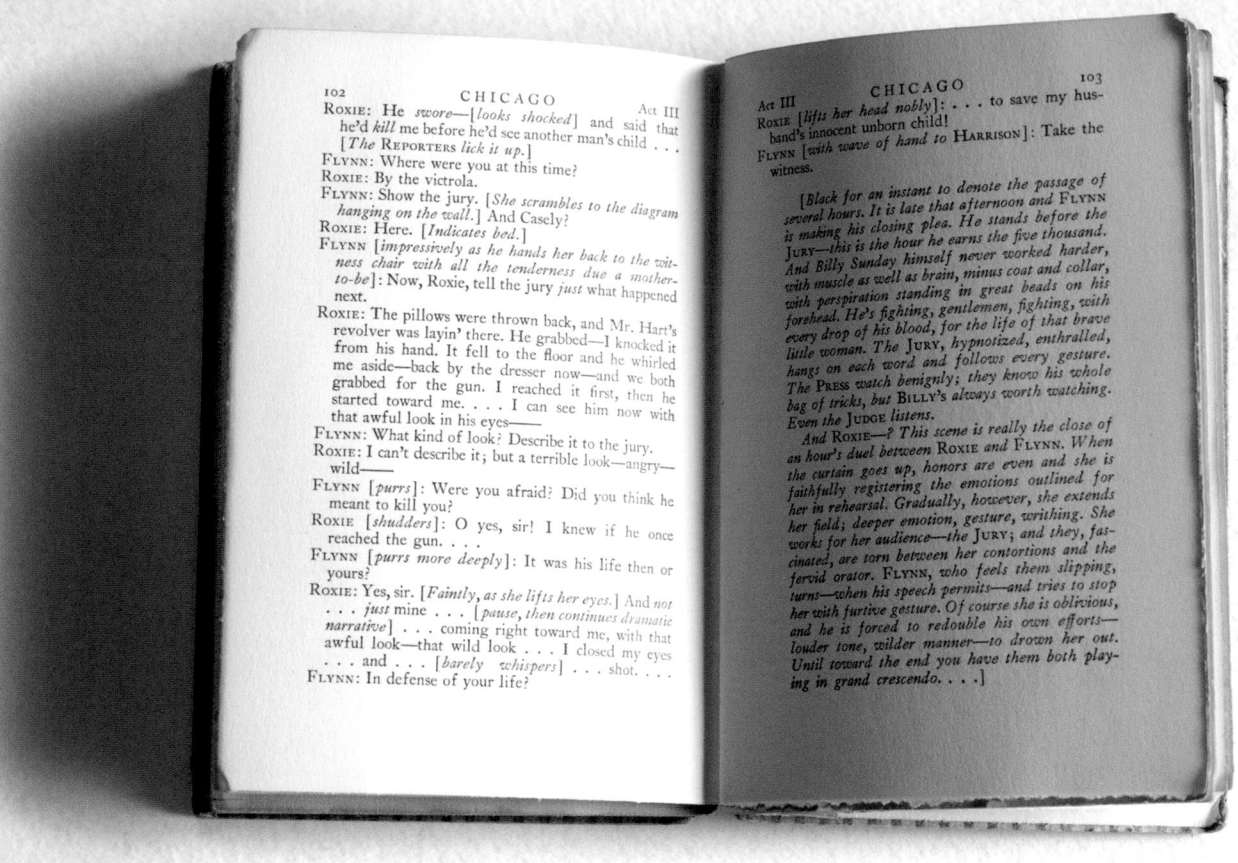

Roxie Hart testifies that she shot her lover to save her husband's unborn child, a development that mirrored Beulah Annan's pregnancy announcement before her murder trial.

detail. Maurine acquired a reporter's ear and eye. Much of her dialogue was punctuated by dashes and sentences left unfinished. If there is such a thing as vampish dialogue to be understood, then it surely came from this play.

Props were precisely described ("a night table with telephone, a stoutish bottle and a couple of glasses, an ash tray and cigarettes"). And Maurine caught many of the so-called feminine details that male writers would have missed. Her Act One was set in the bedroom of "a cheap modern flat on Chicago's South Side" where you could find "a large vanity dresser equipped with imitation ivory toilet articles, bottle with atomizers, perfumes, powder, rouge, eyebrow pencils and lipstick."

To the left stood a Victrola, playing "wild rhythmic jazz."

Maurine also detailed her characters with the same precision. Amos Hart was described as Roxie's "meal-ticket husband" and "an awkward creature of thirty-five with low forehead, snug nose and weak chin," and as "a man who wears a melancholy air."

ROXIE [*grinds out through her teeth*]: God damn you!

SERGEANT: So it was *you*.

ROXIE [*rises, hysterical*]: Yes, it was me! I shot him and I'm damned glad I did! I'd do it again——

JAKE: Once is enough, dearie!

ROXIE [*grinds her teeth in rage*]: "Through!" "Done with me!" I showed him, all right. If I don't have him, nobody does! [*Crumples, sobbing.*]

JAKE: I'm sure glad I met you tonight, sweetheart; to-morrow you'll sing another tune.

SERGEANT: Here's my confession—and the whole damn thing to do over again! [*Shakes* ROXIE.] Here, you. get your rags together! [*To* HARRISON.] We'll get her at the station, but let's finish him [*indicating* AMOS] now.

[*He takes* AMOS *to adjoining room;* HARRISON *starts to follow, but* ROXIE *grasps his arm as h...*

By Act Two, the action has moved from poor Amos' place to the women's ward of the Cook County Jail, a place that Maurine knew well from her work for the *Tribune*. She described a row of cells at the back of the room and, at its center, a long table with chairs, where the jail's matrons and its in-favor prisoners could hang out together and make plans for their own media coverage. There's even a lady boot-legger in the play who shows up every Thursday for the pleasure of the prisoners.

Among Roxie's new friends are Velma Kelly, a fellow murderess whom Maurine turned into both a friend and a rival, and "Crazy Liz," another killer woman working on an insanity defense, even though Maurine made clear that she could be plenty lucid.

"Chicago" painted a picture of a corrupt city with a criminal justice system dominated by payoffs, bribery and the timeless notion of *you scratch my back, I'll scratch yours*. In Maurine's telling, here was a system propped up by all manner of

Hart exclaims, "Yes, it was me! I shot him and I'm damned glad I did!" in the play written by Maurine.

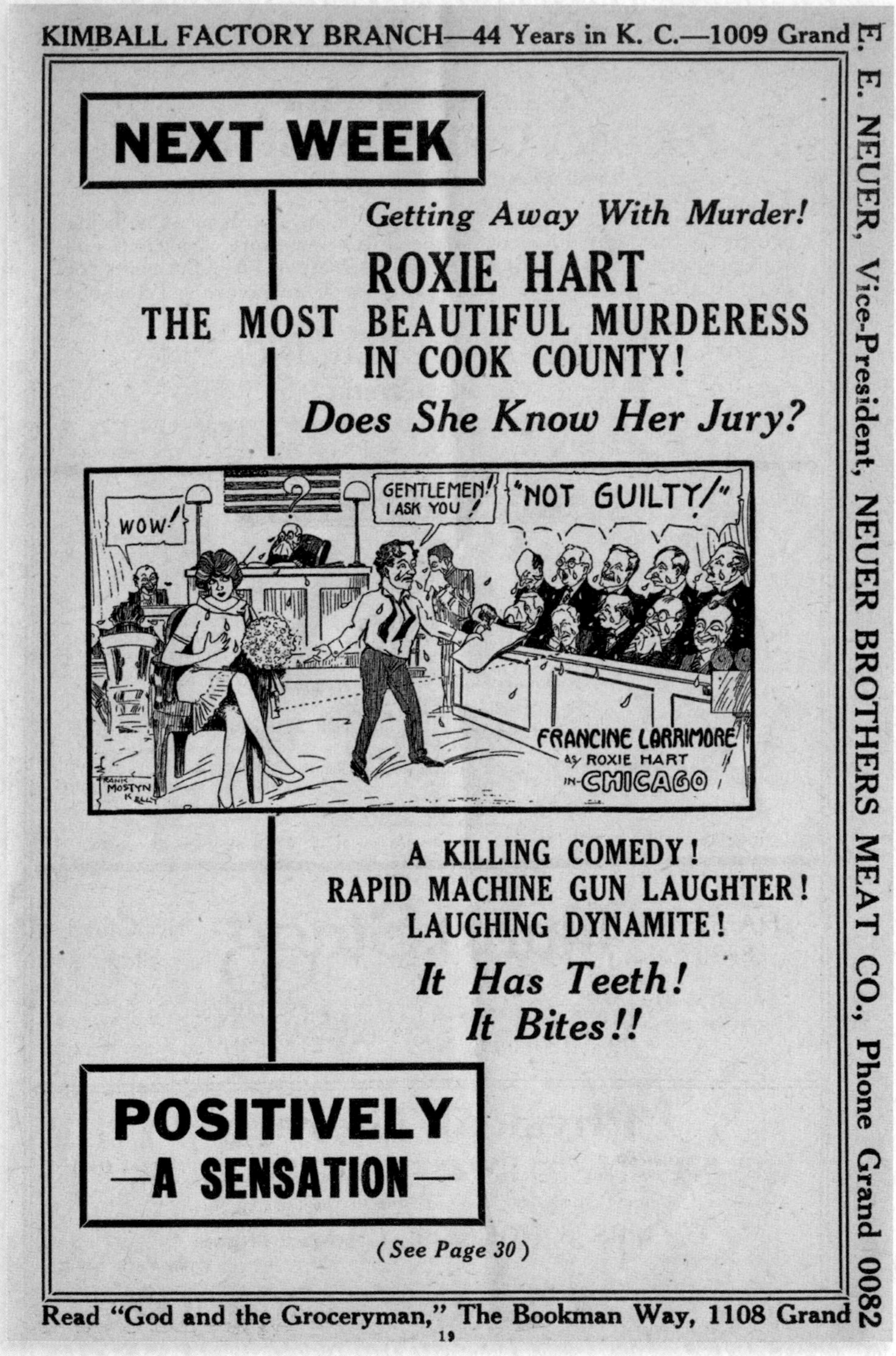

NEXT WEEK

Getting Away With Murder!

ROXIE HART
THE MOST BEAUTIFUL MURDERESS
IN COOK COUNTY!

Does She Know Her Jury?

WOW!

GENTLEMEN!
I ASK YOU!

"NOT GUILTY!"

FRANCINE LARRIMORE
as ROXIE HART
in CHICAGO

FRANK
MOSTYN
KELLY

A KILLING COMEDY!
RAPID MACHINE GUN LAUGHTER!
LAUGHING DYNAMITE!

It Has Teeth!
It Bites!!

**POSITIVELY
—A SENSATION—**

(See Page 30)

19

An advertisement tells of the upcoming performance of the play "Chicago," starring Francine Larrimore as Hart, in November 1927 at the Shubert Theatre in Kansas City, Missouri. The play opened there on November 13, 1927, making Kansas City the third city to see the play.

different people with agendas. The young women wanted to walk free, and they learned to exploit their sexuality. Their guards wanted cash and sex. The local politicians wanted sympathetic headlines. The lawyers wanted publicity and even more cash. And the Chicago media, operating in an era with many competing newspapers all fighting tooth and nail for the same stories, wanted sensational scoops. The need to emotionally engage readers hardly was invented in the twenty-first century: It was very much part of the landscape of Maurine's newspapering era.

And just like today, when aldermanic corruption still makes the headlines, everyone had their price.

In Act Three, Maurine took her readers to the courtroom itself, building on all she had described about the characters and adding the tension of an impending verdict. The play ended with big smiles for the cameras. This is, after all, Chicago.

By September 1927, the touring production of "Chicago" had arrived in Chicago, where it was reviewed at the Harris Theater by the *Tribune*, which thought it exceptionally funny. "Your rightful place is a seat at the Harris for at least one performance of Miss Watkins' gorgeous travesty on what happens to good-looking murderesses in the larger communities of this United States," wrote the semi-pseudonymous theater critic "F.R." (Actually, his name was Frederick Donaghey and he hailed from Philadelphia.)

Warming to his task, F.R. called the play "a screaming apostrophe" to "gallant old Cook County." Maurine surely would have agreed.

Alas, Donaghey would die of a heart attack in 1937, sitting in a dentist's chair awaiting the extraction of a tooth. That was the kind of Chicago story Maurine would have loved.

In the years that followed, Maurine denied permission to most anyone who wanted to adapt her play—some people thought that she had felt some later-in-life remorse for treating these heinous Chicago murderers in so glib and comedic a fashion. And it was only after her death in 1969 that "Chicago" was turned into a musical. But in short measure, "Chicago the Musical"—with a book by Fred Ebb and Bob Fosse, music by John Kander and lyrics by Ebb—greatly exceeded the fame and influence of the play that was its source. Over time it came to be known as the quintessential Fosse musical, the most famous work of the Chicago-born choreographer known for his hyperspecific movement vocabulary of turned-in knees, angled, attitudinal body parts, muscular twitches, sideways shuffling and jazzy, animated hands.

The original Broadway production of "Chicago the Musical" opened in 1975 with Gwen Verdon and Chita Rivera in the two lead roles of Velma Kelly and Roxie Hart. The show ran for nine hundred thirty-six performances over almost two years. By any measure, this was among Kander and Ebb's best work. The pair of sardonic song-smiths, famous for their signature combination of cynicism and longing, caught the paradoxes at the heart of what Maurine always had been writing about. These men knew both Broadway and Chicago. So they knew their way around Big Bamboozlers.

The musical numbers were gorgeously melodic, savvy of lyric and with a lush, dark musical soul. And Ebb's lyrics were singularly witty. "If you want my gravy," he had Mama Morton sing, "pepper my ragout. Spice it up for Mama. She'll get hot for you." Especially when combined with Fosse's physical style, the show simmered and oozed with a sensuality that make a big 1970s splash. When you think about it, Maurine got very lucky: Her play was made into a musical that understood the author's impulses.

But it was Walter Bobbie's 1996 revival—a simpler staging that was based on a concert-style performance but very much in tribute to Fosse—that made the title part of the DNA of the modern Broadway musical.

Much of that was due to its staggering longevity. "Chicago"—which was first produced for the Encores! series of semistaged musicals and featured Fosse-style choreography created by Ann Reinking—became the longest-running revival in Broadway history, eventually playing longer than "Cats" and becoming second only to "The Phantom of the Opera" in terms of its overall longevity.

Facing page: The Broadway production of "Chicago" in 2019.

"If you want my gravy, pepper my ragout. Spice it up for Mama. She'll get hot for you."

—MAMA MORTON, "CHICAGO THE MUSICAL"

Charlotte d'Amboise stars as Roxie Hart in Broadway's record-breaking, Tony Award-winning musical "Chicago" in 2019.

Amra-Faye Wright, front left, performs the song "All That Jazz" as Velma Kelly in the Broadway production of "Chicago."

Its central conceit involved the placement of the band at center stage, thus thrusting the musicians into the telling of the story (and rendering a huge set unnecessary). The staging was a producer's dream—hot, cool and affordable.

Those lead producers, Barry and Fran Weissler, then kept the musical running by casting star after star as the show played on and on across the years, never losing steam.

The celebrities became quite a list: Joel Grey, Sandy Duncan, Chita Rivera, Michael C. Hall, Jasmine Guy, Marilu Henner, George Hamilton, Jennifer Holliday, Ute Lemper, Mel B, Tom Hewitt, John O'Hurley, Eddie George, Brooke Shields, Taye Diggs, Robin Givens, Cuba Gooding Jr., Melanie Griffith, Tom Wopat. They've all done "Chicago."

How apropos. Even in 1926, Maurine had, of course, been writing about the absurd fusion of celebrity and criminality in the American justice system, arguing that some of Chicago's guiltiest and most dangerous women figured out that the way to walk out of jail was to become famous. In the Cook County court system of the 1920s, it was all glitzy show business, profiting those who knew how to play the game.

By the mid-1990s in America—after the rise of people who were famous just for being famous—all of America understood what a 1920s reporter at the *Chicago Tribune* somehow had known all along.

Phyllis Haver stars in the 1927 silent film "Chicago."

'CHICAGO' ON SCREEN

By Michael Phillips

IN THE MOVIE BUSINESS some geese are golden, and they lay golden eggs every time. "A Star Is Born" (four official versions and counting) is one such bird. Terrific adaptations (1937 and 1954), lousy (1976) or merely good (2018), the narrative tells the audience what it wants to believe about love and loss.

Then there's "Chicago." If "A Star Is Born" packages hopes and dreams, tempered by tragedy, "Chicago" sells a wiseacre's game played with loaded dice and a sneer. It's a more jaundiced example of evergreen American hooey, born in the juicy, amped-up 1924 *Chicago Tribune* accounts of a few select and flagrant miscarriages of Cook County justice.

The writer of those columns, Maurine Dallas Watkins, very likely helped acquit a couple of guilty women. Her subsequent stage comedy, "Chicago," premiered in 1926 and played a considerable (though hardly solitary) role in cementing the city's corrosive, alluringly criminal image in the culture.

Later in life, did something like a guilty conscience plague Maurine? It's speculation, but worth speculating: The author probably knew in her heart that both her *Tribune* coverage and Broadway success didn't elevate anyone's sense of justice, her own included.

Maurine's rollicking, cynical, artful *Tribune* reports on the trials of Beulah Annan and Belva Gaertner, the Roxie Hart and Velma Kelly prototypes, suited the mood of a merry, bloody time. It was fun while it lasted, until it wasn't. And the success of Maurine's play led to a lucrative if spotty screenwriting career that lasted a decade.

The sardonic mythology of "Chicago," meanwhile, has long outlived the women who inspired it and the author who capitalized on it, no little thanks to the three film versions.

'CHICAGO' GOES HOLLYWOOD

Hollywood met the "Chicago" phenomenon firsthand in the spring of 1927. The national tour of the Broadway production ran eleven weeks at Hollywood's Music Box Theatre. Nancy Carroll, later an Academy Award nominee and a big star in the pre-Production Code era, played Roxie Hart. A prefamous Clark Gable appeared in the production as well.

The *Los Angeles Times* loved it. Its drama critic said: "Bristling with wicked satire . . . the public is treated to a caricature of itself as a nation of gum-chewing, sensation-seeking addicts who must incessantly be fed faked pictures and hysterical interviews." Well! At least we've moved on since then.

Cecil B. DeMille liked it just fine, too, and produced the silent film version. Lenore J. Coffee adapted Maurine's play for the silent feature. The DeMille "Chicago" retains some, but not much, of the stage version's sass and zingers. "Hang a woman with a face like that?" a reporter cracks via intertitles, sensing the jury is about to acquit a good-looking female killer. "Say, Justice ain't so blind!"

Frank Urson directed the film, a little sluggishly. Producer DeMille reportedly took over while keeping his name off it, so as not to offend audiences who'd come to associate DeMille with the pious yet salacious biblical epic "The King of Kings," a sensation of the time.

Onstage, Maurine's cynicism rarely let up. Onscreen, in 1927, it let up plenty, allowing for sentimental melodrama and conventional romantic interests. In early 1928, the *Los Angeles Times* interviewed "Chicago" film star Phyllis Haver, the onetime Mack Sennett "bathing beauty" who played Roxie. She laid out the

"Bristling with wicked satire . . . the public is treated to a caricature of itself as a nation of gum-chewing, sensation-seeking addicts who must incessantly be fed faked pictures and hysterical interviews."

—LOS ANGELES TIMES

"It is the old story of the necessary appeal for less sophisticated audiences in smaller communities."

—PHYLLIS HAVER

Display ads from the *Chicago Tribune's* March 21 and March 25 editions show the silent film "Chicago" playing at the Roosevelt Theater in 1928.

The Balaban and Katz Theaters ad features the film "Chicago" on March 25, 1928, in the *Chicago Tribune*.

Pathé presents 'CHICAGO' WITH PHYLLIS HAVER

VICTOR VARCONI

VIRGINIA BRADFORD — ROBERT EDESON — JULIA FAYE — MAY ROBSON — T. ROY BARNES —

DE MILLE STUDIO PRODUCTION

PATHÉ EXCHANGE, Inc. DISTRIBUTORS

Legs versus the law

rationale for turning a harsh topical comedy into a softer, more palatable affair. Not mentioning the many concessions DeMille and company made to appease the Hays Office censorship board, Haver preferred to look at it this way: "It is the old story of the necessary appeal for less sophisticated audiences in smaller communities." In the play, Haver said, Roxie got away with murder. "Back in the Middle West," the actress noted, audiences would "sense only the obvious, that Roxie instead of being punished was rewarded for her crime. They would think it is a perfectly terrible example for their young people . . . plays like 'Chicago' are for sophisticated city folk. Movies like 'Chicago' receive the biggest patronage in the hinterlands."

A publicity poster for the silent film "Chicago" shows Haver starring as Hart in 1927.

Hart, played by
Haver, thinks
about what she's
done after killing
her boyfriend
in a scene from
the silent film
"Chicago" in 1927.

D.M. 3-26, HH

Hart, played by Haver, holds a gun in her hand in the silent film "Chicago" in 1927. The Hart character is based on the real-life story of Beulah.

For decades the silent "Chicago" languished in the limbo of apparently lost titles. Then a pristine print turned up in DeMille's private collection. In 2006, the UCLA Film and Television Archive unveiled a restored version, now widely available. Many enjoy it. Few, however, would say it reflects the play's malignant energy.

As the *Chicago Tribune* reviewer (filing under the cloying pseudonym Mae Tinee—matinee, get it?) assessed the DeMille version: "Well, they have slaughtered Maurine Watkins' play . . . the clever, satiric, diabolically human, uproariously funny play that could so well have been made into just such a picture has had all its fine parts ironed out. . . . (T)he result is just a fussy, ordinary melodrama that is rather funny in spots."

Tragically, "Chicago" never got treated to an early talkie adaptation in the pre-Code era, the way Ben Hecht and Charles MacArthur's 1928 newspaper comedy "The Front Page" did in 1931 (among other adaptations). The second time Maurine's property made it to the screen, there was a war on, and 1920s excess and cynicism seemed very much a thing of the Paleolithic era.

Hart, played by Haver, right, pleads with the jury during her murder trial as her lawyer, Billy Flynn, played by Robert Edeson, looks on in a scene from the silent film "Chicago" in 1927.

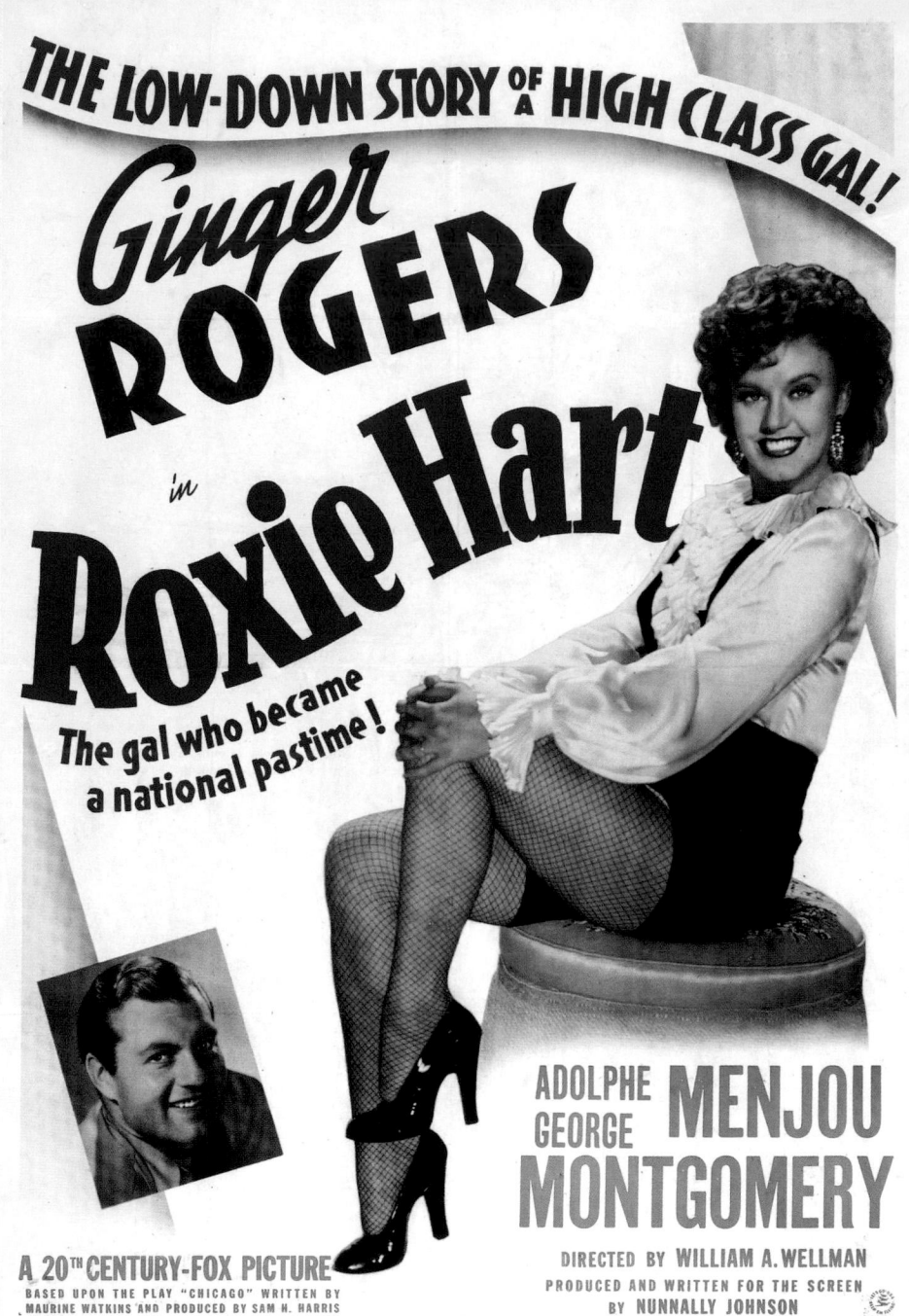

THE LOW-DOWN STORY OF A HIGH CLASS GAL!

GINGER ROGERS

in

Roxie Hart

The gal who became a national pastime!

ADOLPHE MENJOU
GEORGE MONTGOMERY

A 20TH CENTURY-FOX PICTURE
BASED UPON THE PLAY "CHICAGO" WRITTEN BY
MAURINE WATKINS AND PRODUCED BY SAM H. HARRIS

DIRECTED BY WILLIAM A. WELLMAN
PRODUCED AND WRITTEN FOR THE SCREEN
BY NUNNALLY JOHNSON

Ginger Rogers starred in the 1942 film version of the play "Chicago." Rogers played the lead role of Hart.

William Wellman directed that film, titled "Roxie Hart," starring Ginger Rogers and her endlessly exploited dancer's legs. The 1942 release ran a quick and boisterous seventy-five minutes. Maurine had nothing to do with it. By this time her own screenwriting career in Hollywood had run its course, the romantic comedy "Libeled Lady" (1936) one of the highlights on a fairly long resume of story credits, rewrites and lucrative dead ends.

"Roxie Hart" is a total whitewash from one perspective, a fairly pungent variation on the original from another. Journalist-turned-screenwriter Nunnally Johnson wrote the adaptation, told in a series of flashbacks. The present-day early forties scenes feature a garrulous veteran reporter (George Montgomery, gassing on in a role not found in Maurine's play) entertaining a handful of saloon patrons with memories of the dear old Roaring Twenties. In particular, he reminisces about Roxie Hart.

Velma Kelly is nowhere to be found in "Roxie Hart." This is a one-scandal operation. The material's morally improved on screen (though that's hardly an improvement). While the opening credits include a title card dedicating the film to "all those women who shot their men full of holes in a fit of pique," Wellman's picture takes pains to keep Roxie innocent-ish, before consigning her to full-on domestic bliss for a punchline (though she's plainly pissed about it, and misses her old showgirl days). Adolphe Menjou plays this version's Billy Flynn, a little too studied for my taste. But Rogers is pretty terrific.

On YouTube, you can find a one-take Charleston dance sequence, performed by Rogers but cut from the movie. It's swell. So is character actor Lynne Overman as Jake, the reporter with the driest comic delivery imaginable.

Released in the months following Pearl Harbor, "Roxie Hart" did reasonable business. It has its admirers; filmmaker Stanley Kubrick adored it. In 1942, though, it seemed out of sync with the times. *New York Times* critic Bosley Crowther, a wet blanket even when there wasn't a war on, wrote: "This is a most unsuitable time to be calling to mind the follies, the court-room circuses and vulgarities of this brashly eccentric nation during a period which might better be forgotten."

A story in the July 6, 1942, *Chicago Tribune* announced a new movie based on Watkins' play.

Movie Revives Chicago Girl Writer's Play

"ROXIE HART."
Produced by 20th Century-Fox.
Directed by William A. Wellman.
Based upon play "Chicago" by Maurine Watkins.
Presented at the Chicago.
THE CAST.
Roxie Hart.................Ginger Rogers
Billy Flynn.............Adolphe Menjou
Homer Howard.....George Montgomery
Jake Callahan........Lynne Overman
E. Clay Benham.............Nigel Bruce
Babe..........................Phil Silvers
Mrs. Norton................Sara Allgood
O'Malley................William Frawley
Mary Sunshine..........Spring Byington
Stuart Chapman.............Ted North
Velma Wall.........Helene Reynolds
Amos Hart.............George Chandler
Charles E. Murdock....Charles D. Brown
Martin S. Harrison.......Morris Ankrum
Judge...................George Lessey
Gertie......................Iris Adrian
Announcer..............Milton Parsons

By Mae Tinée.

Good Morning!

Some years ago Maurine Watkins—who used to work on THE TRIBUNE, wrote a very swell play called "Chicago" and produced by Sam Harris. . . . "Roxie Hart" is its movie version.

Miss Watkins' heroine was a child of chaos. . . . A 1927 girl in whose veins ran the excited and undisciplined blood of the gangster era, and her story was based on fact.

As the picture opens a gray haired newspaper man of 1942, who had been a hot blooded reporter in 1927, tells the story of Roxie over the bar in one O'Malley's saloon.

Fade-out—and now it's 1927 and one George Chandler is frantically confessing to the murder of a man who had been found dead in his flat. . . The fellow was burglarizing, says Chandler. . . . Mrs. Chandler? O, downtown shopping—or something like that. . . . BUT it turns out that Mrs. Chandler was right there and, at that particular moment is up on the roof, keeping well out of sight.

The corpse is identified as a theatrical agent with whom Roxie Chandler had been having more than business dealings. [You gather.] But, for a good story, the sort of reporters we don't know anything about, persuade her to confess that she has killed to protect her virtue. . . . A famous criminal attorney takes the case. . . . Feature writers and sob sisters get busy and Roxie—who had yearned for her picture in the paper more than anything else in life—becomes famous. . . .

For a day. . . . But, while she awaits trial, a new murder is committed and now everybody's lavishing attention on "Two Gun Bertha." . . . What to do? Roxie thinks up a new one. . . . Never mind what it is —but from here on the little woman is fairly drowned in limelight. . . .

It would have been right nice if the director had known just when to end his epic. For the most part "Roxie Hart" is right clever satire, tho I think a lighter touch might have been employed.

Ginger Rogers is deft. Adolphe Menjou is skilful as the rascally, quick-thinking criminal lawyer. . . . Lynne Overman as the old time newspaper man is just right and there's much good playing by the supporting cast. . . . Didn't care for George Montgomery.

See you tomorrow.

FAST AND LOOSE

Crowther was wrong, again, of course. The building blocks of "Chicago," the material's acidic illustration of what sapheads and star-fornicators we all are, simply needed three more decades to become pertinent again.

Bob Fosse's stage musical, premiering on Broadway in 1975, went for the jugular and all the slinky depravity Fosse could muster. The show ran, but it had the misfortune of opening up against "A Chorus Line."

Just like Roxie, though, it kept adapting and moving on. A stripped-down, scenery-free, dance-forward revival premiered on Broadway in 1996. The timing was exquisite: O.J. Simpson's trial and acquittal, Bill Clinton's affairs—the mood was right. Besides, musical theater audiences had just about had it with British spectacles starring falling chandeliers ("The Phantom of the Opera"), rising helicopters ("Miss Saigon") and annoying cats ("Cats," soon to be a movie!). All those sexy, muscular dancers were like a breath of fresh, nasty air.

It's 2019, and the "Chicago" revival is still running on Broadway. It's still touring, endlessly.

The 2002 film version of the musical played a major part in the sustained

Actress Renée Zellweger, right, portrays Hart with actor Richard Gere in a courtroom scene from the film "Chicago" in 2002.

Facing page: Actress Catherine Zeta-Jones portrays Kelly in a scene from the film "Chicago" in 2002.

Zellweger stars as Hart in the film "Chicago" in 2002.

Is it a great movie musical?
No. Pretty good, though.

interest in "Chicago." Rob Marshall directed it; Bill Condon wrote the screenplay; the songs were, as always, by John Kander and Fred Ebb, and mostly excellent. The choreography was indebted to Fosse.

Renée Zellweger played a Kewpie-doll Roxie; Catherine Zeta-Jones, a former West End chorine with a hungry look in her eyes, won a supporting actress Oscar for her portrayal of Velma Kelly. Richard Gere glided through as Billy Flynn; John C. Reilly and Queen Latifah added a lot as Amos and Mama Morton.

Is it a great movie musical? No. Pretty good, though. And it had been a while since America had seen a pretty good film version of a worthy stage musical. "Chicago" won the top Oscar that year. People were in the mood for it, because the mood now in America, nearly always, is receptive to the simple, facile reminders of this simple, facile Jazz Age fable. Getting away with murder: no problem. Lying: no problem. Cheating: ditto. From Prohibition to Watergate and O.J. to Trump, this country always manages to turn over another rock and mythologize its own corruption.

Miramax financed the screen musical. Through various stages of development, the project was overseen, for years, by studio mogul and serial sexual predator Harvey Weinstein. Weinstein is now well and truly disgraced, a permanent emblem of just how long a bastard with power can get away with nearly anything. He nearly put director Marshall in the hospital with his meddling, though in the end, Weinstein gave up his aggressive bid to share producer's credit with the credited producer, Martin Richards.

"It's great to do the right thing once in a while," Weinstein told the *New York Times* after the film's triumphant completion. "I'm going to have to try to do it more often."

If only Maurine Watkins were still around to write the Harvey Weinstein biopic: the perfect bookend to "Chicago."

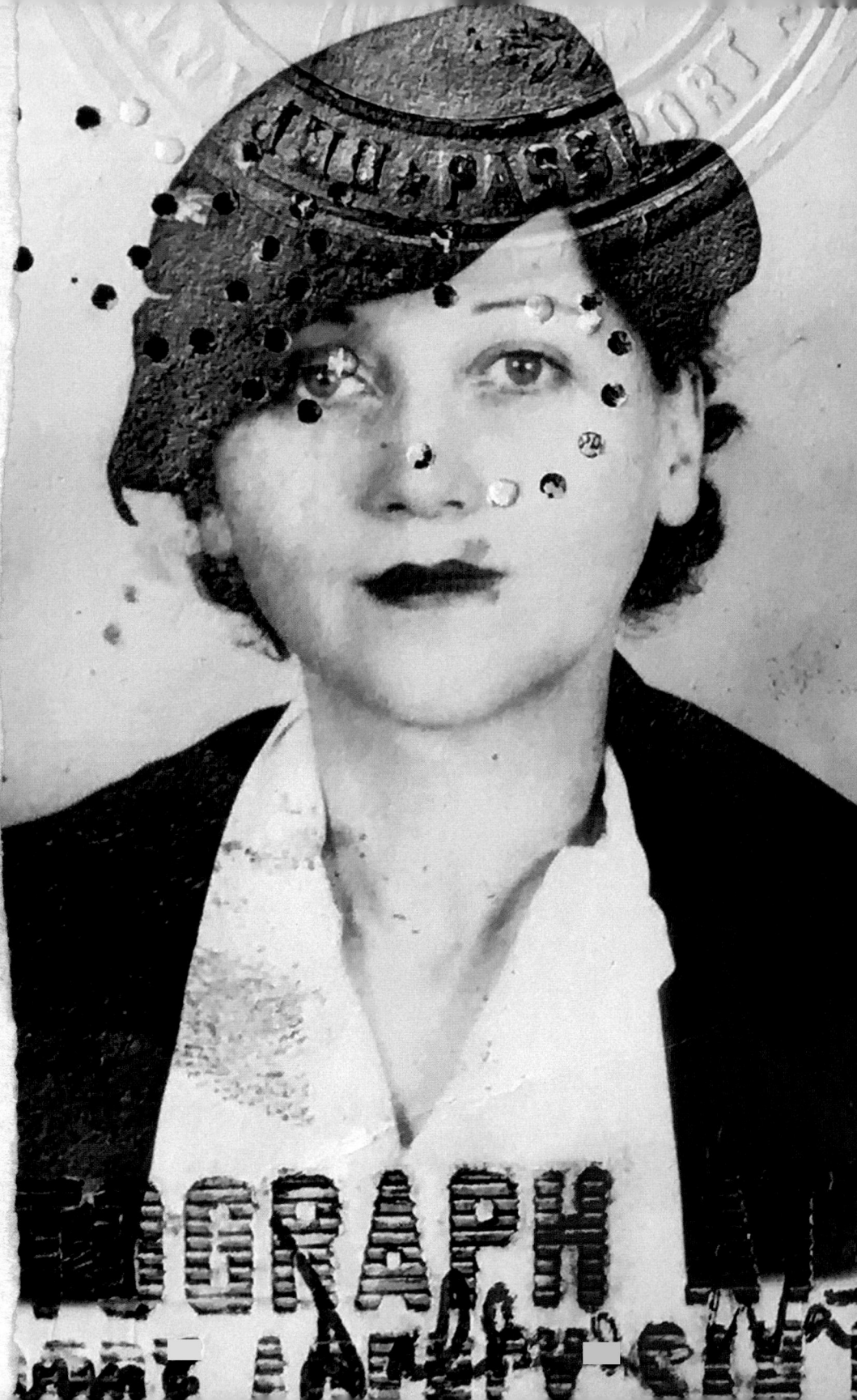

"___" a new play in three ___
___ine Watkins, a second ___
at the Yale School of Drama
___ Francine Larrimore ___
___ at the Shubert Theater ___
___ht by Sam H. Harris. Sta___
___ge Abbott.

___:
Hart, Francine Larrimore;
___asely, Carl Eckstrom; Ja___
___ A. Bickford; Amos Ha___
Halton; Sergeant Murda___
Slattery; Martin S. Harris
Barrat; Babe, Arthur R. ___
___rs. Morton, Isabelle Winto___
Juliette Crosby; Liz, Dare___
___; Billy Flynn, Edward E___
___ Sunshine, Eda Heineman
___he Maggie, Feriki Bocos;
___ Kitty, Edith Fitzgerald; ___
___e Mal; Judge Canton, Mi___
Corbin, G. Albert Smith; ___
___porter, George Cowell; C___
___ Court, Charles Kuhn; ___
___spher, James E. Pall; Sta___
Vincent York; Foreman___
___ W. Anspake.

___ weeks ago, with the f___
___ of the new Yale The___
___mith, a student in the Dep___
___ Drama at Yale Univer___
___ed Yale's first contributio___
___erican stage. The vehicle
___ "The Patriarch" and was ___
___ immediately by John Go___
___ early professional prese___

___ night at the Shubert The___
___aven witnessed Yale's se___
___ution—a travesty on ju___
___en by Maurine Watkins, ___
___ber of the Chicago Tr___
___ now a second year stu___
___ Department of Drama. I___
___ilt on life and apparent___
___ the life role of Beulah ___
___ll and titian-haired. The ___
___ about the arrest, inca___
___nd trial of a beautiful wo___
___etrayed her husband's ___
___ affair with a married ___
___she murdered when he tu___
___er.

___ge as it may seem to ___
___men in close touch with ___
___re in Connecticut, the ve___
___with reality. It is a true ___
___ of conditions as they exi___
___ parts of the country and ___
___ an important message to ___
___an public if it be accep___

___ Larrimore, as Roxie ___
___ress, was excellent in ___
Tough, harsh and moved ___
___raving for publicity and ___
___ty, she adhered so strict___
___rt that it was difficult ___
___ to realize that this lying, ___
___ blood-tainted woman ___
___ything but a cold-blo___

___les A. Bickford, typical ___
___ police reporter, gave a___
___lawless interpretation ___
___ Uni___ he ___
___ but ___
___enti___
real___
even ___ pencil. ___
made ___ an excellent crit___
___ even to his fondness for ___
___rt and demand of "cash ___
___e."

___thy Stickney, in a char___
___ the crazy woman of the ___
___y Jail," was very effecti___
___udly applauded as she le___
___ after her first appearan___
___cago" will be at the S___
___t and tomorrow nigh___

CHAPTER SEVEN

MAURINE WATKINS

"Yet the young woman who wrote 'Chicago' had worked only eight months on any newspaper, and until she got that job on the *Chicago Tribune*, had never seen the inside of a newspaper office nor known a newspaper man. She had never known a killer; nor had seen the inside of a jail."

—"THAT ASTOUNDING YOUNG PERSON!" CLARE OGDEN DAVIS, *SUCCESS MAGAZINE*, DATE UNKNOWN

THE FIRST TIME MAURINE WATKINS' name appeared on the front page of the *Chicago Tribune* was April 5, 1924, under the headline: "Demand Noose for 'Prettiest' Woman Slayer." Maurine wrote about Beulah Annan, a liquored-up woman who shot her equally inebriated lover to death in the apartment she shared with her husband. It might not have been the first story written by Maurine during her eight months at the newspaper, but it was the one that would later garner her fame and fortune.

During the spring and early summer of 1924, the bloody headlines continued.

On May 21, 1924, Robert "Bobby" Franks, fourteen, was kidnapped and murdered. The suspected killers were Richard Loeb and Nathan Leopold, who thought they had planned the perfect murder. Maurine was on the story, reporting from Franks' in-home funeral service on Ellis Avenue in Kenwood.

His tiny white casket had eight pallbearers, all classmates of the young boy, Maurine wrote. She described how Franks' mother, as she walked by her son's friends, "paused and ran her hands hungrily over their faces. Some with the round features of childhood, others slim in adolescence—and four days ago her son had been with them!"

Maurine was part of a gaggle of reporters questioning the highly educated Leopold about "love, philosophy, art, sports" a few days after the Franks boy's funeral. She noted, "If he's not connected with the crime—what an experience! And if he is connected—still it's experience!"

Despite his confession to the murder, one of Loeb's friends couldn't accept the son of a millionaire would commit such a crime for a ransom. "Why, those boys could have had all the money in the world! Why should they do that?" said Richard Rubel.

Yet money and adventure were the reasons the pair gave for committing the crime. Maurine wrote: "Were they bored by a life which left them nothing to be desired, no obstacles to overcome, no goal to attain? Were they jaded by the jazz-life of gin and girls, so that they needed so terrible a thing as murder to give them new thrills?"

Wannabe cabaret dancer Belva Gaertner was also in search of thrills on March 12, 1924, when she and automobile salesman Walter Law pursued a "night of gin and jazz at the Gingham Inn." Just one problem: She claimed not to remember any of it, even after she was charged with Law's murder. That June, while covering the trial, Maurine wrote, "For there were no witnesses: just a man found dead, slumped over the steering wheel of Mrs. Gaertner's car; a bullet in his head from her pistol left lying on the sedan floor; and the woman herself in her apartment at 4809 Forrestville Avenue—hysterical, disheveled and covered with blood."

Maurine also attended the funeral for "good girl gone bad" Wanda Stopa; the acquittal of a fifteen-year-old Italian boy who was accused of murdering his father in his mother's defense; and the robbery of a blind beggar whose $1,100 in pennies was swiped by a supposed friend. The thespian whose bond was set at $1,000 for writing bad checks might have elicited the most comical reaction from any judge whose courtroom Maurine sat in. When the conniving Ray Vorhees asked to say a word, Judge Alfar Eberhardt responded, "You may not! You're too slick a talker and there have been too many suckers already! I've a diamond ring and watch and I want to hold on to them!"

But crime, courts and funerals weren't the only topics Maurine covered for the paper. Thirty of the almost fifty *Chicago Tribune* stories attributed to her were reviews of plays and movies. She also wrote articles on health issues, including birth control and innovations in anesthesiology and child psychiatry; commentary on style; and updates on women leading the pacifism movement.

Maurine covered the opening of a hospital for up to seventy-five unwed mothers and forty children by the Salvation Army, writing, "Although it serves (the lakes) region particularly, many girls come to Chicago from distant points in order to find obscurity."

Two weeks later, she was attending a hairdressers convention where experts were divided on whether cutting a woman's hair would stimulate growth or lead to baldness. She reasoned, "Take your choice! (For you'll pay your money either way!)"

At a clothiers convention, she noted, "The plump woman of middle-age who is shown 'flapper' styles for hours at a time may rejoice in knowing that her choleric spouse has the same experience. Presumably the nation abandons clothes at the age of 25."

From mid-July 1924 to her departure from the paper in August 1924, Maurine only wrote reviews of movies and a few plays appearing in Chicago.

On August 7, 1924, Maurine's byline appeared twice in the *Chicago Tribune*. On Page Two, she interviewed alienist, or psychiatrist, Dr. Bernard Glueck, who testified in court about the mental condition of Leopold and Loeb. Glueck condemned discipline and said parents need to be frank with their children about sex.

On Page Thirteen, she wrote about a publicity stunt in which child actor Jackie Coogan, who starred with Charlie Chaplin in "The Kid" and in later years portrayed Uncle Fester on TV's "The Addams Family," was named mayor of Chicago for ten minutes. Maurine noted the nine-year-old's twelve-hour stay in the city brought in "hundreds of Illinois checks to the Children's Crusade of Mercy."

These stories would be the last she would write for the *Chicago Tribune*.

A PLAYWRIGHT IN THE MAKING

Maurine first made headlines as a playwright at age eleven. She penned the play "Hearts of Gold" for the Ladies' Aid Society of the Crawfordsville Christian Church, where her father, George Watkins, was a minister. She later told the *Indianapolis Star*, "We made $45 with 'Hearts of Gold' and it all went to the heathen, but since then I've become far more mercenary."

It is unclear when and where Maurine, the only child of Watkins and his wife, Georgia, was born. Although various records indicate she was born on July 27 in Kentucky, none agree on whether it was in 1896, 1898 or 1901, or whether it was in Louisville or Lexington. Her original birth certificate is missing from Kentucky's vital statistics files.

The family moved to Crawfordsville, Indiana, when Maurine was young. The small town almost fifty miles northwest of Indianapolis refers to itself as the "Athens of Indiana"—it is home to Wabash College, one of the last all-male liberal arts universities in the United States, as well as to acclaimed authors, most notably retired Civil War General Lew Wallace, who penned "Ben-Hur: A Tale of the Christ" (1880).

Maurine, left, as a freshman at Crawfordsville High School in Indiana in 1911.

Maurine, center seated five from left, with her Crawfordsville High School class in the 1912 yearbook.

In 1911, Maurine entered Crawfordsville High School, which won the state's first basketball championship the same year. She was one of ten founding members of its newspaper, the *Billiken*, which dubbed itself "a racy, newsy, little paper, the first copy of which was given away" and was then distributed every two weeks for the remainder of the school year. She was also secretary of the school's thirty-four-member Press Association.

As a sophomore, Maurine served as secretary of the Sunshine Society, which delivered one hundred fifty blankets and food to hungry families and one hundred dolls to children, "who would otherwise have had very little Christmas cheer."

Their charitable work was aided, in part, by a $25 donation from an anonymous source. The next school year, Maurine became the organization's vice president.

Maurine served during her senior year as president for both the Sunshine Society and German Association. Her final yearbook portrait is accompanied by a quote from the first act of "Romeo and Juliet," a lament about Romeo's unrequited love for the chaste Rosaline: "She'll not be hit with Cupid's arrow."

Maurine graduated from Crawfordsville High School in 1914, ranking at the top of her class of eighty-two students and never scoring below ninety percent through her four years there.

Maurine participated in the Sunshine Society throughout high school. The group collected food and gifts to distribute to families during the holidays. From left, Maurine is second from right in 1912, second from right in 1913, and middle in 1914, her senior year.

Maurine led the honor roll in 1914, her senior year.

Honor Roll for Entire Course

Maurine Watkins	96.23
Lucile Riley	96.2
Marie Ward	95.25
Lois Butler	95.1
Harvey Breaks	95.04
Herman Pugh	94.72
Marguerite Watts	94.49
Byrl Enoch	92.91
Jessie Miller	92.35
Esther Roach	91.6
Forrest Williams	91.57
Herman Rush	90.8

WARD, HAZEL MARIE. "Marie."
Whitesville High School, '10-'11; Literary Editor of ATHENIAN; Social Committee.
Credits, 36.
"There's a language in her eye, her cheek, her lip."

WATKINS, MAURINE DALLAS. "Maurine."
Corresponding Secretary of Sunshine Society, '10-'11; Secretary Press Club, '10-'11; Treasurer Sunshine Society, '11-'12; President "Der Deutsche Verein," '12-'13; Vice-President Sunshine Society, '12-'13; President "Der Deutsche Verein," '13-'14; President of Sunshine Society, '13-'14; Clionian; Charter Member Press Club; "Die Deutsche Gesellschaft"; "Prince Charming"; "C. H. S. Kindergarten"; "Julius Caesar"; "Box of Monkeys"; "The School for Scandal."
Credits, 48.
"She'll not be hit with Cupid's arrow"(?)

WATTS, MARGUERITE ELIZABETH. "Peggy."
C. H. S. Archives; "Nautical Knot"; "Bulbul"; completed course in three and one-half years.
Credits, 36.
"Ripe in wisdom, is she."

WEAVER, BURNEY. "Burney."
Periclean; Clioanian.
Credits, 33.8.
"The conflict is over, the struggle is past."

WILLIAMS, FORREST M. "Forrest."
Polymnian; Periclean; Chairman Program Committee, '13-'14; Class Treasurer, '13-'14; Chairman of Commencement Week Programme Committee; Athletic Editor of ATHENIAN; State Discussion Primary; "Coleman's Coterie"; completed course in three and one-half years.
Credits, 32.6.

WRAY, SARAH ESTHER. "Sarie."
Junior Prom. Committee; Senior Hop Committee; Alumni Editor ATHENIAN; "Suffering Suffragettes"; Sunshine Society; "Nautical Knot"; "Bulbul."
Credits, 35.
"Enthusiasm begets enthusiasm."

A long list of activities and accomplishments is next to Maurine's photo, second from top, in the Crawfordsville High School yearbook in 1914. The photo is accompanied by a quote from "Romeo and Juliet": "She'll not be hit with Cupid's arrow."

PURSUIT OF THE STAGE

Through the years, as Maurine pursued higher education, one theme ruled: She was focused on finding and working with those who could help hone her craft.

She returned to Kentucky in September 1914 to attend Hamilton College, a liberal arts junior college for women connected to Transylvania University, from which her father graduated in 1893. Languages—French, German, Greek, Hebrew, Hindi and Latin—and playwriting were her primary courses of study.

As her freshman year came to a close, Maurine submitted her first application to Radcliffe College, the women's liberal arts college in Cambridge, Massachusetts, that shared facilities and courses with the then all-male Harvard University. In addition to her grades, Hamilton College President E.W. McDiarmid submitted a recommendation on Maurine's behalf, writing, "She has never been under college censure and is a most desirable student."

She continued to complete about seventy hours' worth of courses through Hamilton and Transylvania colleges and served as editor-in-chief of the *Transylvanian* literary magazine. When she graduated with honors in 1916, one of her plays was performed and she was awarded $10 in gold for the best short story.

While awaiting acceptance to Radcliffe, Maurine took a high school teaching position in English and Latin near her parents' Crawfordsville home. She submitted another application on March 30, 1918, to which the secretary of the admissions commission responded that the school was willing to admit her but also encouraged Maurine not to attend Radcliffe: "I think you will lose time in changing as we do not admit students from so-called Junior Colleges."

Instead, Maurine attended nearby Butler University, graduating first in her class with a bachelor's degree in arts in 1919. While at Butler, Maurine worked at the student newspaper, the *Butler Collegian*, and participated in the drama club. During the production of "Green Stockings," a play based on an old English custom in which an older sister wore green stockings to denote a younger sister married first, Maurine was called up to perform the woman's lead role the night before the show's opening. It seems the actress for whom Maurine was an understudy was hospitalized, "suffering from a nervous breakdown." It's one of the few recorded times Maurine appeared on stage.

One performer Maurine admired was a Hungarian immigrant who often wrote

Facing page, from left: Maurine's father, the Rev. George Watkins, submitted an application for her admission into Hamilton College for Women in Lexington, Kentucky. The liberal arts junior college for women was the first college Maurine applied to and attended after high school.

Maurine applied for admission to Radcliffe College in Cambridge, Massachusetts, three times before gaining acceptance. A letter sent to her from Radcliffe warned that the school would "not admit students from so-called Junior Colleges."

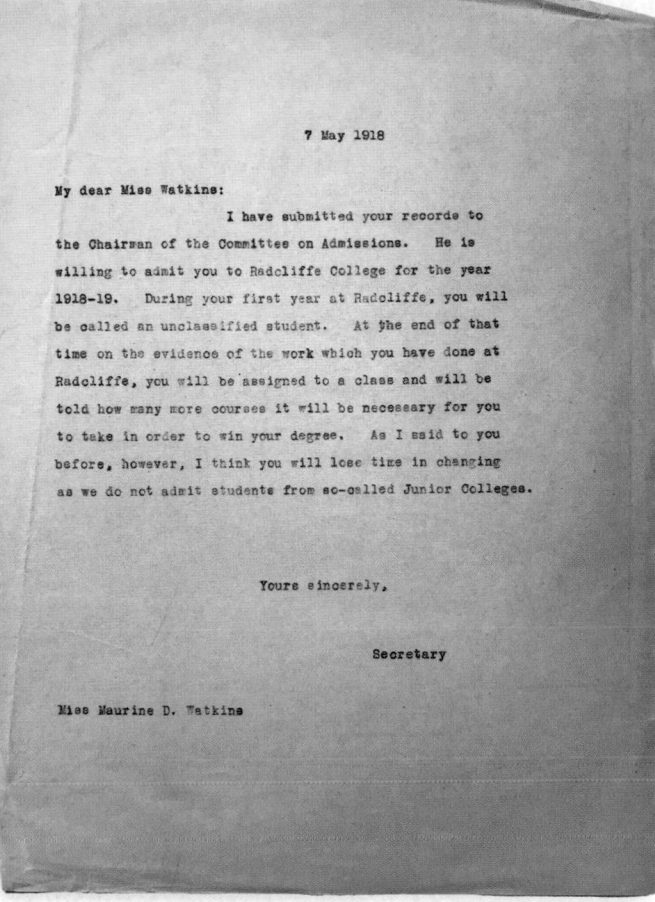

Hamilton College

For Women

Lexington, Ky.

APPLICATION

I desire to enter my daughter as a student in Hamilton College, for the coming session, in conformity to the customs, regulations, and usages of the institution.

Her full name is *Maurine Dallas Watkins*

The date of her birth is *July 27. 1896*

The condition of her health is *Excellent*

Her church membership (or preference) is *Christian Church*

Date *July 14, 1914.*

Parent *Rev. Geo. D. Watkins*

Address *108 W. Franklin St*

Certificate of Admission

I hereby certify that Miss *Maurine Dallas Watkins* #8

has satisfactorily completed in *Crawfordsville* school the studies indicated within. The recitation periods have been *40* minutes long. The passing grade is *75* %.

Anna Wilson Principal

Address *305 E. Wabash Av.*

---

7 May 1918

My dear Miss Watkins:

I have submitted your records to the Chairman of the Committee on Admissions. He is willing to admit you to Radcliffe College for the year 1918-19. During your first year at Radcliffe, you will be called an unclassified student. At the end of that time on the evidence of the work which you have done at Radcliffe, you will be assigned to a class and will be told how many more courses it will be necessary for you to take in order to win your degree. As I said to you before, however, I think you will lose time in changing as we do not admit students from so-called Junior Colleges.

Yours sincerely,

Secretary

Miss Maurine D. Watkins

---

the plays in which he acted, Leo Ditrichstein. The actor-playwright brought the revival of "The Great Lover" to English's Opera House in Indianapolis in March 1917, and Maurine went to see it. "I was so thrilled by his performance that I wrote this play for him. He accepted it and he also asked me to collaborate with him on another play, which was an adaptation from the Hungarian," Maurine recalled in an August 8, 1928, story for Baltimore's *Evening Sun*. But there was a catch: Ditrichstein told Maurine he would not need any new plays for at least two years. "I simply thought of it as a two-year postponement. That was all. I expected, confidently, to write a play for him then," she said.

She submitted her third application to Radcliffe in May 1919, this time for graduate school, and was finally accepted, with a caveat. It would probably take two years for Maurine to earn her master's degree.

"I don't like this life at all. It's fun but I can't feel that I'm getting any place. However, I'm storing up a trunkful of Great American Dramas and counting the days till September."

—MAURINE WATKINS TO HER PROFESSOR, 1920

Radcliffe was an incubator for playwrights. Students in the so-called English 47 class would not only study stagecraft but also put their skills into practice in an experimental theater as part of the 47 Workshop. Each was encouraged to write an original play, have it staged, then receive constructive criticism from their peers and graduates of the program. Students would learn quickly if their ideas would translate to the stage and be coached in how to improve them.

George Pierce Baker, once called "the greatest living authority on the drama" by the *Boston Globe*, was the professor for English 47, which grew out of a request by students to write their own original plays instead of theses about historical dramas. Plays produced in English 47 could be presented in the auditorium of Agassiz House on Radcliffe's campus, since Harvard had no stage at that time. The class attracted not only playwrights but also students interested in pursuing stage decoration and lighting.

As one student wrote about Baker's influence, "He is helping the student to bridge over years of fruitless endeavor, showing him the real essentials that go to make a play and advising him to discard things that have a tendency to weaken the emotional response that is the life-blood of a good play."

Baker, himself a Harvard graduate, lamented the institution didn't provide his boundlessly creative students with the proper facilities to present their work. "Mechanically, the Workshop is laboring in the crudest of amateur conditions," he told the *New-York Tribune* in 1919. "In these it cannot present the type of production which its personnel and training make possible."

Only ten students were permitted to take Baker's English 47 class per semester—each submitting an original play to be considered for inclusion—and Maurine was one of them in fall 1919. She took the course after Eugene O'Neill—who would win the Nobel Prize in Literature in 1937—had already departed for Greenwich Village and before Thomas Wolfe—author of "Look Homeward, Angel"—arrived from North Carolina.

She enrolled in two drama courses that semester taught by Baker, who had just released the book "Dramatic Technique," in which he stated, "I have written for the person who cannot be content except when writing plays." She withdrew, however, halfway through the school year during Baker's absence from the university and returned home to Indiana.

While home, Maurine wrote to Baker, "I don't like this life at all. It's fun but I can't feel that I'm getting any place. However, I'm storing up a trunkful of Great American Dramas and counting the days till September."

She returned to Cambridge in the fall to study again with Baker, but she'd leave Radcliffe before receiving her master's degree. It's not clear why Maurine chose to leave Radcliffe—to which she applied three times before finally gaining acceptance. She moved back to Indiana and stayed there quietly for the next two years. Then, she moved to Chicago.

BECOMING A REPORTER

In 1923, Maurine took a job as assistant manager for outdoor advertising for Standard Oil of Indiana. She lived at the Parkside Hotel in Garfield Park and at 1425 North Dearborn Parkway in the Gold Coast.

She also reconnected with Ditrichstein, the actor-playwright. He renamed the play she wrote for him "The Devil's Diary."

"I'm here in Pittsburgh a few days conferring with Mr. Ditrichstein about a play he has recently accepted," she wrote to Baker on William Penn Hotel stationery. The professor responded on October 23, 1923: "We have a very interesting group who have returned to take English 47. . . . I am sorry you are not among the number, but if you are really selling your plays, what more can I ask?"

Maurine's work with Ditrichstein, however, went nowhere. The actor soon retired and departed for Italy with his wife, saying he preferred to live there because of its lower cost of living. He would stay in Europe until his death June 28, 1928.

"After that," she later recalled, "I thought I'd turn to newspaper work."

Why would a playwright want to become a reporter? Her personnel file, if one ever existed, long ago disappeared from the *Chicago Tribune*. But maybe it was something she remembered from Baker's English 47 class, where a student was taught "how to secure material for the building of plots by watching the daily newspapers for dramatic episodes in real life." Students were required to make

Maurine recalls for
the *New York Times*
the conversation she
had when applying for
a job at the *Chicago
Tribune* in a January
2, 1927, article. After
almost leaving the job
interview, "the manag-
ing editor took an hour
to convince her that
journalism might well
be her life work and
gave her a job," the
Times wrote.

> "What paper have you worked on?"
> "None."
> "Had any newspaper experience at all?"
> "No."
> "Know anything about journalism?"
> "I took it in college."
> "I don't believe you'll like newspaper work."
> "I don't believe I will * * *"

scrapbooks of newspaper clippings, which Baker reviewed "to see if the student has the dramatic instinct for the material."

After eight months working for the paper, however, Maurine was ready to move on. "I left newspaper work because I found it too absorbing," Maurine said in a 1927 interview.

1925: A YEAR OF CHANGE

After she left the *Chicago Tribune*, Maurine's loved ones and mentors seemed to all shift at once, a year of change that laid the groundwork for her most famous work.

Although Maurine's father had been a minister in the Indianapolis area for decades, he decided to leave the church in 1924. In a later interview, Maurine said, "Father is not a baby-kisser nor a handshaker. He adored preaching, but he couldn't do the rest of it."

He had been involved in buying and selling real estate since Maurine was little, and now there was an opportunity for her father to pursue it full time. He and Maurine's mother relocated to Coral Gables, Florida, nicknamed "City Beautiful" by its founder, George Merrick. Himself the son of a minister, Merrick created the planned community whose businesses and residences were constructed in the Mediterranean Revival architecture style and were flanked by spaces desig-nated for parks, golf courses and trails. The Miami suburb was incorporated in 1925—the peak of Florida's land boom—and became home to the newly char-tered University of Miami. An estimated twenty-five thousand people sold real estate in the Miami area at that time. Watkins & Black, an architecture and build-ing firm, joined them.

Their Florida venture was only temporary, however. By June 1926, Maurine's parents had moved back to Indiana, where George gave a speech at a fiftieth wed-ding anniversary celebration for former parishioners David and Emma Clark. It seems the pair left just in time; the building boom was over. Railroads halted de-livering passengers and construction materials to South Florida; the Internal Reve-nue Service began investigating land speculators; and an estimated Category Four hurricane hit Miami on September 18, 1926.

Baker was also seeking a change. His popular English 47 Workshop had opened offices and a scenery studio several years earlier in Harvard's Massachusetts Hall, the oldest building on campus and the oldest collegiate building in the United States. Completed in 1720, the three-story brick structure had been used as a dormitory, housed lecture rooms and administration offices and, most notably, was used as barracks for soldiers during the Revolutionary War.

The facility, still inadequate for Baker's needs, caught fire on the morning of April 6, 1924, with the *Boston Globe* reporting, "flames were leaping through the roof when the firemen arrived." It took two-and-a-half hours to extinguish the blaze, which caused an estimated $10,000 in damage. According to Baker, his group was not responsible for causing the fire.

In late May 1924, administrators announced Massachusetts Hall would be saved and renovated—as a dormitory. Baker's English 47 Workshop was without a home.

The popular professor took some time away from campus. Baker taught two playwriting courses that summer at the University of California at Berkeley. He visited with former students and alumni organizations, toured movie production studios and explored theaters throughout Southern California.

When he returned to Massachusetts, Baker's decision was announced. After thirty-six years as a professor of drama—including ten years leading some of the country's most promising, progressive theater minds—he took a break from Harvard. In a letter to supporters he wrote, "At the moment there is no space available in which the 47 Workshop can be carried on under feasible conditions. This seems, consequently, the right moment at which to take my desired sabbatical year." His sabbatical would last less than two months.

Meanwhile, Edward Harkness, a philanthropist and son of one of the founders of Standard Oil, made a $1 million donation to his alma mater, Yale University. The money would be used to create the School of Drama within Yale's School of Art. Baker was picked to lead the new institution. He resigned from Harvard on November 25, 1924.

Writer Gardner Jackson summed up Baker's influence: "He has made the production of plays a study just as significant in modern life as is the study of poetry, of painting—yes, just as significant as the study of business or industrial engineering."

Meanwhile, Maurine moved to New York City, where she became an associate editor with the Macmillan Company. She also spent time with her parents in

Florida, and it's from there she completed her application to Yale University on October 26, 1925. Interested in pursuing a graduate degree in fine arts, it seemed Maurine was ready to rejoin her beloved professor in his new surroundings.

WRITING 'CHICAGO'

Had Baker and Maurine plotted out a strategy while at Radcliffe for her to move to Chicago to gain material that she could use to craft a play? In a February 22, 1929, letter to a reporter, Baker objected to this notion: "It isn't quite fair to the Yale Department of Drama, is it? To say that out of Miss Watkins' work with me at Radcliffe came 'Chicago.' When she worked with me at Radcliffe, she hadn't the remotest idea of that play. After she had been working for a time with me here, she told me of this play which had its inception in her work as a reporter on the *Chicago Tribune* in the period between her training at Radcliffe and registration here. The play was written and polished here."

In early 1926, Maurine completed "A Brave Little Woman," her first project at Yale. She registered the work with the U.S. Copyright Office on February 26, 1926, under the name "Chicago; or, Play Ball," and retained the rights to it throughout her life.

The three-act play with prologue opened with a murder. Jilted woman Roxie Hart—who personified "the prettiest woman ever charged with murder in Chicago"—gunned down her lover inside the apartment she shared with Amos, "her meal-ticket husband."

Roxie's experiences in the play closely resembled the same plot twists that played out before Maurine's eyes in Cook County court: a pregnancy claim; a defense built on both the murderess and her lover reaching for a gun; an acquittal from a sympathetic, all-male jury; and reporters and photographers at the ready to record the day's drama.

Supporting characters were also inspired by real people. Nicknamed "Moonshine Mary," Polish immigrant Mary Wazeniak was convicted in April 1924 of killing a man to whom she allegedly sold poisoned moonshine. She was an inspiration for "Moonshine Maggie" in Maurine's play.

Liz, nicknamed "God's Messenger," is portrayed in the original "Chicago" as a crazy woman who hears voices and antagonizes her cellmates by howling and admonishing them. Her character was inspired by Elizabeth Unkafer, a middle-aged

Facing page: The front cover of Maurine's play "Chicago" says in her handwriting that it's the "only copy in captivity."

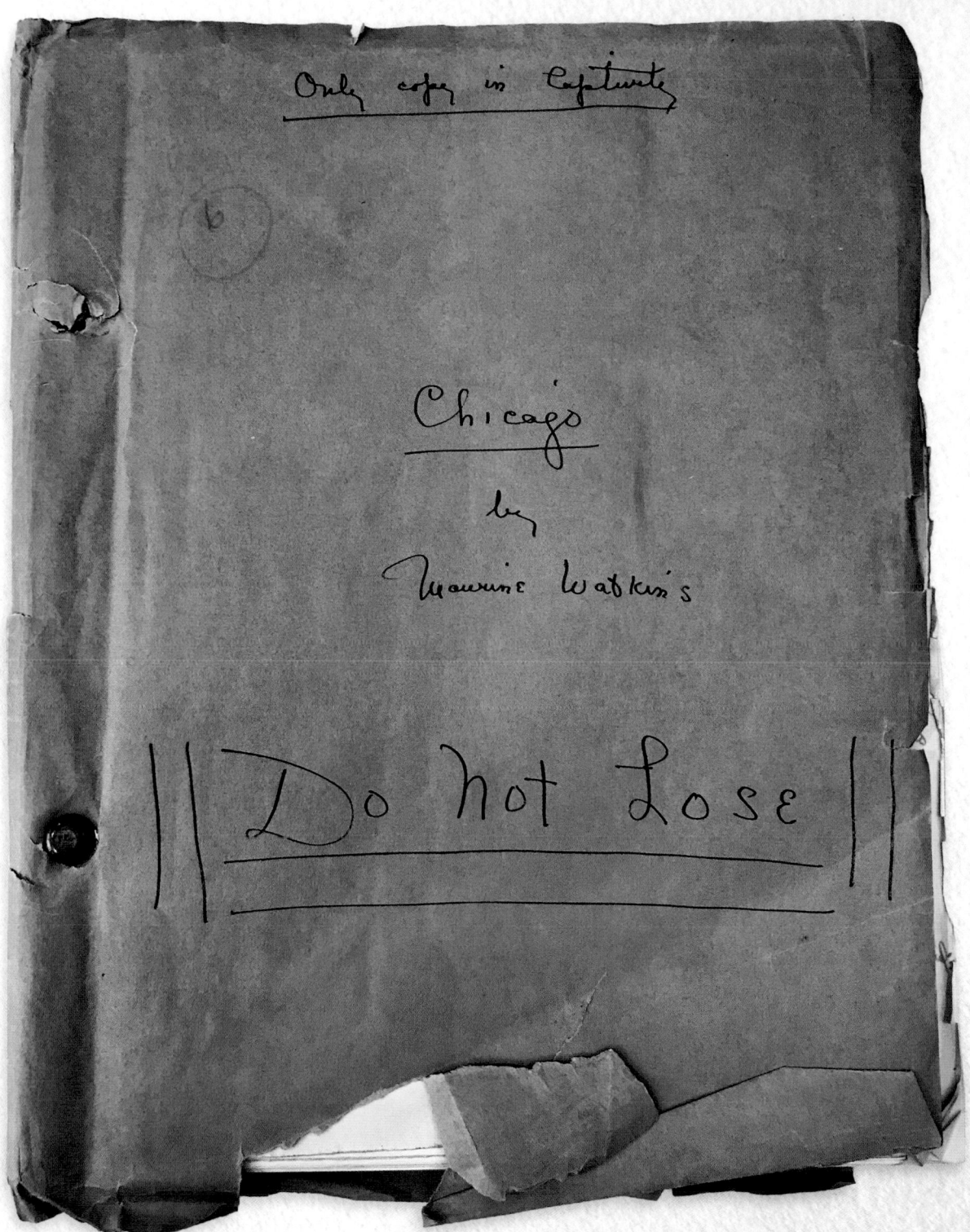

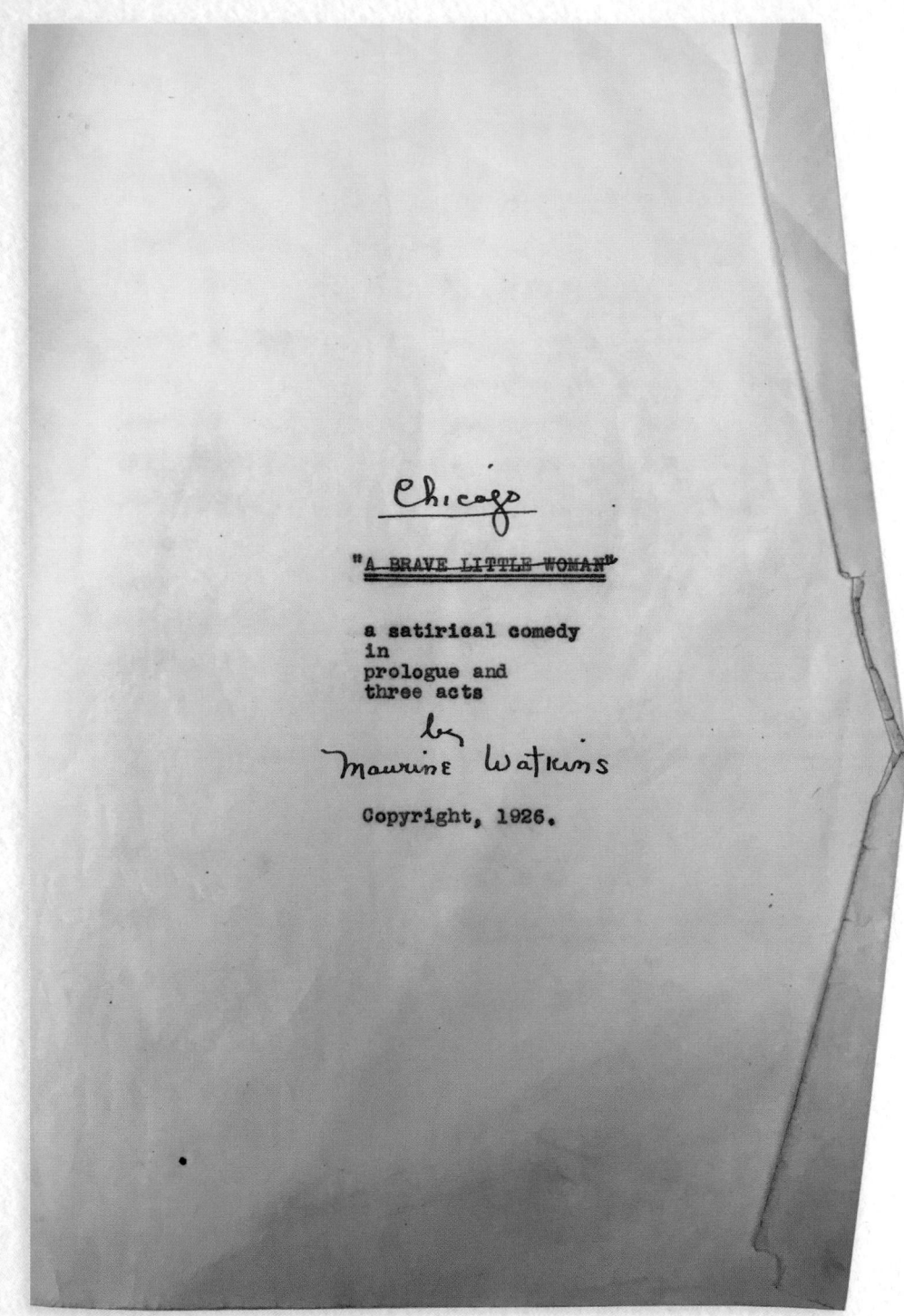

Chicago

"A BRAVE LITTLE WOMAN"

a satirical comedy
in
prologue and
three acts

by
Maurine Watkins

Copyright, 1926.

A front inside page from "Chicago" shows that Maurine crossed out the original name of the play and hand-wrote the new name, "Chicago."

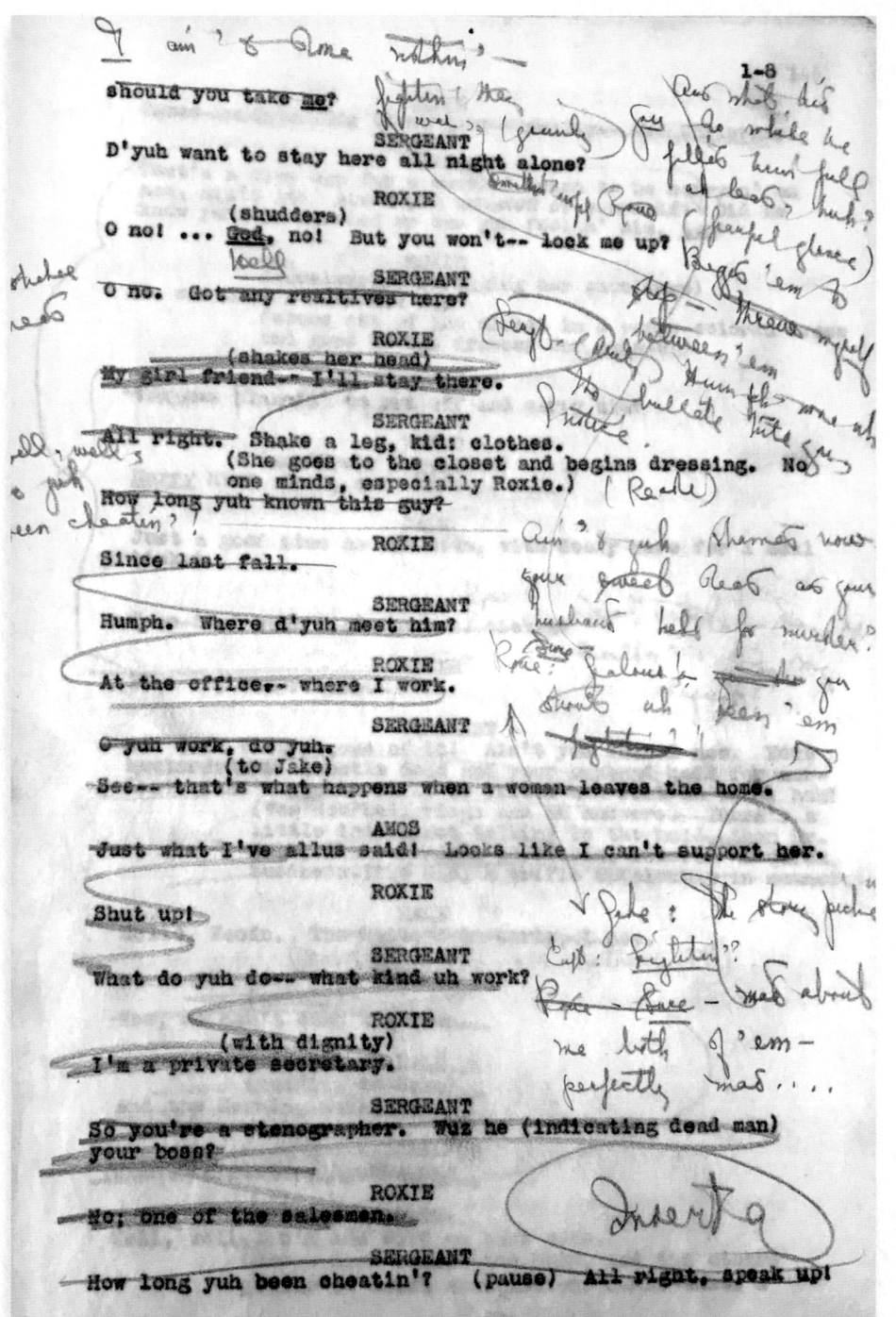

Maurine's handwritten notes cover a page of the play "Chicago," from the original version she wrote in 1926.

MAURINE WATKINS 197

The prologue, including handwritten notes from 1926, shows the setting for the opening scene of "Chicago."

PROLOGUE

Six fifty-eight p.m. Friday, April third.

Bedroom of Amos Hart. A corner room, first floor, in a cheap modern flat on Chicago's South Side, with flowered paper, gaudy rugs, and shiny furniture. Windows at the right and center rear look out on a court. A door (left) opens into a narrow hall, with bath on one side, living-room straight ahead, and outside door (unseen). Another door (left) opens into a small closet.

Between the two windows, with footboard to the front, is a large brass bed, with covers thrown back in confusion and pillows tossed together. At its head is a night-table, with telephone, a stoutish bottle and couple of glasses, an ash-tray and cigarettes. At the right is a large vanity dresser, equipped with imitation ivory toilet articles, bottles with atomizers, perfumes, powder, rouge, eyebrow pencils, and lipstick.

To the left of the center window is a victrola that is playing wild ryhthmic jazz.

~~A man stands in the doorway, pulling on his coat and turned to go.~~ A girl of twenty-three or so, in a flashy negligee of blue georgette with imitation lace, ~~stand by the foot~~ [sits on the edge] of the bed ~~watching him.~~ [and pours herself a drink] She is slender and beautiful, with short upper lip, pouting mouth, dark eyes, and bobbed hair the color of flame.

CHARACTERS

ROXIE HART:	"the prettiest woman ever charged with murder in Chicago"
AMOS HART:	"her meal-ticket husband"
BILLY NASH:	her attorney-- "best in the city, next to Darrow"
MARTIN S. WOODS:	Asst. State's Attorney
JAKE:	reporter on The Morning Gazette
BABE:	photographer on The Morning Gazette
MARY SUNSHINE:	sob sister on The Evening Star
MRS. MORTON:	matron at Cook County Jail
VELMA:	"stylish divorcee")
LIZ:	"God's Messenger") inmates of Murderess Row
MOONSHINE MARY:	"hunyak")
GO-TO-HELL KITTY:	"the Tiger Girl")
SIGNOR Mr. Corbin	Unknown Admirer"

Police Sergeant, Judge, Bailiff, Photographers, Reporters, Jury

The character list from an undated version of "Chicago."

woman who was found guilty in May 1924 of killing her boyfriend after he allegedly told her he was "through with her." Her attorneys claimed her mind was subnormal due to a social disease.

At the play's end, the exonerated Roxie learns she's been upstaged—by another woman who has just committed murder outside the courthouse. When a reporter named Jake Callahan, a character modeled after *Chicago Tribune* crime reporter Jake Lingle but later removed from the musical update of the play, asks her to pose with this new murderess, Roxie refuses.

Jake responds: "Come on, sister, yuh gotta play ball: this is Chicago!" In an earlier version of the play, Jake says: "Gee! Ain't God good to the papers!"

According to Hugh Osborne, Baker's teaching assistant, Maurine was given a score of ninety-eight percent for the first draft of the play. He also told an Associated Press reporter Maurine's work was "one of the most significant in the past several seasons."

'CHICAGO,' ON STAGE

On June 8, 1926, New York City theater owner and producer Sam. H. Harris announced he would stage the newly retitled "Chicago." It would become the first play out of the Yale School of Drama performed professionally.

A preview opened at the Shubert Theatre in New Haven, Connecticut, on December 27, 1926, and was instantly given the kind of publicity its New York City producers might have hoped would lead to increased ticket sales for the show's Broadway premiere three nights later.

It seems one of the people to attend the play's first performance—the first act, anyway, before reportedly storming out of the theater—was John Clark Archer, head of the Department of Missions at Yale Divinity School. Archer was so struck by its content, he immediately penned a statement calling "Chicago" "entirely too vile for public performance." Though he wrote that those familiar with the city may find the content "true to life," he asked, "Why not leave the lid on the sewer and keep the stench from the nostrils of our eastern public?"

Maurine's response to Archer's assessment of her play was swift, as recorded in the December 30, 1926, edition of the *Hartford Courant*:

> *I quite agree with Professor Archer that the situation in the city of Chicago is deplorable. What surprises me is that he of all persons, a divinity school professor, should condemn the action of calling attention to evil. Does he suppose the way to combat it is to ignore it? I wonder whether, in his sermons, Professor Archer pretends that the world is a rose garden and scrupulously avoids the unpleasant side of things.*

> *More than likely he speaks of evil conditions himself. I do the same thing, only the stage enables me to make it more realistic. I take it that he objects to my public portrayal of the matter. Then why, when he evidently thinks my plan an evil, does he do exactly what he criticises me for doing—denounce evil to the public. Professor Archer has not only made a public denunciation of my particular public denunciation, he has made it of the very idea of denouncing publicity. It makes rather a tangle, you see, with Professor Archer at one end of it criticising the very thing he is going himself through other means.*

Stage Comment

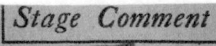

Maurine Watkins is the newest name to rise suddenly on the horizon of successful dramatic authorship with the production in New York of "Chicago," in which Francine Larrimore is starring. Miss Watkins was formerly a reporter on a Chicago paper, the high light of her career being the Leopold-Loeb case which she "covered." In this she picked up some of the background used in "Chicago." She is next to make a play out of the novel, "Revelry," said to tell the inside story of the Harding administration. Sam Harris will again be the producer as he is of "Chicago" and of "Cradle Snatchers," now very popular at the Harris Theater here.

* * *

So valuable does Mr. Harris consider the six leading members of "Cradle Snatchers" that he has insured each of them heavily for the duration of the Chicago run. The lucky players are Mary Boland, Edna May Oliver and Margaret Dale, who enact the venturesome wives, and Humphrey Bogart, Raymond Guion and Raymond Hackett, who hire out to the ladies in question.

*Chicago American,
January 11, 1927*

Chicago's Lady Killers Theme of New Play

New York Crowds Theater Hoping for Shock.

New York, Dec. 30.—[Special.]—A bit of what Miss Maurine Watkins called "Chicago" came to New York tonight in the form of a satirical comedy depicting the methods attributed to shrewd Cook county lawyers to change heartless but beautiful feminine murderers into heroines.

The play came branded by a Yale professor, who saw it in New Haven the other night, as a shocker unfit for human consumption and all Broadway attempted to get into the Music Box where Sam H. Harris staged it. It proved, however, to be a rather realistic and not overly offensive story of the ways of women murderers, newspaper "sob sisters," and the cunning lawyers who ask not whether the defendant is guilty but how much cash can you raise. And at the end it showed how tears and freedom are wrung from the twelve men, good and true, who sit in judgment on Chicago's jury boxes.

There were no

An unidentified Chicago newspaper, circa December 1926

A variety of newspapers announced the anticipated arrival of "Chicago."

STEAMSHOVEL SATIRE RAW BUT RIGHT

Chicago Roars When Chicago, Not London or New York, Is Villain in Play.

THE CAST.

Roxie Hart	Francine Larrimore
Fred Caseley	James Coyle
Jake	Norval Keedwell
Amos Hart	Charles Halton
Sergt. Murdock	William Crimans
Martin S. Harrison	Griffin Crafts
Velma	Millicent Hanley
Liz	Dorothy Stickney
Billy Flynn	Jack Roseleigh
Mary Sunshine	Eda Heineman
Moonshine Maggie	Caroline Morrison
Go-to-Hell Kitty	Stella Larrimore

BY ASHTON STEVENS.

IT used to be London that was the villain in the play. Then it was New York. But last night in the Harris Theater it was Chicago. At last we were a great bad city!

Well, Chicago firstnighters laughed themselves purple over Maurine Watkins' "Chicago," a tough, brittle, convulsing farce written by a former Chicago reporter who throws away her horn and gets a steam shovel. It is satire in the terms of the burlesque wheel; rough, ragged and raw, but always—or nearly always—as funny as a comic strip ought to be.

It is another of those 'inside jobs," only instead of turning up the tent show or the cabaret tragically, it exposes the relations of a murderess with the law and the press comically. Never has so modern passion for "publicity" been so hilariously handled. "Chicago" makes Mr. Mencken, the professional publicity baiter, sound like a corneter in the Salvation Army.

* * *

IT starts like the crack of a pistol. In fact, it starts with the crack of a pistol. "It's too —— demned bad about you!" sneers Francine Larrimore's Mrs Roxy Hart (in her b.v.d.'s) at the gentleman who is, literally, discovered napping with her in her husband's absence.

"Aw, I'm through!" he responds angrily. Whereupon Roxy bets his blankety-blank life he is, and shoots him dead.

Maugham can't be any quicker than that in the play to which Miss Watkins' is said to bear a slight resemblance. Nor can his pick-up be swifter after the dangerously fast start.

Miss Watkins sustains her speed in every scene save that of the ... you look at a Sob Sister such as ...

*Chicago Herald and Examiner,
September 12, 1927*

MISS HAVER MAY BE STAR FOR 'CHICAGO'

BY LOUELLA O. PARSONS,
Universal Service Motion Picture Editor.

LOS ANGELES, May 8.—Possibly Phyllis Haver doesn't know it yet, but there is a strong indication that she is to play the role of the girl who makes staying in jail a positive lark in "Chicago." Cecil De Mille, so rumor says, has purchased the screen rights to Maurine Watkins' famous newspaper play.

Of course, the movie may not be permitted to put in all the ironies that Miss Watkins so deftly injects into her comedy. The screen, you see, is not a privileged character like the stage. The spoken drama can get away with murder in any form. The films, younger and less privileged, have to be careful.

The censor boards throughout the country may find it not within the censorial bounds for the girl to shoot her lover when he threatens to return to his wife and children. Yet it seems difficult to think that any censor board, no matter how hidebound, would refuse to consider comedy in the light of comedy.

This story, which comes to me from an underground channel, makes no mention of the cast, but wouldn't Phyllis Haver be superb as the girl? She has all the allure, all the ingenuousness and all the naive hardness that makes Francine Larrimore and Nancy Carroll so delightful.

*Chicago Herald and Examiner,
May 9, 1927*

'CHICAGO' WILL OPEN HERE SOON

MAURINE WATKINS, former newspaper woman of this city and author of "Chicago," scheduled for a showing at the Harris on September 11, just has finished another play called "The Devil's Diary," in which it is likely Basil Sydney and Mary Ellis will appear. Her adaptation of "Revelry" is to be produced by Robert Milton in the next few weeks.

Francine Larrimore, who will play Roxie Hart in "Chicago," returned last week from Europe, where she arranged for her London appearance in September, 1928.

She also visited Germany, where she attended the Shakespeare festival as a guest of Max Reinhardt.

EDUCATIONAL

on't Know How"

ess advancement e you know nothing above you? Does

*An unidentified newspaper,
circa August 31, 1927*

PAGE TWELVE

Theater

"Chicago," a new play in three acts by Maurine Watkins, a second year student at the Yale School of Drama, featuring Francine Larrimore and presented at the Shubert Theater here last night by Sam H. Harris. Staged by George Abbott.

The cast:

Roxie Hart, Francine Larrimore; Fred Casely, Carl Eckstrom; Jake, Charles A. Bickford; Amos Hart, Charles Halton; Sergeant Murdock, Charles Slattery; Martin S. Harrison, Robert Barrat; Babe, Arthur R. Vinton; Mrs. Morton, Isabelle Winlock; Velma, Juliette Crosby; Liz, Dorothy Stickney; Billy Flynn, Edward Ellis; Mary Sunshine, Eda Heinemann; Moonshine Maggie, Feriki Boros; Go-to-Hell Kitty, Edith Fitzgerald; Bailiff, Carl De Mal; Judge Canton, Milano Tilden; Corbin, G. Albert Smith; Woman Reporter, Wilma Thompson; First Man Reporter, George Cowell; Clerk of the Court, Charles Kuhn; First Photographer, James E. Pall; Stenographer, Vincent York; Foreman of Jury, G. W. Auspake.

Three weeks ago, with the formal opening of the new Yale Theater, Boyd Smith, a student in the Department of Drama at Yale University, furnished Yale's first contribution to the American stage. The vehicle was called "The Patriarch," and was purchased immediately by John Golden for an early professional presentation.

Last night at the Shubert Theater New Haven witnessed Yale's second contribution—a travesty on justice, written by Maurine Watkins, former member of the Chicago Tribune staff and now a second year student in the Department of Drama. It is a play built on life and apparently portraying the life role of Beulah Annan, Chicago's most beautiful slayer, small and titian-haired. The play centers about the arrest, incarceration and trial of a beautiful woman who betrayed her husband's trust for an affair with a married man whom she murdered when he turned from her.

Strange as it may seem to men and women in close touch with court procedure in Connecticut, the vehicle deals with reality. It is a true portrayal of conditions as they exist in many parts of the country and will carry an important message to the American public if it be accepted as fact.

Miss Larrimore, as Roxie Hart, murderess, was excellent in the role. Tough, harsh and moved only by a craving for publicity and more publicity, she adhered so strictly to her part that it was difficult at times to realize that this lying, deceitful, blood-tainted woman could be anything but a cold-blooded killer.

Charles A. Bickford, typical hardboiled police reporter, gave a most flawless interpretation of his role. Unlike the usual stage reporter, he did not carry the proverbial pencil and note-pad, but, like many real news demons, probably didn't even have a pencil. Edward Ellis made an excellent criminal lawyer, even to his fondness for the limelight and demand of "cash in advance."

Dorothy Stickney, in a character role, "the crazy woman of the Cook County Jail," was very effective and was loudly applauded as she left the stage after her first appearance.

"Chicago" will be at the Shubert tonight and tomorrow night with matinee tomorrow.

They call it "a flock of ...

New Haven Evening Register, undated

FEMININE PUNCH IS KNOCKOUT

Where Men Would Have Weakened, Maurine Watkins and Francine Larrimore Rough It All the Way.

By ASHTON STEVENS.

ONLY a woman could be as rough as Maurine Watkins is in that hoarse farce she calls "Chicago." One might even say only a good woman. But I do not wish to be insulting to a lady who only a couple of years ago was, like myself, one of the minor pillars of Chicago journalism. I revel in Miss Watkins' ungloved and roughshod playwriting which leaves no precious brick unflung. I rejoice that no man had a part in the writing of "Chicago." For I know no man who writes as well as Miss Watkins who would not have frequently feinted and side-stepped where she punches straight through.

"Chicago" is a woman's caricature of what used to be one of Chicago's major industries, the private execution by weary women of men that wearied them. With brutal strokes it pictures a murderess all the way ... n sheets to those on news is printed ... arsely

*Chicago Herald and Examiner,
September 18, 1927*

'CHICAGO' ON SCREEN BESTS STAGE PLAY

Phyllis Haver Wins Right to Sit in Ranks of Great by Her Roxie Hart.

"CHICAGO."

Directed by Frank Urson from the play by Maurine Watkins. Presented by Pathe at the Roosevelt Theater.

THE CAST
Roxie Hart .... Phyllis Haver
Amos Hart .... Victor Varconi
Attorney .... Robert Edeson
The Reporter .... T. Roy Barnes
Prosecuting Attorney ....
.... Warner Richmond
The Cop .... Clarence Bradford
Maid .... Virginia Bradford
Matron .... May Robson

BY CAROL FRINK.

"THEY'LL hang me," wails the snappy-looking Roxie Hart as her revolver cools.

"Hang a girl with a face like yours?" counters the reporter, cheerily. "Don't be silly."

And, of course, they don't.

THE pictured "Chicago" is not as ruthless and sordid as Maurine Watkins' play, nor is it, for just that reason, quite as hilarious. But I can see where the changes will

Chicago Herald and Examiner, March 20, 1928

Reviews from the early stage
version of "Chicago"

... is no reason on earth to believe that the woman "on trial" runs any risk of execution.

"Empties Whole Box"

And now a woman has come forward and with magnificent candor and superb contempt emptied the whole box of tricks before the eyes of the world. It has remained for a woman to be the first to tear away the curtains and expose the shams in all their odious idiocy.

She makes the audience howl with laughter, but with the spine-chilling, mist-dispelling laughter that is the sanest thing in this mad world.

This antiseptic young woman is Miss Maurine Watkins. She had some experience on a newspaper, and that is about the quickest laboratory for disillusionment in the world.

Miss Watkins reported murder trials and saw them from the inside. She was inspired to turn them inside out and show the public the whole works. She called her play "Chicago," because the scene is laid there, though exactly the same sort of procedure could be found in every other city, town and village in this glorious republic.

The heroine, Roxy Hart, flawlessly impersonated by Francine Larrimore, has never a good word said for her, says never a good word for herself, except selfishly, and is altogether a hundred per cent American murderess of the utmost fascination.

She is as fascinating and venomous and pretty as a deadly little coral snake, and she crawls out of obscurity, strikes once fatally and is carefully protected from harm till she crawls back into oblivion.

"Starts with a Bang"

The play starts off with a bang. Roxy Hart, the young and pretty wife of a hopeless boob, is revealed in a decided negligee quarreling with another woman's husband who has been her paramour but is now quarreling with her. They exchange a few hot words and he tells her he is through with her. As he is about to leave her, she whips a revolver out of a bureau drawer and shoots him dead. It is as ruthless and inexcusable a crime as could be imagined.

The next scene shows the poor imbecile of a husband trying to shelter the woman who has doubly disgraced him. His chivalry is that required of a husband by our popular barbarianism.

He tells the police and the press that he was with his wife when a strange man entered the window, sure that he was a burglar, the husband killed him. He signs his confession. He is taken into another room and his wife brought in.

She is too big a fool and too ignorant of her husband's self sacrifice to keep from blurting out the dirty facts of her crime. She is frightened almost to death at the thought of being put to death for murder.

A sardonic reporter tells her that she is utterly safe from any punishment except gorgeous publicity: "No woman has ever been hung in Cook County."

The flashlight camera men burst in and Roxy tastes the first sweets of publicity. The prosecuting attorney and the policeman fight for positions in the photograph, and the reporter poses as the dead body by which Roxy kneels to be pictured.

She is shown in jail gloating over her fame and filling a scrap ...

*Chicago Herald and Examiner,
March 27, 1927*

'CHICAGO' SEEN BY NEW YORK

NEW YORK, Dec. 30.—"Chicago," a play about Chicago, based on a murder, of course, and written by a Chicago girl who used to be a reporter there, was launched here tonight. It looks promising.

In the very first act a lady with a lovely profile and a mean disposition grabs her ever-ready pistol and sends a bullet through the heart of the gentleman friend who has been paying her rent and grocery bills. And the names she calls him!

Miss Maurine Watkins, slim, blue-eyed and twenty-six, is the author.

There are two reasons, the wise ones of Broadway say, for predicting this play will bring her a lot of bread and butter.

The first is: New York likes anything that paints Chicago in uncomplimentary colors. And the second is: Miss Watkins already has obtained a vigorous denunciation of her play from the lips of a prominent clergyman, the Rev. John C. Archer, of the Yale Divinity School of New Haven.

"Filth!" he summarized after seeing one act. And he didn't wait to see the rest.

Miss Watkins displayed no undue elation when she heard this comment. But she pulled a venerable line.

"All I have done," said she earnestly, "has been to depict life as it is."

She says the point of the play is to show satirically what people will do for the sake of publicity—police, lawyers, court officers, everybody, even the homicidal lady, clutching at every chance for a line and a picture in the paper.

It might have been called "New York," at that.

As We Are!

SO SHE SAYS!—Miss Maurine Watkins, ex-Chicago reporter, whose new play, "Chicago," depicts life exactly as it is in this city, she asserts.

*Chicago Herald and Examiner,
December 31, 1926*

Young Authoress Buys Ticket for Own Show

"HAVE you a single ticket for tonight?" a young lady in her early twenties asked Jimmy Sheehan of the Harris Theater box office, her voice tingling with excitement.

"Yes, just one," Sheehan answered. "Oh, good!" with a perfect accompaniment of joy as she passed under the ticket wicket. Then she skipped into the theater with the rest of the crowds rushing in to view "Chicago," the mirthfully murderous satire, with Francine Larrimore as its scarlet, quick-shooting heroine, which now enters the last two weeks of its run here.

After the second act the enthusiastic miss slipped back on the stage to sit on the newspaper bench in the courtroom scene. When the curtain went up the visitor's presence so surprised the star that Miss Larrimore's expression of surprise could have made the plain-spoken Roxie, whom she impersonates, blush for modesty. The strange visitor was none other than the celebrated author of the play, Maurine Watkins.

MARVELOUS HUMOR.

That surprising incident gives an excellent picture of this recently risen author. She is a composite bundle of fun, impish, roguish, hard to anticipate, but sporting at all times a delicious sense of humor. She had bought a ticket to her own show just for the fun of it.

Everything is fun for her. That is why she was able to write such an unusual, canny and successful play which is far less satirical and far more actual than the general public may believe. And for her nothing seems impossible.

She hails from Louisville, but has lived mostly in Indianapolis. When ...

*Chicago American,
November 6, 1927*

Reviews out of New York were mostly positive. Critic Burns Mantle wrote, "'Chicago' is devastating satire. Our first audiences have laughed immoderately at it. But I doubt its appeal to a very large public." He later included it in his book "The Best Plays of 1926-1927."

New York World critic Alexander Woollcott's assessment: "Of course, the villain of Chicago is not the preening murderess, nor the gushing sob-sister, not the embattled self-seeking lawyers, nor even the peacock judge. The villain of 'Chicago' is the great fat-headed public from which are drawn both the twelve who acquit the pretty gunwoman and the million readers to whom all that is cheap in every newspaper is addressed."

Novelist Rupert Hughes praised Maurine's work as "a justification of the whole emancipation of her sex. It shows what a crime against humanity was committed for centuries by those thick-headed pompous asses who condemned womanhood to seclusion and household tasks and called the colossal wickedness by pretty names."

Hughes went on to call "Chicago" "the most profound and powerful satire (American theater) has ever known. Best of all it is a satire by a woman on the folly of men in their false homage to woman, their silly efforts to protect her while she dupes them."

One pundit thought "Chicago" could be a candidate for the Pulitzer Prize for Drama, "And even if it fails to gain her the award, the accruing royalties will enable her to laugh in the face of her former city editor."

Baker wrote to her on January 3, 1927, offering his own congratulations but also cautioned, "Now don't let an immediate success or any prospect of it carry you off your feet. You wrote a play with commendable purpose. It was well characterized and actable. Don't let any willingness on the part of anybody to turn it into a play to force as many laughs as possible change you from your original purpose. You wrote something that might have an effect on the conditions you ridicule. It may well be turned into something which will have no such effect."

"Chicago" played at the Music Box Theatre in New York City for twenty-two weeks, earning as much as $20,000 a week—or more than $280,000 in today's dollars. Maurine herself appeared in the one-hundredth performance of her play on March 26, 1927, as a reporter in one of the courtroom scenes.

When the show opened in Los Angeles in the spring of 1927, Clark Gable—who a dozen years later would play Rhett Butler in "Gone With the Wind"—portrayed reporter Jake Callahan. He would continue with the production when it moved to

> "Women—especially newspaper women—stand together more than men. They may be catty in little ways, and make slighting remarks about one another's hair, but in the big things they stick together and help one another."
>
> —MAUREEN MCKERNAN, *DETROIT FREE PRESS*, DECEMBER 25, 1927

San Francisco, where his personification of a newsman was highly praised by the *San Francisco Examiner*: "He carries neither a pencil nor a notebook. He is wise, humorous, slouchy, free-and-easy and dominating. This reporter is the only likeable person in the play."

News of Maurine's success continued to spread. Chicago Mayor William Hale "Big Bill" Thompson offered her a position in his second administration: publicity agent. But that was probably just another effort by Thompson to generate some of his own publicity—like the two rats he carried in a bird cage during his campaign stops, representing his opponents.

In the summer, it was announced a silent film version of "Chicago" would be adapted for the big screen by Cecil B. DeMille. Filming began in the fall of 1927, and the movie was released in theaters that December.

Some wondered if "Chicago" would play in Chicago. In a January 1927 review of the play, Woollcott said he didn't "believe Mr. Sam H. Harris, the entrepreneur of 'Chicago,' will dare to give performances in this city." But play in Chicago it did, beginning on September 11, 1927, at the Harris Theater.

Here's the *Chicago Tribune*'s summation of its namesake play: "It were silly for the most devoted of us, as Chicagoans, to be resentful because the piece is called 'Chicago:' that is, after all, the best of titles for it. And I hope the play is so much of a success here that it will run and run and run: this I hope for the good of the community's soul and for the gratification I should take from thus learning that there is a market here for fun like this is."

Before the year concluded, "Chicago" staged in Cincinnati, St. Louis, Detroit and Berlin, where The Associated Press noted, "The critics praised it and accepted it as a satire on American justice. They do not take the play over-seriously, however."

Maurine hired her former *Chicago Tribune* co-worker, Maureen McKernan, to help manage her publicity. The two reporters had covered the Leopold and Loeb trial together and now were navigating the theatrical world in sync. McKernan, a Kansas native, said, "Women—especially newspaper women—stand together more than men. They may be catty in little ways, and make slighting remarks about one another's hair, but in the big things they stick together and help one another."

McKernan wrote a profile of Maurine that was sent to local papers for publication before the play premiered in a city. The piece focused not only on the female playwright, but also the other women involved in the production, both on stage and behind the scenes: "And while this play has some 30 men characters, against the nine women, it might almost be classed as a 'woman' play, for the leading character is a woman, the author is a woman, the play was marketed by a woman play broker and it is press agented by a woman."

'BEGIN AGAIN'

How to follow up such an undeniable success at such a young age?

Soon after the Broadway premiere of "Chicago," Maurine signed on to adapt for the stage Samuel Hopkins Adams' novel "Revelry," a fictional version of the corruption involving the Ohio Gang within the Warren G. Harding administration.

The show opened on August 29, 1927, in Philadelphia, but quickly closed. A review in the *Baltimore Sun* noted, "Miss Maurine Watkins, who has dramatized the novel, hasn't done such a swell job, but these Philadelphia objectors know more about their politics then their dramaturgy."

She toyed with returning to Yale. She wrote "Victory" and "Butterfly Goes Home," including her New York City address on their covers.

While "Chicago" was playing in New York City and preparing for its Los Angeles premiere in April 1927, Maurine was hired by the *New York Telegram* to cover the trial of Ruth Snyder, who had an affair with a married corset salesman then convinced him to help her strangle her husband to death in an attempt to collect several insurance policies on his life. Maurine would "draw parallel between her play and this murder" and take the "'sob' out of sob sisters."

This jury, unlike those Maurine previously observed, took no pity on the woman. Snyder and her lover were both found guilty of murder and sentenced to the electric chair. In January 1928, a Chicago-based photographer, Thomas "Tom"

Howard, covertly captured a now iconic image of Snyder during her execution in Sing Sing prison. (Howard was the grandfather of actor and Beverly native George Wendt and great-grandfather of actor Jason Sudeikis.)

Maurine's assessment of divorce in light of Snyder's fate was surprisingly nuanced, "I believe too strict divorce laws are responsible for many love crimes. Divorce should be granted speedily, to either applicant in a marital divorce. But make marriage so difficult that only the fittest survive."

In November 1927, Maurine received a message from Baker:

When are you going to cease to be a refugee in Canada and give us a new play? I am disturbed because I believe, as I have told you more than once, that you have a special gift in writing for the Theatre in your ability to see serious things comically. This, I believe, you should capitalize to the utmost, particularly now that your recent success is still in the mind of the public, especially the theatrical world of New York. I can understand that you may not have had a wholly happy experience in spite of your success in the theatre world, but you cannot afford not to have something worthy of you on the New York stage within a year. Otherwise, you will have to begin again. Therefore, forgive this letter if I am saying just what you do not want to hear, and charge it to an old teacher who believes heartily in your powers if properly guided by you, and who wants to see you going on increasing the reputation for really significant work which you have already won.

She retreated to Indiana for the holidays, with a local newspaper reporting she "has exchanged for a brief interval, the scenery of the stage for the snow-covered hills and bare trees that make up the scenery of the country, and is enjoying it intensely."

Meanwhile, the silent film version of "Chicago" premiered to mixed reviews. "(I)t is doubtful if the picture will qualify as good entertainment in the minds of those who know nothing about the original," critic Norbert Lusk wrote in the *Los Angeles Times*. The *New York Daily News* reported it was "equally brilliant a motion picture production, save for a couple of sequences which were not in the play and have been injected into the movie." The *Chicago Tribune*'s critic, writing under the pseudonym Mae Tinee, wrote, "Well, they have slaughtered Maurine Watkins' play to make a De Mille holiday. . . . Some of the play's most pungent parts have been left out and in their place incidents introduced that the author, being a bright girl, would never have dreamed of."

> "Well, they have slaughtered Maurine Watkins' play to make a De Mille holiday. . . . Some of the play's most pungent parts have been left out and in their place incidents introduced that the author, being a bright girl, would never have dreamed of."
>
> —*CHICAGO* TRIBUNE ON THE 1927 SILENT FILM VERSION OF 'CHICAGO'

Maurine continued to write plays but had difficulty connecting with audiences. "An Old-Fashioned Girl" was tried out in 1929 but, "for one reason or another, adjudged unsatisfactory." "So Help Me God!" went into rehearsals but fizzled after premiering off-Broadway. And the Dramatic League of Chicago canceled its announcement of "The Devil's Diary" because "it seems that Miss Watkins has forgotten to finish the play."

After the stock market crash of 1929, Maurine headed west. She was hired by Fox Films to create, adapt and rewrite screenplays. For the next decade, she would bounce around studios—including Warner Brothers, Paramount, RKO Pictures and Metro-Goldwyn-Mayer. "I'd love to write a novel with the cinema scene as a background but I'm quite sure that if I told the unvarnished, unexaggerated truth no one would believe it," Maurine told the *New York Daily News* in a story published September 22, 1920. \She arrived on the Fox lot at the same time as University of Southern California football star and recipient of a long-term acting contract John Wayne.

Maurine worked continuously but was credited with few hits. Her original screenplay "Up the River" was picked up by director John Ford and released the same year she was hired by Fox. Actors Spencer Tracy, in his first starring movie role, and Humphrey Bogart, in his second film, brought to life the comical tale of two Sing Sing inmates who escape prison to help their friend on the outside. It was a comedy that the *Chicago Tribune* gave three stars with this advice: "Don't let the fact that 'Up the River' has no big names keep you from seeing the picture."

The 1936 screwball comedy "Libeled Lady," which Maurine wrote with two others, was probably Maurine's most critically successful film. Featuring Jean

Harlow, William Powell, Spencer Tracy and Myrna Loy, the film was nominated for an Academy Award for Best Picture in 1937, but lost to another Powell and Loy picture, "The Great Ziegfeld."

Maurine earned a reputation as a dependable writer who enjoyed sitting on the floor cross-legged, scribbling furiously with big, soft black pencils while munching candy. She steered clear of romantic entanglements and hearsay, with New York City gossip columnist Sidney Skolsky noting, "Of all the yarns that have drifted back from the cinema city, not once has Maurine's name been connected with a male or a piece of gossip. It seems she didn't go Hollywood, either. Pretty and charming—a strange person."

Though she didn't appear to chase clout in Hollywood, she used her screen-writing earnings to invest in prime stocks, purchase luxury items and travel the world. The pages of her 1933 passport are covered in visa stamps from Germany, Italy, Argentina, France and Greece. She mailed postcards to family members from Tahiti, Fiji, Tanzania and Singapore. One photo, a twentieth-century selfie, shows the author in a light-colored jacket and pith helmet during one stop in her travels. She captioned it, "The Perfect Lady Tourist—camera under my arm, lunch-box under the other, black glasses, umbrella, sun-helmet. I'm certainly working hard and having the world's best time! Love, Me." A custom Louis Vuitton desk with space for a portable typewriter and a Louis Vuitton lingerie trunk accompanied her on these expeditions as well.

She purchased hats—sometimes buying a new model each week—and staged a "hat luncheon" in 1937 for friends in Hollywood. Maurine also amassed an expansive jewelry collection worth tens of thousands of dollars that included rings, earrings and necklaces sporting sapphires, emeralds and diamonds.

Her living quarters in California mostly consisted of hotels, from which she penned original work between her studio commitments. "Mardi Gras" and "Thistle" were written at the Beverly Wilshire Hotel; "Home Free" and "The Same Boat" were produced at the Chateau Elysee, which is better known today as The Manor Hotel or the Church of Scientology's Celebrity Centre International.

Once described as "rather old-fashioned, she does not smoke, nor drink; neither has she bobbed her hair," Maurine did not conform to society's standards of what a professional, single woman should look like and be. She was setting her own.

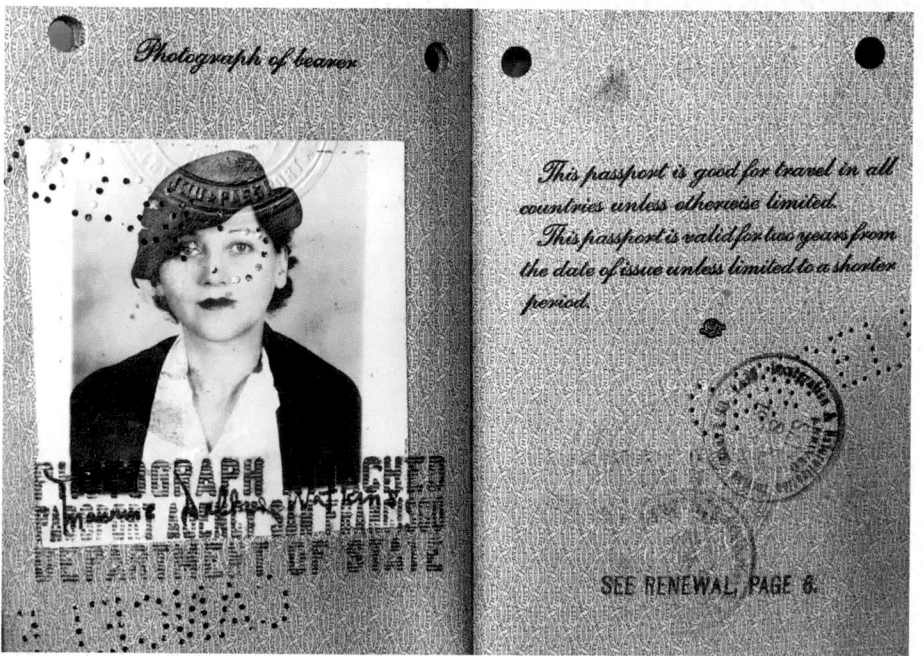

Maurine's 1933 passport is a key document showing the use of her middle name, Dallas, something she did not incorporate into her signatures or bylines in her early life.

Maurine's passport, circa 1937, shows she traveled often after becoming famous for writing the play "Chicago."

Native Street, Zanzibar

Maurine's postcards, from 1934 and 1936, show the variety of places she traveled to after becoming famous for writing the play "Chicago."

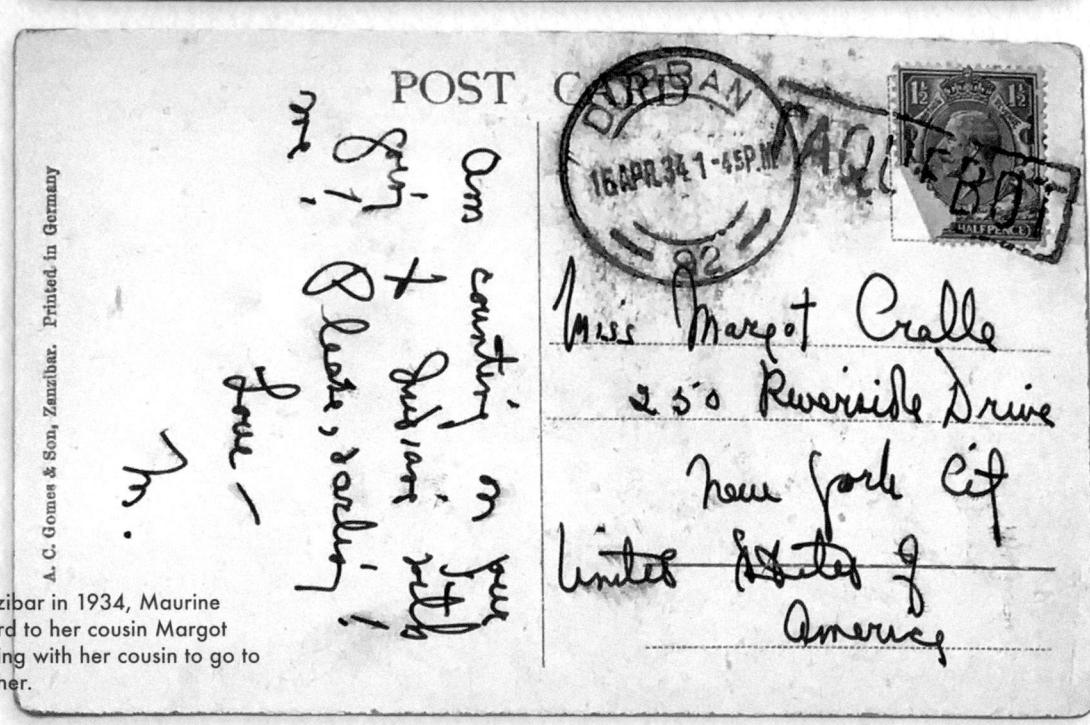

POST CARD

A. C. Gomes & Son, Zanzibar.   Printed in Germany

Miss Margot Cralle
250 Riverside Drive
New York City
United States of
America

While in Zanzibar in 1934, Maurine sent a postcard to her cousin Margot Cralle, pleading with her cousin to go to Indiana with her.

GRAND PACIFIC HOTEL, SUVA, FIJI ISLANDS

773A:—Chateau Marmont, Hollywood, Calif.

FADING FROM VIEW

Following a long illness, Maurine's beloved father died on February 15, 1941, at age seventy. Funeral services were held in Indianapolis, and his body was buried in his hometown of Buffalo, Missouri. It wasn't the first time the man had faced death. He dictated his own obituary prior to a major operation in June 1940, and that's the version that was used in his hometown newspaper, the *Buffalo Reflex*, on February 20, 1941.

In it, Watkins gave a detailed history of his early years, which he described as "very much the same as that of any other boy raised in the Ozark hills." He went on to describe why he felt compelled to preach and how he met Maurine's mother, "who at all times has been a loyal and loving companion." But he saved the kindest words for his only child, "who, at all times, has been a bright and shining star."

Neither Maurine nor her mother traveled to Missouri to attend Watkins' burial. Maurine sent a telegram, but it arrived too late to be read at the service. It said, "Be sure to tell Dallas County churches that Father was sure their prayers gave him additional months of life and happily thankful we are. Our very great love to all. Maurine Dallas Watkins."

Maurine stopped writing plays and traveling the world. She was no longer mentioned in Hollywood stories and made no public comment following the 1942 release of "Roxie Hart," the Twentieth Century Fox film starring Ginger Rogers. From her father's death in 1941, there's no record of where she lived for almost a decade—until her name appeared in the 1951 city directory for Jacksonville, Florida.

At first, Maurine shared an apartment with her mother in a seventeen-story high-rise in downtown Jacksonville, but by 1954, Maurine moved to her own unit on the same floor. She would rent this same apartment until her death fifteen years later. As the fortunes of those inside the apartment building declined—as evidenced by a history of foreclosures, liens and frequent changes in ownership—so, too, possibly, did Maurine's health. But the only real evidence of this are a handwritten note to her mother dated August 23, 1955, and will titled "My Last Will and Testament" dated September 2, 1955.

If she was in ill health in 1955, then that might explain why Maurine chose her mother, who was decades her senior, as executor of her estate. Her "Letter to Mother (to Accompany Will)" included specific instructions for distribution of her jewelry, coins, art, luggage, books, housewares, furs and clothing. Control

FR 360 P541-548

My Last Will and Testament

I, Maurine Dallas Watkins (of St. Johns Apartments, Jacksonville, Florida), being of sound and disposing mind and memory, do make this my Last Will and Testament, and do revoke all other wills and codicils heretofore made by me.

I

I hereby nominate and appoint as Co-executors of my Will and any codicile thereto hereafter made: (1) Georgia M. Watkins (my mother) and Ann Carpenter (410 N. Meridian, Indianapolis, Indiana), jointly or survivor, and (2) such national bank as they may designate — in default of effective appointment by them within Thirty (30) days after my death, the Florida National Bank, Jacksonville; and I give to each personal Co-executor the power, exercisable at her discretion, in event of death or inability of other to serve, to name and appoint a successor personal Co-executor to serve in event of her own death, and for this possible eventuality I recommend whichever of the feminine beneficiaries named herein can most conveniently serve. It is my desire that the personal Co-executors particularly facilitate administration by supplying information, caring for personal effects, and exercising the judgment called for in Clause IX (a), page 8, but that my corporate Co-executor shall be responsible for all ministerial and administrative duties required by law and custom.

II

I hereby direct my Co-executors, after payment of all my just debts, including the expenses of my last illness and funeral, to place any money, other than cash needed for essential expenses, into federal government bonds and federal tax-notes. And I further direct my Co-executors to pay all death duties — estate-tax, inheritance (by whatever name called) — which shall have become payable by reason of my death; and I further direct that no charge for such be made against any personal beneficiary, whether of Will, insurance, or other form of transfer, but should a change in tax laws or other circumstance render

2

Included in her last will and testament was a letter Maurine wrote to her mother, Georgia Watkins, stating her wish for personal items like Bibles, suitcases, jewelry and clothing to go to family and friends. Maurine signed the letter, "Love Always! Maurine."

Letter to Mother (to accompany Will)

I am not including these items in Will since (1) I may have effected distribution of same prior to my death and (2) I wish to give you leeway to change at your convenience and in event certain items are not readily ascertainable during period of administration. But if they do show up, I should like to give —

(1) to Johnson Bible College — encyclopedias, bibles, and books on the Holy Land [in Hogans]

(2) to St. Meinrad's Abbey — crimson alter cloth, silver crucifix, ivory rosary [in American vault]; bust of Socrates [Shellhouse], Taylor's translation of Plato [Hogans] and of Aristotle [Delcher's], any coins (except aureus of Marcus Aurelius) of numismatic interest [in Atlantic box]

(3) to Harley Arthur Long [540 North Orange Drive, Los Angeles 36, California] — the above aureus of Marcus Aurelius, Socrates-cameo ring [both in Atlantic box], L.Y. luggage (secretarial suitcase — Suddath's, hand book-case — Shellhouse, regular suitcase — Shellhouse or Suddath's), and contents of book-boxes or storage: Delcher's #607, Hogans 2A, exclusive of books disposed of above

(4) to Margaret Long Brown — portraits of Robert E. Lee and Stonewall Jackson (Hogans), six place-settings of Royal Danish silver [in Barnett or Atlantic vault], two barrels of curios's [Hogan's]: #2, marked with broad red stripe from top to bottom, #3 — marked "3742-WT75," triangle black opal ring [possibly with me, otherwise in Atlantic box], light green jade set [Fletcher-box]

(5) to Dorotha Watkins Jacobsen — my father's Bible, six place sets of Sovereign silver [both in Atlantic vault — or Barnett], my mother's engagement ring, one barrel of curios [Hogan's]: #1 — marked "3742, E-J-J," beaver cape and hat, cabochon emerald ring [in Fletcher] 10

(6) to Freda Honie — dark green jade set [Fletcher], old manuscript (fr. sentiment — no value) of Chicago as Devil's Diary [American vault], oblong emerald ring [probably with me], curios and souvenir of choice [American vault]

(7) to Ann Carpenter — flat, uncut-stone medallion (with chain) from Ceylon, topaz necklace, star-ruby ring [all in Fletcher], choice of curios

(8) to Mary and Georgia Daugherty — cultured pearls [Fletcher], dark blue set [Barnett], choice of curios, choice of typewriters, bedding, other household items

General: give to Sarah, Nills, Florence, and any of the above, as you think they's like and as convenient for you — flat pieces of silverware, scarves, hand bags, luggage, etc.; give appliances, furniture, clothing not otherwise disposed of to Goodwill or Salvation Army

Note: destroy all old manuscripts (no value), notes, clippings, letters, etc.

(Of course keep anything you'd like for yourself — such as black hand bags, fur capelet, etc.)

Love always!
Maurine (Dallas Watkins)

Tuesday, August the twenty-third
nineteen hundred and fifty-five

SCHEDULE "C"

of Maurine's literary properties—including the U.S. and worldwide copyrights to "Chicago"—were bequeathed to her mother, according to this letter.

Maurine also named a laundry list of cousins and acquaintances to whom she earmarked specific items: portraits of Robert E. Lee and Stonewall Jackson for Aunt Margaret; her father's Bible for Dorotha Watkins Jacobsen, her first cousin on her father's side; old manuscripts for "Chicago" and "The Devil's Diary"—of which she wrote "no value"—to friend and fellow writer Freda Hiner; a star ruby ring to good friend Ann Carpenter; Louis Vuitton luggage for California friend Harley Arthur Long; and choice of typewriters for cousin Mary Daugherty. Though Maurine owned no real estate, an exhaustive inventory of items found in multiple storage spaces in Jacksonville and Indianapolis was compiled by the office of attorney for the executor, Stephen P. Smith, following her death.

A variety of schools and organizations, many of them with religious ties, were also included in Maurine's letter to her mother: books about the Holy Land for Johnson Bible College (now Johnson University) in Tennessee, and a crimson altar cloth and bust of Socrates for St. Meinrad Archabbey in Spencer County, Indiana.

Maurine gave her mother the power to amend her daughter's wishes: "Of course keep anything you'd like for yourself—such as black hand bags, fur capelet, etc." But Maurine was firm in regard to what should happen to her writings: "Note: Destroy all old manuscripts (no value), notes, clippings, letters, etc." She signed it "Love always! Maurine (Dallas Watkins)"

It is the eight-page, handwritten will that shows the breadth of Maurine's estimated more than $2 million estate (or about $14 million in today's dollars)—a 1969 inventory broke it down to include more than $1.7 million in stocks, $164,376 in checking and savings accounts and $84,003 in miscellaneous assets. She gave her mother one-third of her stocks and any of her father's sermons, notes and personal papers with the recommendation "that she dispose of all items, except those desired for sentiment or personal use." The remaining two-thirds of stock—including shares in Eastman Kodak, Libbey-Owens-Ford, Honeywell, Merck, Monsanto, Pfizer and others—was to be divided in equal shares to five named family members and friends.

Proceeds from the sale of six hundred eighteen shares in Standard Oil of California could be given to "one, or more than one, church or library in such amounts and for such purposes as my mother may designate." Other religious organizations—particularly those teaching classical languages—would benefit from

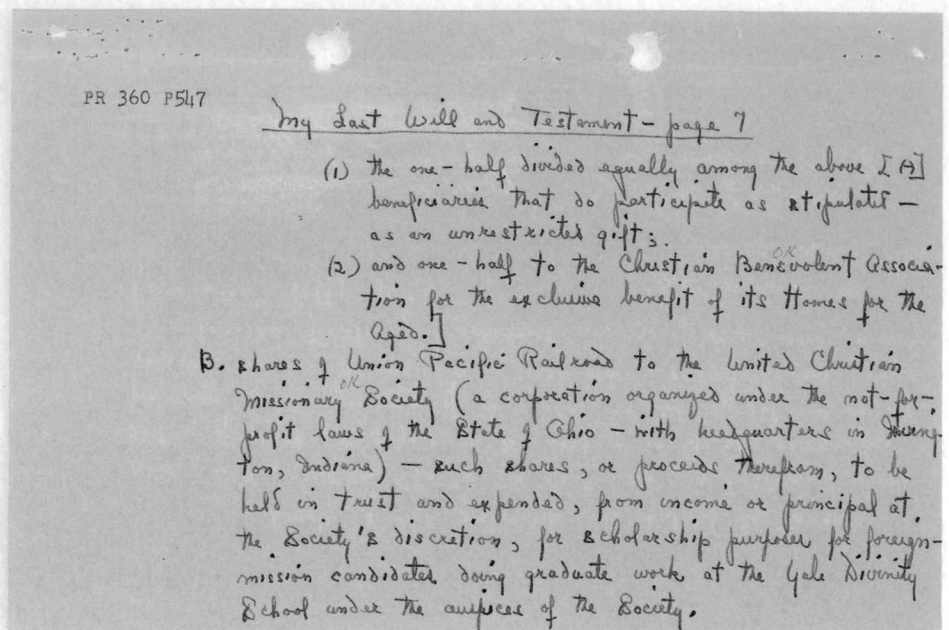

The handwritten last will and testament of Maurine Dallas Watkins, dated September 2, 1955, shows how she divided and handed out her assets to many Christian organizations.

Maurine's charity, too: sales of shares of Texas Gulf Sulphur to create a scholarship in the name of her father at Johnson Bible College; $2,500 to create a Latin award at Academy of the Visitation in St. Louis; $10,000 for a Greek contest going to St. Louis University; $10,000 to the college honorary fraternity Eta Sigma Phi for a Greek translation contest; $10,000 to St. Meinrad Archabbey; and $10,000 to her father's alma mater, Transylvania University.

Maurine lived for another fifteen years but never amended this letter to her mother nor her will.

One of the schools named in her will was Abilene Christian College (now Abilene Christian University) to which she bestowed three hundred shares of Johns Manville, a manufacturer of insulation and roofing materials. In 1956, Maurine began a roughly thirteen-year letter-writing campaign with the school's vice president, W.R. Smith. It's some of the last known correspondence Maurine had with someone other than a family member during her life. She wrote Smith of her interest in providing financial aid to students pursuing preaching vocations; prize money for writing contest winners; and a donation for the creation of a library of study materials for graduate students.

She was also vocal about the type of students she wanted to receive her gifts. In a May 1957 letter to Smith, Maurine expressed concern about giving scholarship money to students who were also pursuing a significant other. "I believe that training for the ministry (or any profession—or just plain life!) is so important that it's a full-time job and that matrimony is so important that it deserves mature judgment, and that any attempt to combine the two at the undergraduate level can be done only at the detriment of one or both." Yet she marked the letter "Personal," telling Smith "I wouldn't want it read by anyone it might hurt."

In her letters, Maurine appeared upbeat and reflective, but always deflected attempts to meet in person. She often used her work or health as excuses to avoid human contact. When Smith wrote Maurine on June 13, 1959, to say the school's president, Don H. Morris, would be in Florida and could meet with her, Maurine declined. Just a few days later she wrote back to Smith, "I wish the suggested meeting were possible—or practicable—but I'm so committed in SO many directions that, in good conscience, I don't dare even think of it!"

Periods of quiet often lingered between the pen pals, as mentioned in this June 3, 1963, letter from Maurine to Smith: "partly because am fighting an allergy battle—a chronic condition that now and then gets out of control under too much stress-and-strain, of which I've had plenty in the past several months. (Not an illness but a condition— no 'get well' cards indicated!) Am planning a semi-sabbatical . . ."

THE RIGHTS

Maurine died of carcinoma of the right lung at Jacksonville's Methodist Hospital on August 10, 1969. Her body was cremated and her ashes scattered over the Atlantic Ocean at her request. A headstone was placed in her memory next to her father's grave in Buffalo, Missouri. It had been more than forty-one years since "Chicago" was last staged on Broadway and twenty-seven years since the movie "Roxie Hart." Yet her famous work didn't expire with her.

On the contrary, her estate was inundated with requests for it. As C.R. Leonard, a trust officer for the bank representing Maurine's estate, recalled in a May 2018 interview with the *Florida Times-Union*, "A number of people came out of the woodwork wanting to acquire the rights."

It's unknown if Maurine, in her later years, had opposed the sale of her play, which could explain its extended absence from the stage and screen. In a 1997 interview with the *Chicago Tribune*, Sheldon Abend, owner of the American Play Company, said he found a file of correspondence going back to 1952. In it, Maurine

	CERTIFICATE OF DEATH	STATE FILE NO. `69-046641`

STATE BOARD OF HEALTH
BUREAU OF VITAL STATISTICS

CERTIFICATE OF DEATH
FLORIDA

STATE FILE NO. `69-046641`

REGISTRAR'S NO. `69` `2794`

RTH NO.

LACE OF DEATH COUNTY	Duval	CODE NO. 26-083	2. USUAL RESIDENCE (Where deceased lived. If institution: Residence before admission) a. STATE Florida	b. COUNTY Duval

CITY, TOWN, OR LOCATION Jacksonville	c. IS PLACE OF DEATH INSIDE CITY LIMITS? YES ☒ NO ☐	c. CITY, TOWN, OR LOCATION Jacksonville	e. IS RESIDENCE INSIDE CITY LIMITS? YES ☒ NO ☐

NAME OF HOSPITAL OR INSTITUTION Methodist Hospital

d. STREET ADDRESS 311 West Ashley Street

AME OF DECEASED Type or print)	First Maurine	Middle D.	Last Watkins	4. DATE OF DEATH	Month August	Day 10,	Year 1969

EX Female	6. COLOR OR RACE White	7. ☐ MARRIED ☐ WIDOWED ☐ DIVORCED ☒ NEVER MARRIED	8. DATE OF BIRTH July 27, 1901	9. AGE (In years last birthday) 68	IF UNDER 1 YEAR Months Days	IF UNDER 24 HRS. Hours Min.

USUAL OCCUPATION (Give kind of work done during most of working life, even if retired) Playwright	10b. KIND OF BUSINESS OR INDUSTRY Movies & Theatre	11. BIRTHPLACE (State or foreign country) Lexington, Kentucky	12. CITIZEN OF WHAT COUNTRY? USA

FATHER'S NAME George W. Watkins	14. MOTHER'S MAIDEN NAME Georgia M. Long

SOCIAL SECURITY NO.	17. INFORMANT'S SIGNATURE Mrs Robert H. Brown, P.O. Box 223, Coopers Station, New York City, N.Y.	Address

18. CAUSE OF DEATH [Enter only one cause per line for (a), (b), and (c).]

PART I. DEATH WAS CAUSED BY:
IMMEDIATE CAUSE (a) Carcinoma of the Right Lung.

INTERVAL BETWEEN ONSET AND DEATH
Not known

Conditions, if any, which gave rise to above cause (a), stating the underlying cause last.

DUE TO (b) _____

DUE TO (c) _____

PART II. OTHER SIGNIFICANT CONDITIONS CONTRIBUTING TO DEATH BUT NOT RELATED TO THE TERMINAL DISEASE CONDITION GIVEN IN PART I(a)

19. WAS AUTOPSY PERFORMED?
YES ☐ NO ☒

20a. (Probably) ACCIDENT ☐	SUICIDE ☐	HOMICIDE ☐	20b. DESCRIBE HOW INJURY OCCURRED (Enter nature of injury in Part I or Part II of item 18.)

20c. TIME OF INJURY	Hour a. m. p. m.	Month, Day, Year	61

20d. INJURY OCCURRED WHILE AT WORK ☐ NOT WHILE AT WORK ☐	20e. PLACE OF INJURY (e. g., in or about home, farm, factory, street, office bldg., etc.)	20f. CITY, TOWN, OR LOCATION	COUNTY	STATE

21. I attended the deceased from 7/4/69 , to 8/10/69 and last saw her alive on 8/10/69
Death occurred at 7:10 P. m on the date stated above; and to the best of my knowledge, from the causes stated.

22a. SIGNATURE (Degree or title) M.D.	22b. ADDRESS Jacksonville, Fla.	22c. DATE SIGNED 8/11/69

23. BURIAL, CREMATION, REMOVAL (Specify) Cremation	23b. DATE 8/13/69	23c. NAME OF CEMETERY OR CREMATORY East Coast Crematorium	23d. LOCATION (City, town, or county) Jacksonville Beach, Florida	(State)

FUNERAL DIRECTOR'S SIGNATURE Gordon Hardage ADDRESS Hardage & Sons, 517 Park St, Jax, Fla.	25. DATE RECD. BY LOCAL REG. Aug 12, 1969	26. REGISTRAR'S SIGNATURE

Maurine's death certificate shows she died of carcinoma of the right lung on August 10, 1969.

thanked the company, which she paid $500 per year to serve as her agent, for keeping producers away from the play. Abend himself attempted to buy "Chicago" from Maurine but never worked out an agreement before her death. He died in 2003, but American Play Company still serves as the agent for Maurine's original play, which is now known as " 'Chicago' aka 'Play Ball.' "

Dancer/actress Gwen Verdon asserted in several interviews that it was her idea to adapt Maurine's play into a musical. Verdon said she purchased the rights to "Chicago," but there's no proof of this.

Though Maurine's mother was due to inherit all of her daughter's copyrighted work, there were complications. Court records from Duval County, Florida, show

Maurine's mother fractured her hip in June 1969, underwent an operation and was bedridden in a nearby nursing home. To protect her health, relatives did not tell her of Maurine's death. Georgia's sister, Margaret Brown, asked the court to be appointed administrator of Maurine's estate. The court granted her request and also placed Florida National Bank of Jacksonville as co-executor. As Brown would later say during a court deposition, "I am the only one in our family alive."

Since Maurine's will was handwritten and not notarized, litigation ensued. It would take years—and even the Florida Supreme Court—to sort out ambiguities.

Maurine's mother died on September 2, 1970. After an order of partial distribution was granted by the court on April 20, 1972, Brown and Florida National Bank of Jacksonville hired Abend to manage offers for new productions of "Chicago."

On May 31, 1972, Brown and the bank gave the court notice that they intended to execute an agreement with Robert Fryer and James Cresson for "Chicago" to become "a Broadway musical in New York City." Fryer's previous Broadway productions included "A Tree Grows in Brooklyn," "Sweet Charity," "Redhead" and "Mame" starring Angela Lansbury. The agreement gave Fryer and Cresson two years to produce the play in New York City first, then "on other stages throughout the United States and the world." In return, the producers would give the estate a $2,500 payment (or roughly $15,000 in today's dollars), a percentage of the ticket sales for any major production of the play and additional proceeds from the sale of its rights. Here's how it was written in the contract:

> One and one-half (1½%) percent of the gross weekly box office receipts from all first class stage presentations, and all other stage presentations of the play in the United States of America and throughout the world, said Agreement also provides for other sums to be paid for the sale, lease or disposition of other rights in the play.

Other stipulations of this contract stated all materials promoting the new production—programs, billboards, posters, advertisements—would include the phrase "Based on the play by Maurine Dallas Watkins." Publication rights and any royalties and proceeds from them "remain the sole property of the Estate of Georgia M. Watkins, her heirs and legal representatives." Another benefit for Watkins' heirs was four pairs of tickets in the first 10 rows of the orchestra's center section guaranteed to them for each Broadway performance—with an additional four pairs of similar seats for the musical's opening night.

Trust officer Leonard said he also negotiated for the heirs to receive one-and-a-half

OFFICIAL RECORDS.

ESTATE GEORGIA M. WATKINS

Annual Accounting from 12/10/71 through 12/9/72

SCHEDULE "A" - BEGINNING INVENTORY

The Accountant charges itself with the principal balance as set forth in Schedule "I" of the previous Annual Accounting heretofore filed $ 201,501.45

SCHEDULE "B" - ADDITIONS

Date	Description	Amount	Total
Various dates	From Income Account		$ 8,318.24
1/7/72	From Estate Maurine D. Watkins, Deceased, 1/3 proceeds sale of 50 Shrs. General Motors Corp. $5.00 Pfd. Stock per specific bequest under Item III of Will		1,315.31
1/13/72	From Estate Maurine D. Watkins, partial distribution of estate as follows:		
	one brown mink full length coat (old and worn)	150.00	
	one sealed box purporting to contain collection of stamps	361.77	
	Three sealed boxes purporting to contain U.S. & foreign Gold & silver coins	2,656.37	3,168.14
5/17/72	From Estate Maurine D. Watkins partial distribution of estate as follows:		

Copyrights - valid worldwide except U.S.:
1. A Lady of Glamour
2. Against The Day
3. Marsh - Land
4. The Devil's Dairy
5. Glory, or, The Angel -Girl
6. Henrietta's Mother
7. Velvet

Copyrights - valid in U.S. and worldwide
1. Gesture
2. Mardi Gras
3. Chicago, or Play Ball
4. Snatch The Day or Grotesque
5. So Help Me God
6. Tinsel Girl

Date	Description		Total
	All carried for control purposes at		1.00
5/13/72	From C. R. Leonard, refund excess advance		70.00
7/11/72	From Robert Fryer and James Cresson, initial payment to acquire stage rights to play "Chicago"		2,500.00
8/18/72	From Merchants National Bank of Indianapolis, Indiana, proceeds checking Account		5,467.82
11/28/72	From County Judges Court, refund court deposit		89.65
			$ 20,930.16

SCHEDULE "C" - PURCHASES, SALES, GAINS, LOSSES

Date		Description	Cost or Inv.	Proceeds	Gains	Losses
1/5/72	Purchase	Florida First Ntl. Bank of Jacksonville Savings Account (additional deposit) purchased from Company at 100	463.12	463.12	--	--

In 1972, Broadway producers Robert Fryer and James Cresson made the first payment of $2,500 to acquire the stage rights to the play "Chicago." The acquisition made the musical version of the play that we know today possible.

percent of all box office receipts for any movie made from Maurine's play. "Chicago"—released in 2002 and the winner of six Academy Awards, including Best Picture—grossed more than $170 million in the U.S. and $306 million total worldwide.

After the contract had been redrafted fourteen times, the sale of "Chicago" to Fryer and Cresson was approved on June 8, 1972. Leonard traveled to New York City with an attorney to witness the producers sign the contract.

The estate's administrators granted the producers an extension after director and choreographer Bob Fosse needed open-heart surgery in 1974. "Chicago: A Musical Vaudeville" premiered on June 3, 1975, starring Fosse's estranged wife Gwen Verdon as Roxie Hart, Chita Rivera as Velma Kelly and Jerry Orbach as Roxie's attorney, Billy Flynn. The musical ran for nine hundred thirty-six performances before closing on August 27, 1977.

Maurine's heirs, most of whom never met her, continue to reap the financial benefits of her famous work through both the licensing of her original play and the musical production.

$2 BILLION LEGACY

The Tony- and Oscar-winning musical versions of "Chicago" for the stage and screen have earned more than $2 billion worldwide, likely making Maurine's work the most financially successful piece of writing ever produced by a *Chicago Tribune* reporter in the paper's more than 170 years of history.

And the money continues to roll in. "Chicago the Musical" is the second longest running show on Broadway (behind "The Phantom of the Opera"), with more than nine thousand three hundred performances as of April 2019. International and U.S. tours have visited four hundred eighty-five cities in at least thirty-five countries and productions have been performed in twelve languages.

Maurine held only one professional journalism job during her lifetime, as a *Chicago Tribune* reporter for eight months in 1924. Yet almost a century after her arrival in the newsroom, there are no indications she ever worked for the *Chicago Tribune*. No major awards won. No conference rooms named in her honor. Only after a deep dive into the paper's archives were her bylines revealed, almost a century later.

Her August 10, 1969, death, too, went barely noticed. The *Chicago Tribune*, Maurine's former employer, like many newspapers around the country, failed to run her obituary. A nine-line paid death notice appearing on Page C-8 in the *Florida*

The three-sentence-long obituary for Maurine that ran on August 12, 1969, never mentions she wrote the famous play "Chicago."

Times-Union on August 12, 1969, would be the only recognition of her passing in Jacksonville, Florida. Though this eulogy mentioned Maurine was a playwright, it failed to include the name of her famous work.

Much about Maurine is unknown and may never be understood. Though she continued to write for the stage and screen after "Chicago," she was never able to replicate her blazing initial success. She was close with her parents and cousins, but Maurine never married nor had children. Her final years, spent self-sequestered, only make her more of an enigma.

Yet parts of her life—especially her early years—are well documented and show Maurine's commitment to earning an education, perfecting her art and defying social norms of what was expected of a woman during the early years of the twentieth century. Her story is that of an immensely driven, immensely talented woman, and her seminal work stands among the most iconic and valuable the city of Chicago has ever produced.

ACKNOWLEDGMENTS

THIS PROJECT WOULD not have been possible without the generous support of:

- Our families, especially Patrick and Boone Finley and Brian and River Morgan.
- *Chicago Tribune* managing editor Christine W. Taylor and directors of content Jonathon Berlin, Todd Panagopoulos and Amy Carr.
- The staff of the *Chicago Tribune* newsroom, especially Jennifer Day, Chris Jones, Rick Kogan, Kathleen B. O'Malley, Michael Phillips, Scott Powers, Soren Smith, Heidi Stevens and our colleagues in the data visualization and photography departments who generously juggled workloads while we toiled away in the newspaper's archives.
- Agate Publishing founder Doug Seibold and staffers Morgan Krehbiel, Helena Hunt, and Jacqueline Jarik.
- Cousins of Maurine Dallas Watkins.
- Elliot S. Blair, Esq., of the American Entertainment Holding Company.
- At Yale University: Michael Frost and Genevieve Coyle of the manuscripts and archives department at Sterling Memorial Library; Elizabeth Frengel, head of research services at the Beinecke Rare Book and Manuscript Library; and the staff of Beinecke.
- At Harvard University: the reference staff at Harvard University Archives at Pusey Library in Harvard Yard; reference librarian Susan Halpert and the staff at Houghton Library; and research librarian Sarah Hutcheon at the History of Women in America at the Radcliffe Institute.

- Supervisor Fred W. Hill and the staff of the probate department at the Duval County Clerk of Courts.
- Brian Corrigan, the public information officer and senior manager of the public records department at Duval County Clerk of Courts.
- McGarvey Ice, the director of special collections and archives, and Carisse Berryhill, the special collections librarian, at Abilene Christian University.
- Supervisors Catheryne Popovitch and John Reinhardt and the staff at the Illinois State Archives.
- Chief Deputy Clerk Phil Costello and the staff of the archives department at the Clerk of the Circuit Court of Cook County.
- Dellie J. Craig, the local history specialist at the Crawfordsville District Public Library, and the library's reference services staff
- Susan "Tracie" Schneider, archivist at the State Archives of Florida.
- Sandy Leitheiser, county clerk of Montgomery County, Illinois.
- Thomas H. Pauly, author of "Chicago: With the *Chicago Tribune* Articles That Inspired It."
- Emilie Le Beau Lucchesi, author of "Ugly Prey: An Innocent Woman and the Death Sentence That Scandalized Jazz Age Chicago."
- Louise Kiernan, editor-in-chief of ProPublica Illinois, whose 1997 piece for the *Chicago Tribune* on Maurine Watkins' life provided inspiration and clues to begin our research.
- Murray Weiss, literary manager at Catalyst Literary Management.
- Heath Schwartz, Broadway production representative for "Chicago" at Boneau/Bryan-Brown.
- John Wilson, librarian at the Jacksonville Public Library, and the library's special collections staff
- Lisa Sheppard, planner at the Planning and Development Department of the City of Jacksonville, Florida.
- Giselle Alonso, Florida and genealogy librarian for the Helen Muir Florida Collection at the Miami-Dade Public Library System.
- Walter Bowman of archives and records management at the Kentucky Department for Libraries and Archives.

- Andrea Glenn, Indiana Division librarian at the Indiana State Library.
- Amanda LeVasser, archivist at the Valdes-Fauli Coral Gables in the Historical Resources and Cultural Arts Department of the City of Coral Gables, Florida.
- Katelyn Kraunelis, communications associate at Christie's.
- Stephanie Fletcher, e-resources/reference librarian at the Ryerson and Burnham Libraries at the Art Institute of Chicago.
- Dallas County Library in Buffalo, Missouri.
- Sarah Revell, spokeswoman for the Florida Department of State.
- Genevieve Maxwell, reference librarian at the Margaret Herrick Library at the Academy of Motion Picture Arts and Sciences.
- Libby Smigel, dance curator and archivist in the music division of the Library of Congress.
- Mitchell Hemann, archivist at the Jacksonville Historical Society.
- Michelle Leonard, associate university librarian at the Marston Science Library, George A. Smathers Libraries at the University of Florida.
- Theresa Mier of the Office of Public Affairs at the California Department of Public Health.
- Gary J. Sammet, administrator of public health statistics and medical classification at the Bureau of Vital Statistics at the Florida Department of Health.
- Brenda S. Lovold, guidance counselor at Crawfordsville High School.
- Lindsey Beckley, outreach manager at the Indiana Historical Bureau.
- Ruthie Cobb, author of "A Place We Called Home: A History of Illinois Soldiers' Orphans' Home, 1864-1931, Illinois Soldiers' and Sailors' Children's School, 1931-1979."
- Maarten Kooij of ICM Partners.
- Mary Callahan, project manager at the Verdon Fosse Legacy.
- Matthew Yongue of clip and still licensing at Twentieth Century Fox.
- John Schauerman, director of licensing at Visual Icon.
- Tim Samuelson, cultural historian for the City of Chicago.

Belva, left, and Beulah, center, prepare to go before a jury with Sabella's statement in their minds: "You no hang, you too pretty." Sabella, once sentenced to hang, had been granted a new chance to prove her claimed innocence. All three prisoners pose while in court for their arraignment on April 21, 1924. With them are Deputy Sheriffs Paul Dasso, William Sullivan, John Buffo and Sam Annoreno.

NOTES

CHAPTER 2: BEULAH ANNAN

The pair were intimate through "the prettiest woman ever accused of murder in Chicago": Maurine Watkins, "Demand Noose for 'Prettiest' Woman Slayer," *Chicago Tribune*, April 5, 1924.

She was pregnant: Maurine Watkins, "Beulah Annan Awaits Stork, Murder Trial," *Chicago Tribune*, May 9, 1924.

(John) treated her cruelly: "Fierce Temper Is Allegation," the *Twice-A-Week Messenger* (Owensboro, Kentucky), Dec. 18, 1907.

Beulah married for the first time: Spencer County, Ind., Index to Marriage Record 1850-1920 Inclusive Vol., original record located: County Clerk's Office Roc, Book: 19, Page: 177; "Married in Rockford," The Passing Throng, the *Owensboro Messenger* (Owensboro, Ky.), Feb. 12, 1915.

It's likely Beulah lied about her age: Dorothy Stevens, death certificate, March 11, 1928, registered no. 7501, Illinois Department of Public Health—Division of Vital Statistics, copy in possession of author.

Beulah gave birth: Perry W. Stephens, birth certificate, Kentucky, Birth Index, 1911-1999, accessed via Ancestry.com.

"Games and music were enjoyed": "Varied Interests," Society Events, *Messenger-Inquirer* (Owensboro, Ky.), Aug. 13, 1918.

"She was never mentioned": Karen Owen, "The Woman Too Pretty to Hang," *Messenger-Inquirer* (Owensboro, Ky.), Dec. 7, 1992.

She was married again: Cook County, Ill., Marriages Index, 1871-1920, Illinois Department of Public Health—Division of Vital Statistics, accessed via Ancestry.com.

earned up to $60 a week: "Demand Noose for 'Prettiest' Woman Slayer," *Chicago Tribune*.

Small would win reelection: Stephan Benzkofer, "Len Small: Perhaps the Dirtiest Illinois Governor of Them All," Flashback, *Chicago Tribune*, June 19, 2011, https://www.chicagotribune.com/news/opinion/ct-per-flashback-small-0619-20110619-sto-ry.html.

Albert Annan tried to shoulder the blame: "Mrs. Annan Has Lonesome Day Behind the Bars," *Chicago Tribune*, April 7, 1924.

"I was nervous, you see": "Woman Plays Jazz Air as Victim Dies," *Chicago Tribune*, April 4, 1924.

Irish-born W.W. O'Brien: Michael Lensy, "Chicago's Deadly Decade," excerpt from "Murder City: The Bloody History of Chicago in the Twenties" (W.W. Norton, 2007), *Chicago Tribune*, Jan. 21, 2007, https://www.chicagotribune.com/news/ct-xpm-2007-01-21-0701210517-story.html.

"Darned good reason: I shot him": "Demand Noose for 'Prettiest' Woman Slayer," *Chicago Tribune*.

"I've been a sucker": Ibid.

Beulah "powdered her nose": Ibid.

Albert Annan immediately returned to work: "Mrs. Annan Has Lonesome Day Behind the Bars," *Chicago Tribune*.

"he had nothing to offer me": Maurine Watkins, "Beulah Annan Sobs Regret for Life She Took," *Chicago Tribune*, April 6, 1924.

Beulah's actions didn't deter admirers: "Mrs. Annan Has Lonesome Day Behind the Bars," *Chicago Tribune*.

"If I had not shot him": "Relatives Cheer Prettiest Killer in Cell at Jail," *Chicago Tribune*, April 8, 1924.

a speedy trial was promised: "Judge Promises Speedy Hearing for Mrs. Annan," *Chicago Tribune*, April 16, 1924.

she was expecting a baby: "Beulah Annan Awaits Stork, Murder Trial," *Chicago Tribune*.

A poll of women on Murderess Row: Ibid.

twelve jury members were chosen: Maurine Watkins, "Select Jury to Pronounce Fate of Beulah Annan," *Chicago Tribune*, May 23, 1924.

Kalstedt threatened Beulah: Maurine Watkins, "Judge Admits All of Beulah's Killing Stories," *Chicago Tribune*, May 24, 1924.

Watkins wrote: Maurine Watkins, "Jury Finds Beulah Annan Is 'Not Guilty'; Self-Defense Plea Gains Her Freedom," *Chicago Tribune*, May 25, 1924.

"You have seen that face, gentlemen": Ibid.

Beulah was not guilty: Ibid.

She packed her belongings: "Beulah Annan Fades Away to Seclusion," *Chicago Tribune*, May 26, 1924.

"I will never marry again": "Beulah Annan to Get Divorce, Judge Indicates," *Chicago Tribune*, Aug. 21, 1926.

The latest husband: "Beulah Annan Reported About to Be Married," *Chicago Tribune*, Jan. 18, 1927.

He had already purchased a new home: "Beulah Annan, Beauty Freed of Murder, Is Bride," *Chicago Tribune*, Jan. 19, 1927.

Beulah's third marriage ended: "Beulah Annan Harlib Wins Divorce from Second Mate," *Chicago Tribune*, May 12, 1927.

Beulah entered the Chicago Fresh-Air Hospital: Dorothy Stevens, death certificate.

The simple funeral: Kathleen McLaughlin, "Beulah Annan, Chicago's Jazz Killer, Is Dead," *Chicago Tribune*, March 14, 1928.

Maurine Watkins used Beulah's life: Ibid.

Meet the Deceased: Harry Kalstedt

living in the city's Fifth Ward: US Census 1910, Chicago Ward 5, Cook, Ill., Roll T624_245; Page 12B; Enumeration District: 0298; FHL Microfilm: 1374258.

They had a child: Archives of the Evangelical Lutheran Church in America, Elk Grove Village, Ill., Parish: First Lutheran Church, ELCA Film Number: M23, SSIRC Film Number: E-23.

The couple was married: Ibid.

Kalstedt moved back to Chicago: WWI draft card, Cook County, Ill.; Roll: 1439693; Draft Board: 12.

Kalstedt met Beulah Annan: "Demand Noose For 'Prettiest' Woman Slayer," *Chicago Tribune*.

Naming Roxie Hart

the young female witness: "Demand Noose for 'Prettiest' Woman Slayer," *Chicago Tribune*.

Walter Runyan shot friend and hired farmhand Artie Stull: "Kills Employee at Farm Home," *Indianapolis Star*, Oct. 25, 1913.

"Gossip and scandal ran a race": W.H. Blodgett, "Acquits Runyan of Charge of Murder," *Indianapolis News*, Feb. 20, 1914.

he mentioned his illegitimate birth: "Roxie Hart Coming to Defend Her Name," *Fort Wayne Daily News*, Jan. 29, 1914.

Hart wrote a letter: "Acquits Runyan of Charge of Murder," *Indianapolis News*.

"every subscriber on the line listened": Ibid.

overflow seating for 500 people: "Jam Court Room," *Princeton Clarion News* (Princeton, Ind.), Jan. 23, 1914.

Robbers took advantage of homes: "Acquits Runyan of Charge of Murder," *Indianapolis News*.

Roxie said she visited the Runyan home several times: United Press, "Runyan to the Witness Stand," *Seymour Daily Republican* (Seymour, Ind.), Feb. 4, 1914.

"It was just Walter's way": "Tells of Kisses Given by Runyan During Her Visit," *Indianapolis Star*, Feb. 4, 1914.

Walter Runyan took the witness stand: United Press, "Runyan Takes Stand in His Own Behalf," *Huntington Herald* (Huntington, Ind.), Feb. 6, 1914.

not guilty verdict for Walter Runyan: "Acquits Runyan of Charge of Murder," *Indianapolis News*.

CHAPTER 3: BELVA GAERTNER

husbands always cause women trouble: "No Sweetheart Worth Killing—Mrs. Gaertner," *Chicago Tribune*, March 14, 1924.

Belva's Nash sedan: "Mystery Victim Is Robert Law; Hold Divorcee," *Chicago Tribune*, March 12, 1924.

"(G)in and guns": "No Sweetheart Worth Killing—Mrs. Gaertner," *Chicago Tribune*.

"I liked him and he loved me": Ibid.; Maurine Watkins, "Beulah Annan Sobs for Life She Took," *Chicago Tribune*, April 6, 1924.

Though no birth certificate exists: Sandy Leitheiser (clerk, Montgomery County, Illinois), in email with the author, Feb. 28, 2019; Belva E. Gaertner, death certificate, local registration district 7003, certificate number 20051, California, County of Los Angeles Registrar-Recorder/County Clerk, copy in possession of author.

The town was known for its railroad junctions: "History of Litchfield Illinois," Historical Society of Montgomery County Illinois, June 15, 2009, http://history.montgomeryco.com/Archives/History /ID/61/History-of-Litchfield-Illinois.

Belva and a younger sister, Malinda: Illinois Soldiers' and Sailors' Children's School, "Register of Children," Record Series 255.004, Illinois State Archives.

Belva married for the first time: Belle Boosiner and Harry Peepo, marriage certificate, number 13154, County Clerk of Montgomery County, Illinois, copy in possession of author.

he moved to Bloomington, Illinois: "Harry W. Peepo," Second Ward, the *Pantagraph* (Bloomington, Ill.), Jan. 18, 1934.

she couldn't recall the exact date: Oberbeck v. Oberbeck, 1917, case number S-327058, Superior Court of Cook County in Chancery, accessed at the Archives Department of the Clerk of Circuit Court of Cook County.

"I was angry": Ibid.

Belva married William Gaertner: Belva Eleanor Boosinger and William Gaertner, marriage registration, Indiana, Marriages, 1810-2001. Salt Lake City, Utah, accessed via FamilySearch, 2013.

mutual love for horseback riding: "Scientist and Singer to Test Remarriage Law," *Chicago Tribune*, Sept. 16, 1917.

Those who violated the law: H.S., "Indiana Marriages in Contravention of the Illinois Act of 1905," *Illinois Law Review* (now named *Northwestern University Law Review*), Volume 1, 1906-1907.

question not tackled previously: "Scientist and Singer to Test Remarriage Law," *Chicago Tribune*.

This time legally: Belle Oberbeck and William Gaertner, marriage certificate, Cook County, Illinois, Marriages Index, 1871-1920. Salt Lake City, Utah, accessed via FamilySearch, 2013.

Each spouse hired private investigators: "Gaertners' Life Just One Sleuth after Another," *Chicago Tribune*, April 9, 1920.

"My divorce left me with $3,000": "She's Taxi Driver Now—Her Own Boss," *Chicago Tribune*, July 10, 1920.

Her blood-drenched karakul coat: "State Launches Trial of Belva for Law Killing," *Chicago Tribune*, June 5, 1924.

"We were sitting there talking": "Mystery Victim Is Walter Law; Hold Divorcee," *Chicago Tribune*.

two men unleashing a stench bomb: "Hold Divorcee as Slayer of Auto Salesman," *Chicago Tribune*, March 12, 1924.

Belva was charged with Law's murder: "Mrs. Gaertner Indicted as Walter Law's Slayer," *Chicago Tribune*, March 22, 1924.

"That was bum": "No Sweetheart Worth Killing—Mrs. Gaertner," *Chicago Tribune*.

Her legal bills were paid: R.T. O'Connor, "William Gaertner, 1864-1948," *Popular Astronomy* 57 (1949); "Hold Divorcee As Slayer of Auto Salesman," *Chicago Tribune*.

"'Class'—that was Belva": Maurine Watkins, "Mrs. Gaertner Has 'Class' as She Faces Jury," *Chicago Tribune*, June 4, 1924.

Dr. Joseph Springer: "State Launches Trial of Belva for Law Killing," *Chicago Tribune*.

"Her sultry eyes": Ibid.

"Belva wore a new dress": Maurine Watkins, "Jury Finds Mrs. Gaertner Not Guilty," *Chicago Tribune*, June 6, 1924.

"Oh, I'm so happy!": Ibid.

"I'm going to rewed William": "Belva Gaertner Marries Former Husband 3D Time," *Chicago Tribune*, May 3, 1925.

Belva went to her former cell: "Murderess Row Loses Class as Belva Is Freed," *Chicago Tribune*, June 7, 1924.

She apparently fainted: "Jury Finds Mrs. Gaertner Not Guilty," *Chicago Tribune*.

A "terrible strain": "Murderess Row Loses Class As Belva Is Freed," *Chicago Tribune*.

Gaertner and Belva did remarry: "Thrice Married," *Chicago Tribune*, May 3, 1925.

Traveling together to exotic destinations: New York, Passenger Lists, 1820-1957, accessed via Ancestry.com.

Gaertner did file for divorce through **"Yes, of course"**: "Belva Gaertner Will Fight Rich Husband's Suit," *Chicago Tribune*, Aug. 2, 1926.

Yet, Gaertner stuck with Belva: "Belva Gaertner Held for Driving While Intoxicated, *Chicago Tribune*, Nov. 3, 1926.

She reported thieves: "Mrs. Gaertner's Home Is Looted of Cigarets," *Chicago Tribune*, April 9, 1927.

William dies at his home: "Leaves Firm in a Trust to Aid Workers," *Chicago Tribune*, Dec. 15, 1948.

He's buried in Mount Greenwood Cemetery: "William Gaertner," https://www.findagrave.com /memorial/136782246/william-gaertner.

Belva moved to the Los Angeles area: California, Voter Registrations, 1900-1968, accessed via Ancestry.com.

Belva dies of cardiovascular disease: Belva E. Gaertner, death certificate, California, County of Los Angeles Registrar-Recorder/County Clerk, copy in possession of author.

Her ashes are interred: "Belva Boosinger Gaertner," https://www.findagrave.com/memorial/178410143 /belva-gaertner.

Meet the Deceased: Walter Law

the youngest of five children: U.S. Census 1920, Chicago Ward 2, Cook, Ill.; Roll: T624_242; Page: 2A; Enumeration District: 0206; FHL Microfilm: 1374255.

Law registered for the World War I Draft: WWI draft card, Cook County, Ill., Roll: 1452384, Draft Board: 3.

He married Freda Orton: Cook County, Ill., Marriage Indexes, 1912-1942, Illinois Department of Public Health—Division of Vital Statistics, accessed via Ancestry.com.

Paul E. Goodwin: "Hold Divorcee as Slayer of Auto Salesman," *Chicago Tribune*.

CHAPTER 4: KATHERINE BALUK

"Not a word": Genevieve Forbes, "Savage Mother Cries Out from Gun Girl's Soul," *Chicago Tribune*, Nov. 29, 1923.

"Do you want me?": "Mrs. Malm Surrenders; Admits Share in Slaying," *Chicago Tribune*, Nov. 28, 1923.

she waved off Malm's confession: "Savage Mother Cries Out from Gun Girl's Soul," *Chicago Tribune*.

"I thought for sure they would give me the rope": "Kitty Admits She Expected 'Rope' Verdict," *Chicago Tribune*, Feb. 28, 1924.

Katherine Walter was born: Katherine Walter, death certificate, Dec. 27, 1932, registered No. 099063, Illinois Department of Public Health—Division of Vital Statistics, copy in possession of author.

Katherine's father died: Secretary of State, "Executive Section. Executive Clemency Files," Record Series 103.096, Illinois State Archives.

"So I went to work": "Savage Mother Cries Out from Gun Girl's Soul," *Chicago Tribune*.

he was at least 20 years her senior: Cook County, Ill., Marriage Indexes, 1912-1942, Illinois Department of Public Health—Division of Vital Statistics, accessed via Ancestry.com.

The bright spot in the marriage: Katherine Baluk, birth certificate, Cook County, Ill., Birth Index, 1916-1935, accessed via Ancestry.com.

"God, I could kill a woman" through **Katherine left her husband**: "Savage Mother Cries Out from Gun Girl's Soul," *Chicago Tribune*.

During the late summer of 1923: Ibid.

Malm was a convicted felon: "Youthful Bandit Admits a Murder," *Rock Island Argus* (Rock Island, Ill.), March 1, 1915; and "Homicide in Chicago, 1870-1930" interactive database, http://homicide .northwestern.edu/database/.

He was paroled again: "Kitty Malm and Husband Given Life in Prison," *Chicago Tribune*, March 9, 1924.

obtained a marriage license: Indiana, Marriages, 1810-2001, accessed via Ancestry.com.

"Get Bockelman": "Youth Finds Her Jimmying Door; Slain," *Chicago Tribune*, Nov. 5, 1923.

"a 19-year-old waitress": Genevieve Forbes, "Girl Confesses Bandit Raid That Ended in Slaying," *Chicago Tribune*, Nov. 7, 1923.

Bockelman was arrested: "Blames Escape of Mrs. Malm on Policemen," *Chicago Tribune*, Nov. 25, 1923.

"I never heard of Bockelman in my life": "Confession of Slayer Clears Man in Cell: Tells How He and His Wife Killed Lehman," *Chicago Tribune*, Nov. 24, 1923.

Beck immediately recanted her confession: Ibid.

surveillance on the home of Katherine's mother: "Suspends Police Blamed for Gun Girl's Escape," *Chicago Tribune*, Nov. 26, 1923.

"I'll tell you what I did": "Mrs. Malm Surrenders; Admits Share in Slaying," *Chicago Tribune*.

all four were indicted: "Rival 'Slayers' All Indicted in Lehman Case," *Chicago Tribune*, Dec. 6, 1923.

"God help me to kill her": "Quiz 'Killers' Face to Face: One Pair Slew Lehman; Which? State Puzzled," *Chicago Tribune*, Nov. 29, 1923.

"Why didn't you let me alone?": "Malm Woman Tries Suicide in Her Cell," *Chicago Tribune*, Dec. 1, 1923.

Malm stepped forward: "Malm Wants to Plead Guilty to Lehman Slaying," *Chicago Tribune*, Feb. 5, 1924.

Katherine projected confidence: Genevieve Forbes, "Angel Wings for Malm If I Hang, Says Lone Kitty," *Chicago Tribune*, Feb. 19, 1924.

"I know it almost by heart": Ibid.

"I want to go to mommie": Ibid.

"The evidence will show": "Jury Completed to Decide Fate of Kitty Malm," *Chicago Tribune*, Feb. 21, 1924.

They would continue to use animalistic terms: "Kitty Is 'Tiger' Again at Sight of Cherry Pie," *Chicago Tribune*, Feb. 25, 1924.

King testified that Katherine carried two guns: Genevieve Forbes, "Mrs. Malm Has Collapse after State Surprise," *Chicago Tribune*, Feb. 22, 1924.

Crediting $600 to Tootsie: Ibid.

Malm proposed breaking into the Delson plant: "'I'm Not Scarc't,' Says Kitty, but She Cries a Bit," *Chicago Tribune*, Feb. 24, 1924.

Katherine took the stand through "No sir. I never carried or fired a gun": "'Tiger Girl,' on Stand, Accuses Malm of Killing," *Chicago Tribune*, Feb. 26, 1924.

Katherine was found guilty through She fainted again in her cell: "Guilty; Malm Girl Gets Life: Courage Fails over Verdict; She Collapses," *Chicago Tribune*, Feb. 27, 1924.

"I thought for sure they would give me the rope": "Kitty Admits She Expected 'Rope' Verdict," *Chicago Tribune*.

"This woman's rights were fully protected": "Kitty Malm and Husband Given Life in Prison," *Chicago Tribune*.

sued Katherine for divorce: "Kitty Malm's Legal Husband Seeks Divorce," *Chicago Tribune*, March 13, 1924.

Malm killed another man: "Slayer Kills Prison Mate; Robber Flees," *Chicago Tribune*, July 19, 1925; "Kitty Malm 'Tiger Girl' of Sensational Murder Case, Is Dead," *Chicago Tribune*, Dec. 28, 1932.

Katherine entered prison: Katherine Walter, death certificate, Dec. 27, 1932.

She became a proficient stenographer: "Kitty Malm 'Tiger Girl' of Sensational Murder Case, Is Dead," *Chicago Tribune*.

"She got life in prison. Why not give it to her?" through Katherine's pardon request was denied: Secretary of State, "Executive Section. Executive Clemency Files," Record Series 103.096, Illinois State Archives.

She fell ill within a week: "Kitty Malm 'Tiger Girl' of Sensational Murder Case, Is Dead," *Chicago Tribune*.

Katherine died of the flu: Katherine Walter, death certificate, Dec. 27, 1932; "Katherine Walter Baluk," https://www.findagrave.com/memorial/146856359/katherine-baluk.

Meet the Deceased: Edward Lehmann

who had been working as a chauffeur: Edward Lehmann, death certificate, Illinois, Deaths and Stillbirths Index, 1916-1947, accessed via Ancestry.com.

Lehmann was the son of Paul and Margaret Lehmann: U.S. Census 1920, Chicago Ward 24, Cook County, Ill.; Roll: T625_335; page 9B; Enumeration District: 1343.

CHAPTER 5: SABELLA NITTI

She shifted her stocky legs: Genevieve Forbes, "Mrs. Nitti and Consort Given Noose Penalty," *Chicago Tribune*, July 10, 1923.

Her distinctive Bari dialect: Supreme Court of Illinois, "Case Files," Record Series 901.001, Illinois State Archives.

"Three frantic interpreters": Genevieve Forbes, "Dialect Jargon Makes 'Em Dizzy at Nitti Trial," *Chicago Tribune*, July 7, 1923.

"dumb, crouching animal-like Italian peasant": Ibid.

"That was just": "Mrs. Nitti and Consort Given Noose Penalty," *Chicago Tribune*.

"They chokes me?": "Oct. 12 Is Set as Date to Hang Woman Slayer," *Chicago Tribune*, July 15, 1923.

it's a disgrace to us: Genevieve Forbes, "Jury Foreman's Wife Rebels at Nitti Verdict," *Chicago Tribune*, July 11, 1923.

Isabella Maria Travaglio was born: Illinois, Federal Naturalization Records, 1856-1991, accessed via Ancestry.com.

She arrived in New York City: Ibid.

Her husband, Francesco Nitti: New York, Passenger and Crew Lists (including Castle Garden and Ellis Island), 1820-1957, accessed via Ancestry.com.

He lived a relatively humble life: Supreme Court of Illinois, Case Files, Record Series 901.001, Illinois State Archives.

two daughters would join the family: Illinois, Federal Naturalization Records, 1856-1991, accessed via Ancestry.com.

Francesco Nitti had a temper: "Father Killed by Hired Man, Says Nitti Boy," *Chicago Tribune*, Sept. 22, 1922.

asked his father for $500: Supreme Court of Illinois, Case Files, Record Series 901.001, Illinois State Archives.

One neighbor, Mike Travaglio, testified: Ibid.

his "bum son" did it: Ibid.

take the children and go to bed: Ibid.

he visited with the man later that night: Ibid.

She went to the home of Louis Kral: Ibid.

Sabella wept: Ibid.

he was told Nitti was missing: Ibid.

Michael Nitti stayed away: Ibid.

Lucchesi's research reveals: Emilie Le Beau Lucchesi, "Ugly Prey: An Innocent Woman and the Death Sentence That Scandalized Jazz Age Chicago" (Chicago Review Press, 2017), 45-46.

membership in the Cook County Democratic Marching Club: "City and County Notes," *The Inter Ocean* (Chicago, Ill.), July 13, 1897.

He resigned the position: "Summary of the Daily Tribune: Local," *Chicago Tribune*, Jan. 31, 1900.

charges of cruelty used against the boys in his charge: "Bridewell Whipping Room and the Spankers: Uses Wooden Paddle First," *Chicago Tribune*, Dec. 4, 1898.

Dasso spoke Italian: Le Beau Lucchesi, "Ugly Prey," 45-46.

They were taken into custody: Ibid.

Sabella's sons: "Farmer's Body Thrown in River, Girl of 7 Says," *Chicago Tribune*, Sept. 19, 1922.

James, Sabella's oldest son, used his mother's incarceration: Supreme Court of Illinois, Case Files, Record Series 901.001, Illinois State Archives.

James had been living in Wisconsin: Ibid.

he began selling off pieces of his father's estate: Estate of Francesco Nitti, case number 84083, Probate Court of Cook County, accessed at the Archives Department of the Clerk of Circuit Court of Cook County.

she had seen her father's body: "Farmer's Body Thrown in River, Girl of 7 Says," *Chicago Tribune*.

Charles refused at first: "Father Killed by Hired Man, Says Nitti Boy," *Chicago Tribune*.

"He hit father on the head with a sledgehammer": Ibid.

his mother knew nothing: "Nitti Murdered, Son Confesses; Absolves Widow," *Chicago Tribune*, Sept. 26, 1922.

Crudelle bludgeoned him: "Nitti's Widow, Prudella, Held to Grand Jury," *Chicago Tribune*, Oct. 15, 1922.

"Whatever Charlie said, that is true": Supreme Court of Illinois, Case Files, Record Series 901.001, Illinois State Archives.

Police stopped looking for Nitti's body: "Believe Nitti's Body Swept into Illinois River," *Chicago Tribune*, Sept. 28, 1922.

James was named administrator: Estate of Francesco Nitti, case number 84083, Probate Court of Cook County, accessed at the Archives Department of the Clerk of Circuit Court of Cook County.

Sabella's attorney, Eugene Moran: Ibid.

With no body and no evidence: Le Beau Lucchesi, "Ugly Prey," 295.

the court ordered James to return his father's estate to his mother: Estate of Francesco Nitti, case number 84083, Probate Court of Cook County, accessed at the Archives Department of the Clerk of Circuit Court of Cook County.

James had already sold $235: Ibid.

the probate court awarded Sabella about $800: Ibid.

Sabella and Crudelle were married: "Boy Tells How 'Star Boarder' Slew His Father," *Chicago Tribune*, May 10, 1923.

a decomposed body was found in a storm drain: The Associated Press Leased Wire, "Missing Man's Body Found in Catch Basin," the *Dispatch* (Moline, Ill.), May 9, 1923.

From the waistline up, it was just a skeleton: Supreme Court of Illinois, Case Files, Record Series 901.001, Illinois State Archives.

"by means of a pair of shoes and ring": "Boy Tells How 'Star Boarder' Slew His Father," *Chicago Tribune*.

On July 12, 1923, jury selection took place: "Woman, Son, and Husband Tried for Nitti Murder," *Chicago Tribune*, July 3, 1923.

the waterlogged pair of shoes: "Identify Nitti's Shoes at Trial for His Murder," *Chicago Tribune*, July 4, 1923.

"alleged husband-killer who acknowledges 39 years and possesses 46": "Dialect Jargon Makes 'Em Dizzy at Nitti Trial," *Chicago Tribune*.

James testified on July 5, 1923: "Son Testifies His Own Mother Killed Father," *Chicago Tribune*, July 6, 1923.

"Gentlemen, this is a disgrace": "Dialect Jargon Makes 'Em Dizzy at Nitti Trial," *Chicago Tribune*.

David questioned Moran's competence and understanding: Supreme Court of Illinois, Case Files, Record Series 901.001, Illinois State Archives.

Charges against Charles were dropped: "Son Is Freed in Nitti Trial as Defense Rests," *Chicago Tribune*, July 8, 1923.

"She hadn't understood the words": "Mrs. Nitti and Consort Given Noose Penalty," *Chicago Tribune*.

"Verdicts seem to be inversely proportional": "Jury Foreman's Wife Rebels at Nitti Verdict," *Chicago Tribune*.

return to her mother's home: Ibid.

Sabella's cellmates in Cook County Jail drafted a letter: Genevieve Forbes, "Mrs. Nitti's Tragedy Melts Hearts of Women in Jail," *Chicago Tribune*, July 12, 1923.

The congregation of Olivet Institute: "Church Offers Ray of Sunshine for Mrs. Nitti," *Chicago Tribune*, July 14, 1923.

However, the *Chicago Tribune* supported the sentence: "Discouraging Gunwomen," *Chicago Tribune*, July 12, 1923.

"the first woman in Illinois to be hanged": "Italians Move to Save Woman from Gallows," *Chicago Tribune*, July 13, 1923.

the youngest woman to ever pass the test: "Girl Wins Degree at Law, but Must Wait a Year to Practice," *Chicago Tribune*, June 17, 1920.

she attempted suicide twice: "Mrs. Nitti's Tragedy Melts Hearts of Women in Jail," *Chicago Tribune*.

"a mother has never been hanged in the history of this country": "Oct. 12 Is Set as Date to Hang Woman Slayer," *Chicago Tribune*.

"I will not listen to such stuff": Ibid.

"They should go back or be sent back to Italy": "Racial Inequality," *Chicago Tribune*, July 17, 1923.

Sabella yearned for her daughters: "Strive to Save Mrs. Nitti by Legal Loophole," *Chicago Tribune*, July 28, 1923.

"if I got to die, they die with me": "Mrs. Nitti Fails to Get Freedom on Court Writ," *Chicago Tribune*, July 31, 1923.

Judge Joseph Sabath of Superior Court: Ibid.

"I feel that I am doing the right thing for the community": "Denies New Trial to Doomed Nitti Woman and Mate," *Chicago Tribune*, Aug. 30, 1923.

There were "only two places left open": Ibid.

Illinois Supreme Court Justice Orrin Carter stayed the execution: "Justice Carter Orders Stay of Nitti Hangings," *Chicago Tribune*, Sept. 26, 1923.

After a substantial defense fund for Sabella and Crudelle was raised: "Supreme Court Asked to Annul Nitti Hangings," *Chicago Tribune*, Dec. 16, 1923.

Amongst the claims presented through The trial judge failed: Supreme Court of Illinois, Case Files, Record Series 901.001, Illinois State Archives.

Sabella and Crudelle were spared the gallows: "Supreme Court Saves Mrs. Nitti from Gallows: Remands Her Case and Three Others," *Chicago Tribune*, April 15, 1924.

Sabella and Crudelle were failed by an incompetent lawyer: Supreme Court of Illinois, Case Files, Record Series 901.001, Illinois State Archives.

Cirese encouraged Sabella to learn English: Le Beau Lucchesi, "Ugly Prey," 216-217.

she affixed her signature to an official document: "Mrs. Crudelle, Back on Nitti Farm, Rejoices," *Chicago Tribune*, June 17, 1924.

Crudelle was released the next day: "Crudelle, Mrs. Nitti's Aid, Released on $12,500 Bond," *Chicago Tribune*, June 18, 1924.

the couple moved to a small farm in Maywood: "Woman Who Once Escaped Noose Hunts Husband," *Chicago Tribune*, Sept. 10, 1925.

"Please help me find him": Ibid.

Sabella married a third time: Illinois, Federal Naturalization Records, 1856-1991, accessed via Ancestry.com.

she received citizenship five years later: Northern District, Ill., Naturalization Index, 1926-1979, accessed via Ancestry.com.

In 1949, she moved to Los Angeles: Isabelle Campobasso, death certificate, registration number 7053, registrar's number, 23105, California, County of Los Angeles Registrar-Recorder/County Clerk, copy in possession of author.

The once despised farmworker was buried: "Isabella Maria Travaglio Campobasso," https://www.findagrave.com/memorial/197163481/isabella-maria-campobasso.

Meet the Deceased: Francesco Nitti

In honor of our grandfather: "Francesco 'Frank' Nitti," https://www.findagrave.com/memorial/153614335/francesco-nitti.

At the time of his supposed death: Estate of Francesco Nitti, case number 84083, Probate Court of Cook County, accessed at the Archives Department of the Clerk of Circuit Court of Cook County.

Helen Cirese

Cirese thought she would become a reporter: "Woman's Right to Change Mind Fully Justified: Ascends to J.P.'s Seat on Legal Ladder," *Chicago Tribune*, May 6, 1945.

her plans changed when an older brother left: Ibid.

She studied law at DePaul University: Helen Cirese papers, Special Collections and University Archives, University of Illinois at Chicago.

Cirese was named a commencement speaker: "Girl Wins Degree at Law, But Must Wait a Year to Practice," *Chicago Tribune.*

In her address, entitled "Youth and loyalty": Helen Cirese papers, Special Collections and University Archives, University of Illinois at Chicago.

Cirese became the youngest woman to pass the Illinois Bar exam: "Girl Wins Degree at Law, But Must Wait a Year to Practice," *Chicago Tribune.*

"William the Conqueror has been dead": "Illinois Women Suing for Right of Jury Service: Fight 'Men Only' Ruling of 1006 A.D.," *Daily News* (New York, N.Y.), June 12, 1921.

After pleading Sabella's case at age twenty-four: "Woman's Right To Change Mind Fully Justified: Ascends to J.P.'s Seat on Legal Ladder," *Chicago Tribune.*

She helped acquit Lela Foster: "White Wife Is Freed as Killer of Negro Mate," *Chicago Tribune*, July 17, 1924.

Cirese ran for justice of the peace in Oak Park: Helen Cirese papers, Special Collections and University Archives, University of Illinois at Chicago.

"A wisp of a girl": "Young Portia Asks Oak Park Votes for J.P.," *Chicago Tribune*, April 6, 1925.

She was, however, defeated in a 2-to-1 ratio: "Evanston and Oak Park Swat Sunday Movie," *Chicago Tribune*, April 8, 1925.

She was elected president of the Women's Bar Association of Illinois: "Helen Cirese New Head of Women Lawyers' Group," *Chicago Tribune*, June 6, 1930.

"It's an awful thing to admit, I suppose": Virginia Gardner, "Do Women Like To Cook? Some Do, Some Don't: Here Are Viewpoints of a Few of Them," *Chicago Tribune*, Oct. 10, 1930.

He filed for a quickie divorce: "Divorce Trial Set for Pair Wed Here," *Indianapolis Star*, May 30, 1933.

A judge tossed the divorce request: "Court Throws Out Hunnewell Divorce: Rules Rich Husband's Residence in Reno Not Bona Fide," the *Boston Globe*, July 14, 1933.

Hunnewell's extramarital affairs may have contributed: "Unfaithfulness Is Charged in Suit of Mrs. Hunnewell," *Nevada State Journal* (Reno, Nev.), July 12, 1933.

Cirese was elected president: "Portias Will Honor Leader: Chicagoan to Be Guest of Women Lawyers at Luncheon Today," *Los Angeles Times*, July 25, 1939.

On her second attempt in 1945: "Woman's Right to Change Mind Fully Justified: Ascends to J.P.'s Seat on Legal Ladder," *Chicago Tribune.*

She served in that capacity until 1961: "Helen M. Cirese Endowed Scholarship," DePaul.AcademicWorks .com, https://depaul.academicworks.com/donors/helen-m-cirese-endowed-scholarship.

She died in Florida: Ibid.

CHAPTER 7: MAURINE WATKINS

Beulah Annan, a liquored up woman: Maurine Watkins, "Demand Noose for 'Prettiest' Woman Slayer," *Chicago Tribune*, April 5, 1924.

The suspected killers: Ron Grossman, "The Original 'Affluenza' Case: Leopold and Loeb," *Chicago Tribune*, March 31, 2016, https://www.chicagotribune.com/news/opinion/commentary/ct-clarence -darrow-leopold-loeb-perspec-0403-jm-20160329-story.html.

His tiny, white casket had eight pallbearers: Maurine Watkins, "Simple Funeral Service Is Held for Franks Boy," *Chicago Tribune*, May 26, 1924.

"And if he is connected—still it's experience!": Maurine Watkins, "Big Experience Either Way, Is Nathan's View," *Chicago Tribune*, May 31, 1924.

"Were they jaded by the jazz-life of gin and girls": Maurine Watkins, "'Dick Innocent,' Loebs Protest; Plan Defense," *Chicago Tribune*, June 1, 1924.

she claimed to not remember any of it: Maurine Watkins, "Mrs. Gaertner Has 'Class' as She Faces Jury," *Chicago Tribune*, June 4, 1924.

"You're too slick a talker": Maurine Watkins, "Court Immune to Taking Way of Bad Actor," *Chicago Tribune*, July 9, 1924.

Maurine covered the opening of a hospital: Maurine Watkins, "First Hospital for Unmarried Girls Dedicated," *Chicago Tribune*, April 13, 1924.

"Take your choice!": Maurine Watkins, "Bobbed Wigs or Wigged Bobs Is Fashion Decree," *Chicago Tribune*, April 24, 1924.

"The plump woman of middle-age": Maurine Watkins, "Step Up Men; Read What Style Arbiters Say You Must Wear," *Chicago Tribune*, April 29, 1924.

Glueck condemned discipline of children: Maurine Watkins, "Know Children, Expert's Word to All Parents," *Chicago Tribune*, August 7, 1924.

named mayor of Chicago for 10 minutes: Maurine Watkins, "Jackie Coogan Is Mayor for Ten Minutes," *Chicago Tribune*, August 7, 1924.

Maurine first made headlines: Mary E. Bostwick, "Maurine Watkins, Playwright at 11, Returns after Greater Achievements," the *Indianapolis Star*, Jan. 6, 1928.

her original birth certificate is missing: Walter Bowman, archivist/research room supervisor, Kentucky Department for Libraries and Archives, email message to author, Jan. 23, 2019.

"Athens of Indiana": "Crawfordsville: The Athens of Indiana," compiled and published for the City of Crawfordsville by the Chamber of Commerce, 1929, accessed via Hathi Trust Digital Library, https://catalog.hathitrust.org/Record/006000137; "The Athens of Indiana," produced by Indiana Public Media on July 9, 2012, https://indianapublicmedia.org/momentofindianahistory/athens-indiana/.

won the state's first basketball championship: "The First State Basketball Champs: Crawfordsville High School 1911," Indiana History Blog, Indiana Historical Bureau of the Indiana State Library, March 10, 2016, https://blog.history.in.gov/tag/1911-state-champs/.

She was one of ten founding members: 1911 Crawfordsville High School yearbook, courtesy of the Marian Morrison Local History Collection at Crawfordsville District Public Library.

Maurine became the organization's vice president: 1912 and 1913 Crawfordsville High School yearbooks, courtesy of the Marian Morrison Local History Collection at Crawfordsville District Public Library.

"She'll not be hit with Cupid's arrow": 1914 Crawfordsville High School yearbook, courtesy of the Marian Morrison Local History Collection at Crawfordsville District Public Library.

Maurine graduated from Crawfordsville High School: "Maurine Dallas Watkins," Crawfordsville District Public Library, http://www.cdpl.lib.in.us/services/reference/Watkins; Radcliffe College student files, 1890-1985, Watkins, Maurine Dallas, 1919-21, RG XXI, Series 1, Radcliffe College Archives, Schlesinger Library, Radcliffe Institute, Harvard University, Cambridge, Mass. https://id.lib.harvard.edu/ead/sch01143/catalog.

She returned to Kentucky in September 1914: Alumni Records Office, Yale University, Records of Alumni from the Classes of 1701-1978 (RU 830), Manuscripts and Archives, Yale University Library.

"She has never been under college censure": Radcliffe College student files, 1890-1985, Radcliffe Institute, Harvard University.

she was awarded $10 in gold: "Chancellor for Transylvania," the *Courier-Journal* (Louisville, Ky.), June 9, 1916; "118th Annual Commencement," the *Courier-Journal* (Louisville, Ky.), June 5, 1916.

"So-called Junior Colleges": Radcliffe College student files, 1890-1985, Radcliffe Institute, Harvard University.

Maurine attended nearby Butler University: "39 Candidates for Degrees at Butler," the *Indianapolis News*, March 17, 1919; Radcliffe College student files, 1890-1985, Radcliffe Institute, Harvard University.

Maurine was an understudy: "Butler Students in Play," the *Indianapolis Star*, May 3, 1919.

"I was so thrilled by his performance": Lillian G. Genn, "No. 3—Maurine Watkins: The Girl Who Put 'Chicago' on the Boards," Women Who've Won, the *Evening Sun* (Baltimore, Md.), Aug. 8, 1928.

"I simply thought of it": "War and Peace on Stages," *St. Louis Post-Dispatch*, Nov. 20, 1927.

She submitted her third application to Radcliffe: Radcliffe College student files, 1890-1985, Radcliffe Institute, Harvard University.

"the greatest living authority on the drama": "Record-Breaking Enrollment: Harvard Summer School of Arts and Sciences," the *Boston Globe*, July 10, 1916.

request by students: "Surprises Theatrical and Academic World by Turning Out Successful Dramatists," the *Sun* (New York, N.Y.), Nov. 9, 1913.

Harvard had no stage at the time: Hayden Talbot, "The Best Show Town in the World—Berlin," *New-York Tribune* (New York, N.Y.), Sept. 28, 1919.

"the life-blood of a good play": "Turning Out Playwrights: Brooklyn Man at Harvard Describes Professor Baker's Courses in Dramaturgy," the *Brooklyn Daily Eagle*, March 24, 1912.

"the Workshop is laboring in the crudest of amateur conditions": "The Best Show Town in the World—Berlin," *New-York Tribune*.

Maurine was one of them in fall 1919: Radcliffe College student files, 1890-1985, Radcliffe Institute, Harvard University.

She took the course after Eugene O'Neill: John D. Leonard, "George Pierce Baker: Prism for Genius," the *Harvard Crimson*, Nov. 6, 1957.

"I have written for the person who cannot be content": George Pierce Baker, "Dramatic Technique" (Cambridge, 1919; Project Gutenberg, July 2, 2011), http://www.gutenberg.org/files/36580/36580-h/36580-h.htm.

Reconnected with Ditrichstein: "Maurine Watkins, Playwright at 11, Returns after Greater Achievements," the *Indianapolis Star*.

"I'm here in Pittsburgh": Maurine Watkins, correspondence with George Pierce Baker, 1923 and undated, George Pierce Baker papers, MS Thr 639, (2861), Houghton Library, Harvard College Library.

"We have a very interesting group": Ibid.

He would stay in Europe: "Leo Ditrichstein, 63, Dies in Austria," *Chicago Tribune*, June 30, 1928.

"I thought I'd turn to newspaper work": "No. 3—Maurine Watkins: The Girl Who Put 'Chicago' on the Boards," the *Evening Sun*.

"These he must cut out": "Turning Out Playwrights: Brooklyn Man at Harvard Describes Professor Baker's Courses in Dramaturgy," the *Brooklyn Daily Eagle*.

"I wrote a letter to the city editor": "No. 3—Maurine Watkins: The Girl Who Put 'Chicago' on the Boards," the *Evening Sun*.

"Father is not a baby-kisser": Clare Ogden Davis, "That Astounding Young Person!", *Success Magazine*.

Merrick created: Stacey Steig, "A History of Coral Gables," Coral Gables Chamber of Commerce, https://coralgableschamber.org/a-history-of-coral-gables/.

25,000 people sold real estate: Stuart McIver, "Florida's First Boom—and Bust," *South Florida Sun-Sentinel*, March 10, 1991, https://www.sun-sentinel.com/news/fl-xpm-1991-03-10-9101120716-story.html.

Watkins & Black: Giselle Alonso, Florida and genealogy librarian, Helen Muir Florida Collection, Miami-Dade Public Library System, email message to author, Oct. 26, 2018.

George gave a speech: "Couple Honors Golden Wedding with Ceremony," *Indianapolis Star*, June 15, 1926.

the building boom was over: "Florida's First Boom—and Bust"; "Great Miami Hurricane of 1926," National Weather Service Miami-South Florida, https://www.weather.gov/mfl/miami_hurricane.

barracks for soldiers: "Blaze in Historic Harvard Building," the *Boston Globe*, April 7, 1924.

estimated $10,000 in damage: Ibid.

his group was not responsible: "Space Not Available for 47 Workshop," the *Boston Globe*, Sept. 25, 1924.

without a home: "Massachusetts Hall to Be Dormitory," the *Boston Globe*, May 27, 1924.

Baker taught two playwriting courses: "Professor Says Radio Will Be Stage Device," *Oakland Tribune* (Oakland, Calif.), July 6, 1924; Ibid.

He resigned from Harvard: "Severe Criticism of Harvard Authorities," the *Boston Globe*, Nov. 26, 1924.

"yes, just as significant": Gardner Jackson, "How Prof Baker Made Place for His Work—If Not at Harvard," the *Boston Globe*, Nov. 30, 1924.

she completed her Yale application: Alumni Records Office, Yale University.

"It isn't quite fair": George Pierce Baker papers, Houghton Library, Harvard College Library.

She registered the work: "Petition for Authority to Execute Agreement for Sale of Play 'Chicago,'" June 7, 1972, Estate of Georgia M. Watkins, Deceased, Case Number 34767-D, Probate Department, Duval County, Fla.

Nicknamed "Moonshine Mary": "Moonshine Mary Sent to Prison for Man's Death," *Chicago Tribune*, April 6, 1924.

Her attorneys claimed her mind was subnormal: "Woman Given Life in Jail as Murderess," *Chicago Tribune*, May 8, 1924.

Jake Lingle: "Walter Winchell on Broadway," *Tampa Times*, June 18, 1930.

In an earlier version of the play: Maurine Watkins Papers, Yale Collection of American Literature, Beinecke Rare Book and Manuscript Library, https://archives.yale.edu/repositories/11/resources/5459.

"one of the most significant": The Associated Press, "'Chicago' Author Makes Reply to Her Play's Critic," *Hartford Courant* (Hartford, Conn.), Dec. 30, 1926.

first play out of the Yale School of Drama: "Indianapolis Woman Sells Play 'Chicago,'" the *Indianapolis Star*, June 9, 1926.

"entirely too vile": The Associated Press, "Calls New Play Vile and Leaves after First Act," *Hartford Courant* (Hartford, Conn.), Dec. 28, 1926.

Maurine's response to Archer's assessment: "'Chicago' Author Makes Reply to Her Play's Critic," *Hartford Courant* (Hartford, Conn.).

Critic Burns Mantle wrote: Burns Mantle, "Two Gun Chicago Is Subject of Satire," *Chicago Tribune*, Jan. 9, 1927.

"the villain of Chicago": Alexander Woollcott, "Man's Taste for Murder Trials Razzed in New Play," the *Baltimore Sun*, Jan. 9, 1927.

Novelist Rupert Hughes: Rupert Hughes, "A Young Woman Our Foremost Satirist," *Dayton Daily News*, March 13, 1927.

Candidate for the Pulitzer Prize: R.M. Harrison, "The Theatre and Its People," *Windsor Star* (Ontario, Canada), March 4, 1927.

"Now don't let an immediate success": Wisner Payne Kinne, "George Pierce Baker and the American Theatre" (Harvard University Press, 1954), 267.

"Chicago" played at the Music Box Theater: "'Chicago' Ends New York Run," the *Messenger* (Owensboro, Ky.), June 5, 1927; "Shows in N.Y. and Comment," *Variety*, Jan. 26, 1927.

Maurine, herself, appeared: "News and Comment of the Dramatic World—Screen Items," the *Brooklyn Daily Eagle*, March 31, 1927.

"He is wise": Idwal Jones, "Lovely Jazz Slayer Saved from Noose in 'Chicago,' Crime Burlesque at Lurie," the *San Francisco Examiner*, June 26, 1927.

publicity agent: United Press International, "Thompson Is Going to Have Publicity Agent," *Des Moines Tribune*, April 9, 1927.

In the summer: "Closeups," *Chicago Tribune*, July 18, 1927.

If "Chicago" would play in Chicago: Frederick Donaghey, "This Thing and That Thing of the Theater," *Chicago Tribune*, Jan. 23, 1927.

"It were silly": "Theater: 'Chicago,'" *Chicago Tribune*, Sept. 12, 1927.

Before the year concluded: The Associated Press, "Berlin Likes 'Chicago,' Maurine Watkins' Play," *Chicago Tribune*, Nov. 21, 1927.

"Women—especially newspaper women": "Makes Good," the *Emporia Gazette* (Emporia, Kan.), Dec. 23, 1927.

"the play was marketed by a woman": Maureen McKernan, "'Chicago' Case Throws Light on Co-Eds," *Detroit Free Press*, Dec. 25, 1927.

Samuel Hopkins Adams' play, "Revelry": Martin Hayes, "The Drama Here and Elsewhere," the *Scranton Republican* (Scranton, Pa.), Jan. 17, 1927.

but quickly closed: Robert F. Sisk, "Revelry, on Stage, Brings Out Groans and Invective," the *Baltimore Sun*, Sept. 4, 1927.

She toyed with returning to Yale: "Theater," *Chicago Tribune*, March 31, 1927.

She penned "Victory": Maurine Watkins Papers, Yale Collection of American Literature, Beinecke Rare Book and Manuscript Library.

hired by the New York Telegram: "Murder without Sobs," *Pittsburgh Press*, April 21, 1927.

Snyder and her lover were both found guilty: Chris Jones, "Review: A Stunning Young Woman in 'Machinal' at the Greenhouse Theater," *Chicago Tribune*, Aug. 20, 2017, https://www.chicagotribune.com/entertainment/theater/reviews/ct-ent-machinal-greenho se-review-0821-story.html.

"Tom" Howard: Rick Kogan, "Loretta M. Wendt, 1922-2010," *Chicago Tribune*, July 28, 2010, https://www.chicagotribune.com/living/ct-xpm-2010-07-28-ct-met-wendt-obit-0729-2010 728-story.html.

Maurine's assessment of divorce: Grant Dixon, "Lights of New York," *Hartford Courant* (Hartford, Conn.), April 24, 1927.

"When are you going to cease to be a refugee": Kinne, "George Pierce Baker and the American Theatre," 268.

She retreated to Indiana: "Maurine Watkins, Playwright at 11, Returns after Greater Achievements," the *Indianapolis Star*.

"(I)t is doubtful": Norbert Lusk, "'Chicago' Is Melodrama," *Los Angeles Times*, Jan. 1, 1928.

"(E)qually brilliant": "Old Year Goes Out in Blaze of Cinematic Glory," *New York Daily News*, Jan. 1, 1928.

"they have slaughtered Maurine Watkins' play": Mae Tinee, "Our Maurine's Fine Play Is Film-Flammed," *Chicago Tribune*, March 20, 1928.

"An Old-Fashioned Girl": William J. McNally, "'RioRita' Opens Metropolitan Engagement Today; Shubert Presents 'No, No, Nanette,'" *Star Tribune* (Minneapolis, Minn.), Nov. 3, 1929.

"So Help Me God!": "Another Watkins Play," the *Brooklyn Daily Eagle*, Aug. 27, 1929.

"forgotten to finish the play": "The Stage," *Chicago Tribune*, Aug. 15, 1930.

"I'd love to write a novel": Florabel Muir, "Maurine Finds Filmland Novel Beyond Belief," *New York Daily News*, Sept. 22, 1930.

John Wayne: Louella O. Parsons, "Jim Tully Collaborating on Film Take for Jack Gilbert," the *San Francisco Examiner*, April 30, 1930.

two Sing Sing inmates: Mae Tinee, "Satiric Comedy of Prison Life Evokes Mirth," *Chicago Tribune*, Nov. 9, 1930.

"The Great Ziegfeld": Andrea Passafiume, "Behind the Camera on Libeled Lady," TCM.com, http://www.tcm.com/this-month/article/615680%7C0/Behind-the-Camera-Libeled-Lady.html.

a dependable writer: Mollie Merrick, "Author Has Day as Hollywood Realizes Value," the *Atlanta Constitution*, Dec. 4, 1932.

"a strange person": Sidney Skolsky, "Impressions of People," Behind the News, *New York Daily News*, May 19, 1932.

Her 1933 passport: Maurine Watkins Papers, Yale Collection of American Literature, Beinecke Rare Book and Manuscript Library.

Louis Vuitton desk: Sandra Hayes-White, email message to author, Dec. 28, 2018.

Staged a "hat luncheon": "Writer Gives Luncheon to Show Off Her New Hat," Star Tribune (Minneapolis, Minn.), May 2, 1937.

expansive jewelry collection: Katelyn Kraunelis, communications associate, Christie's New York, email message to author, Oct. 25, 2018.

Her living quarters in California: Maurine Watkins Papers, Yale Collection of American Literature, Beinecke Rare Book and Manuscript Library.

"she does not smoke": "That Astounding Young Person!" *Success Magazine*.

He dictated his own obituary through "Our very great love to all": "Geo. W. Watkins," Deaths, *Buffalo Reflex* (Buffalo, Mo.), Feb. 20, 1941.

Maurine moved to her own unit: Jacksonville city directory, 1951, viewed at the Jacksonville Public Library.

the only real evidence through All her household goods: Estate of Georgia M. Watkins, Deceased, Case Number 34767-D, Probate Department, Duval County, Fla.

more than $2 million estate: Maurine Watkins Papers. Yale Collection of American Literature, Beinecke Rare Book and Manuscript Library.

She demanded any cash through Additional universities: Estate of Georgia M. Watkins, Probate Department, Duval County, Fla.

In a May 1957 letter through Periods of quiet: Correspondence with Maurine D. Watkins (1956-1965), William Roy Smith Papers, 1951-1969, Center for Restoration Studies MS #446, Milliken Special Collections, Brown Library, Abilene Christian University, Abilene, Texas.

Her body was cremated: "Petition," Feb. 3, 1970, estate of Maurine Dallas Watkins, deceased, Case Number 34603-D, Probate Department, Duval County, Fla.

C.R. Leonard: Charlie Patton, "Author of Original 'Chicago' Lived, Died in Jacksonville," *Florida Times-Union* (Jacksonville, Fla.), May 17, 2018, https://www.jacksonville.com/news/20180517/author-of-original-chicago-lived-died-in-jacksonville.

Maurine thanked the company: Louise Kiernan, "Murder, She Wrote," *Chicago Tribune*, July 16, 1997.

it was her idea: Linda Winer, "Verdon and Rivera Bring N.Y. Sass to 'Chicago,'" *Chicago Tribune*, April 5, 1978.

Verdon said she purchased the rights: Robert Wahls, "The Old Razzle Dazzle," *New York Daily News*, Feb. 6, 1977.

The court granted her request: "Petition for Letters of Administration," Aug. 21, 1969, estate of Maurine Dallas Watkins, deceased, Probate Department, Duval County, Fla.

"I am the only one in our family alive": Estate of Maurine Dallas Watkins, deceased, Probate Department, Duval County, Fla.

Maurine's will was handwritten: Elliot S. Blair, Esq., phone conversation with the author, Nov. 12, 2018.

Maurine's mother died: Estate of Georgia M. Watkins, deceased, Case Number 34767-D, Probate Department, Duval County, Fla.

They intended to execute an agreement: "Notice," May 31, 1972, estate of Georgia M. Watkins, deceased, Probate Department, Duval County, Fla.

Fryer previously produced: Dorothy Manners, "Robert Fryer Becoming Known for Best Seller Screening," *Anderson Daily Bulletin* (Anderson, Ind.), Feb. 25, 1969.

a $2,500 payment through **an additional four pairs:** "Petition for Authority to Execute Agreement for Sale of Play 'Chicago,'" June 7, 1972, estate of Georgia M. Watkins, deceased, Probate Department, Duval County, Fla.

Trust officer Leonard: "Author of Original 'Chicago' Lived, Died in Jacksonville," *Florida Times-Union.*

$306 million total: "Chicago," Box Office Mojo, https://www.boxofficemojo.com/movies/?id=chicago.htm.

redrafted 14 times: "Petition for Allowance of Attorneys' Fees," Dec. 3, 1974, estate of Georgia M. Watkins, deceased, Probate Department, Duval County, Fla.

ran for 936 performances: "Chicago: Broadway, Musical Original" *Playbill*, http://www.playbill.com/production/chicago-46th-street-theatre-vault-0000003096.

$2 billion worldwide: Calculation of data from Box Office Mojo and Playbill Pro.

"Chicago the Musical": Statistics provided by Heath Schwarz, Broadway production representative for "Chicago," Boneau/Bryan-Brown, email to the author, Oct. 17, 2018.

PHOTO CREDITS

Most newspaper clippings are in the collection of the *Chicago Tribune* except for those accessed through Newspapers.com. All photos are in the *Chicago Tribune* photo collection, which includes the *Chicago Herald and Examiner* and *Chicago American*, except those noted below.

Page x: E. Jason Wambsgans/*Chicago Tribune*
Page 4: Newspapers.com
Page 14: U.S. Census Bureau
Page 15, top: Spencer County Clerk's Office via Ancestry.com
Page 15, bottom left: *Owensboro Messenger-Inquirer*
Page 15, bottom right: *Owensboro Messenger-Inquirer*
Page 34: Illinois Department of Public Health
Page 37: *Indianapolis News*
Page 42: Montgomery County clerk
Page 44: Archives Department of the Clerk of the Circuit Court of Cook County
Page 45: Archives Department of the Clerk of the Circuit Court of Cook County
Page 67: Los Angeles County Registrar—recorder/county clerk
Page 98: Secretary of State, "Executive Section. Executive Clemency Files," record series 103.096, Illinois State Archives
Page 99: Secretary of State, "Executive Section. Executive Clemency Files," record series 103.096, Illinois State Archives
Page 102: Secretary of State, "Executive Section. Executive Clemency Files," record series 103.096, Illinois State Archives
Page 109: Supreme Court of Illinois, "Case files," record series 901.001, Illinois State Archives
Page 111: National Archives at Chicago via Ancestry.com
Page 117: Archives Department of the Clerk of the Circuit Court of Cook County
Page 118, middle: Archives Department of the Clerk of the Circuit Court of Cook County
Page 118, right: Supreme Court of Illinois, "Case files," record series 901.001, Illinois State Archives
Page 120: Supreme Court of Illinois, "Case files," record series 901.001, Illinois State Archives
Page 125: Supreme Court of Illinois, "Case files," record series 901.001, Illinois State Archives
Page 130: Supreme Court of Illinois, "Case files," record series 901.001, Illinois State Archives

Page 136, right: Supreme Court of Illinois, "Case files," record series 901.001, Illinois State Archives
Page 138: Supreme Court of Illinois, "Case files," record series 901.001, Illinois State Archives
Page 139, left: Newspapers.com
Page 145: National Archives of Chicago via Ancestry.com
Page 150: DeMille Pictures Corporation
Page 152: Photographed by E. Jason Wambsgans/*Chicago Tribune*. Collection of Chicago Cultural Historian Tim Samuelson
Page 154: Photographed by E. Jason Wambsgans/*Chicago Tribune*. Collection of Chicago Cultural Historian Tim Samuelson
Page 156: Photographed by E. Jason Wambsgans/*Chicago Tribune*. Collection of Chicago Cultural Historian Tim Samuelson
Page 157: Photographed by E. Jason Wambsgans/*Chicago Tribune*. Collection of Chicago Cultural Historian Tim Samuelson
Page 158: Collection of Chicago Cultural Historian Tim Samuelson
Page 161: Jeremy Daniel
Page 162: Jeremy Daniel
Page 163: Jeremy Daniel
Page 164: DeMille Pictures Corporation
Page 169: DeMille Pictures Corporation
Page 170–171: DeMille Pictures Corporation
Page 172: DeMille Pictures Corporation
Page 173: DeMille Pictures Corporation
Page 174: 20th Century Fox Films
Page 176: Miramax Films
Page 177: Miramax Films
Page 178: Miramax Films
Page 180: Maurine Watkins Papers. Yale Collection of American Literature, Beinecke Rare Book and Manuscript Library
Page 185, top: Marian Morrison Collection at the Crawfordsville District Public Library
Page 185, bottom: Marian Morrison Collection at the Crawfordsville District Public Library

Page 186, left: Marian Morrison Collection at the Crawfordsville District Public Library

Page 186, middle: Marian Morrison Collection at the Crawfordsville District Public Library

Page 186, right: Marian Morrison Collection at the Crawfordsville District Public Library

Page 186, bottom: Marian Morrison Collection at the Crawfordsville District Public Library

Page 187: Marian Morrison Collection at the Crawfordsville District Public Library

Page 189, left: Schlesinger Library, Radcliffe Institute for Advanced Study

Page 189, right: Schlesinger Library, Radcliffe Institute for Advanced Study

Page 192: *The New York Times* from the Alumni Records Office, Yale University, Records of Alumni from the Classes of 1701-1978 (RU 830). Manuscripts and Archives, Yale University Library

Page 195: Maurine Watkins Papers, Yale Collection of American Literature, Beinecke Rare Book and Manuscript Library

Page 196: Maurine Watkins Papers, Yale Collection of American Literature, Beinecke Rare Book and Manuscript Library

Page 197: Maurine Watkins Papers, Yale Collection of American Literature, Beinecke Rare Book and Manuscript Library

Page 198: Maurine Watkins Papers, Yale Collection of American Literature, Beinecke Rare Book and Manuscript Library

Page 199: Maurine Watkins Papers, Yale Collection of American Literature, Beinecke Rare Book and Manuscript Library

Page 209: Maurine Watkins Papers, Yale Collection of American Literature, Beinecke Rare Book and Manuscript Library

Page 210–211: Maurine Watkins Papers, Yale Collection of American Literature, Beinecke Rare Book and Manuscript Library

Page 213: Estate of Georgia M. Watkins, Duval County Clerk of Courts, Florida

Page 214: Estate of Georgia M. Watkins, Duval County Clerk of Courts, Florida

Page 216: Estate of Georgia M. Watkins, Duval County Clerk of Courts, Florida

Page 218: Estate of Georgia M. Watkins, Duval County Clerk of Courts, Florida

Page 220: Estate of Georgia M. Watkins, Duval County Clerk of Courts, Florida

Page 222: *The Florida Times-Union* via Jacksonville Public Library